Barcelona

Shortlist

timeout.com / barcelona

116

155

Contents

98

Introduction	**5**
Welcome to Barcelona	7
Highlights	10
Sightseeing	19
Eating & Drinking	25
Shopping	31
Entertainment	37
Barcelona Day by Day	**45**
Itineraries	46
Diary	53
Barcelona by Area	**61**
Getting Started	62
Barri Gòtic & La Rambla	67
Born & Sant Pere	85
Raval	99
Barceloneta & the Ports	111
Montjuïc & Around	121
Eixample	133
Gràcia & Other Districts	153
Barcelona Essentials	**167**
Accommodation	168
Getting Around	174
Resources A-Z	178
Spanish Vocabulary	186
Catalan Vocabulary	187
Index	188

ABOUT THE GUIDE

The *Time Out Barcelona Shortlist* is one of a series of pocket guides to cities around the globe. Drawing on the expertise of local authors, it distils their knowledge into a handy, easy-to-use format that ensures you get the most from your trip, whether you're a first-time or a return visitor.

Time Out Barcelona Shortlist is divided into four sections:

Welcome to Barcelona introduces the city and provides inspiration for your visit.

Barcelona Day by Day helps you plan your trip with an events calendar and customised itineraries.

Barcelona by Area is the main visitor section of the guide. It includes detailed listings and reviews for the very best sights, museums, restaurants ⑩, bars ⑩, shops ⑩ and entertainment venues ⑩, all organised by area with a corresponding street map. To help navigation, each area of Barcelona has been assigned its own colour.

Barcelona Essentials provides practical visitor information, including accommodation options and details of public transport.

Shortlists & highlights

We have selected a Shortlist of stand-out venues in each area, which are marked with a heart ♥ in the text. The very best of these appear in the Highlights feature (*see p10*) and receive extended coverage in the guide.

Maps

There's an overview map on *p8* and individual street maps for each area of the city. Venues featured in the guide have been given a grid reference so that you can find them easily on the maps and on the ground.

Prices

All our **restaurant** listings are marked with a euro symbol (€-€€€€) indicating the average price you should expect to pay for a main course in Barcelona: € = under €10; €€ = €10-€20; €€€ = €20-€30; €€€€ = over €30.

A similar system is used in our **Accommodation** chapter, based on the hotel's standard prices for one night in a double room: Budget = under €100; Mid-range = €100-€200; Expensive = €200-€300; Luxury = over €300.

Introduction

Barcelona has a panache that is all its own. A radiant pop art sculpture by Lichtenstein towers alongside a dark and sombre neoclassical arcade; serried ranks of apartment blocks in the Eixample occasionally explode in a proliferation of Modernista colour and pizzazz; and local festivals incorporate both the *sardana*, a sedate traditional Catalan dance involving gentle bouncing on tiptoes, and the *correfoc*, a reckless, firework-wielding rampage through the streets.

The city is captivated by all things modern but never turns its back on the past. Much of its appeal stems from a respect for heritage that gives it the best-preserved medieval quarter in Europe. You could spend a day mooching around this labyrinth, escaping the heat in shadowy alleyways while seagulls wheel overhead in an azure sky, without ever feeling the need to tick off museums or head for the beach.

In fact, we suggest you do just that. This pocket guide gives you a selection of the best sights and museums large and small, famous and obscure. But to really appreciate what keeps visitors returning time and again, you won't always need it.

Welcome to Barcelona

10   **Highlights**
19   **Sightseeing**
25   **Eating & Drinking**
31   **Shopping**
37   **Entertainment**

Park Güell

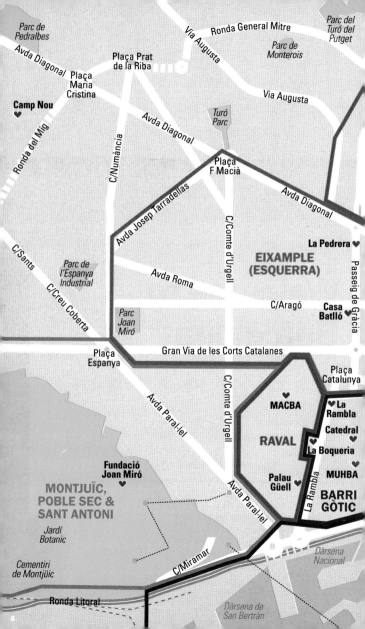

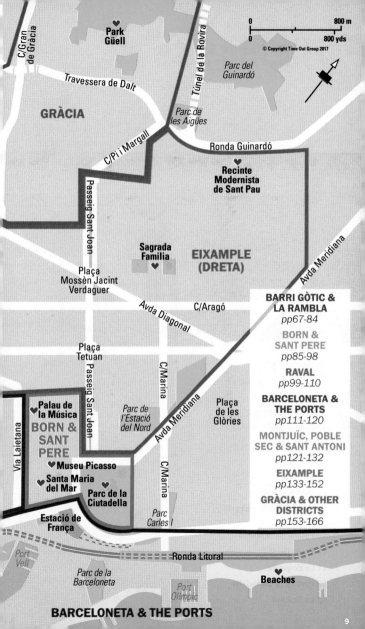

0   800 m
0   800 yds
© Copyright Time Out Group 2017

C/Gran de Gràcia

Park Güell ♥

Túnel de la Rovira

Parc del Guinardó

Travessera de Dalt

GRÀCIA

Parc de les Aigües

C/Pi i Margall

Ronda Guinardó

Recinte Modernista de Sant Pau ♥

Passeig Sant Joan

Sagrada Familia ♥♥

EIXAMPLE (DRETA)

Avda Meridiana

Plaça Mossèn Jacint Verdaguer

Avda Diagonal

C/Aragó

BARRI GÒTIC & LA RAMBLA
pp67-84

BORN & SANT PERE
pp85-98

Plaça Tetuan

C/Marina

Passeig Sant Joan

Parc de l'Estació del Nord

Avda Meridiana

Plaça de les Glòries

RAVAL
pp99-110

BARCELONETA & THE PORTS
pp111-120

MONTJUÏC, POBLE SEC & SANT ANTONI
pp121-132

Via Laietana

Palau de la Música ♥

BORN & SANT PERE

♥ **Museu Picasso**

♥ **Santa Maria del Mar**

Parc de la Ciutadella ♥

C/Marina

Parc Carles I

EIXAMPLE
pp133-152

GRÀCIA & OTHER DISTRICTS
pp153-166

Estació de França

Port Vell

Ronda Litoral

Parc de la Barceloneta

Port Olímpic

Beaches

BARCELONETA & THE PORTS

9

Highlights

From La Pedrera to La Mercè, and Camp Nou to Park Güell, we count down the highlights of this multifaceted city. Other destinations may flit in and out of vogue, but Barcelona remains eternally popular: here's why.

01 **Sagrada Família**
02 **Museu Picasso**
03 **Camp Nou Experience**
04 **Casa Batlló**
05 **Beaches**
06 **Palau de la Música Catalana**
07 **La Rambla**
08 **Park Güell**
09 **Fundació Joan Miró**
10 **Catedral de Barcelona**
11 **MUHBA**
12 **Santa Maria del Mar**
13 **MACBA**
14 **Recinte Modernista de Sant Pau**
15 **Festes de la Mercè**
16 **Palau Güell**
17 **La Boqueria**
18 **Parc de la Ciutadella**
19 **La Pedrera**

01

Sagrada Família *p142*

Gaudí's unfinished basilica is a fantastic riot of colour and maverick architecture, its walls erupting with flora and fauna. Love it or hate it, it is Barcelona's most emblematic building and a must-see. The plans for its completion were burnt by anarchists long after Gaudí's death, but decades of research have gone into making the building as faithful as possible to his designs.

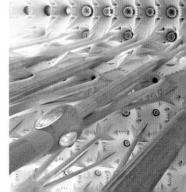

02

Museu Picasso *p90*

Though born in Málaga, Picasso moved to Barcelona as a teenager, and this museum focuses on those early years. With the exception of the entire *sala* devoted to his spectacular *Las Meninas* series, these rooms do not contain a parade of his greatest hits, but instead give a fascinating insight into his development as a young artist, and the accomplishment of some of his very early paintings is jaw-dropping.

03

Camp Nou Experience *p159*

The huge and hallowed Barça stadium – where the likes of Messi, Ronaldinho and Maradona have worked their magic – is a must for die-hard footie fans (and appears every year in the top three most-visited Barcelona attractions). Entrance includes the club museum and a tour of the players' tunnel and dug-outs, along with a peek into the President's box.

04

Casa Batlló *p138*

There are many interpretations of the fantastical façade of Gaudí's Casa Batlló, but most agree that its shimmering tiles represent the scales of the dragon slain by St George (Catalonia's patron saint), and the skeletal balconies are intended to evoke the bones of its victims. Nowadays you can visit the interior, which is predictably more sober than its shell, but its sinuous curves are still unmistakeably the work of Gaudí.

05

Beaches *p116*

There are a few valiant souls who brave the water around Christmas time, but for most, the sea is warm enough to swim in from late spring to early autumn. Seven kilometres of sand await, with something for everyone, whether your bag is kayaking, gay nudism, rock pooling or volleyball. Barceloneta's *xiringuitos* (beach bars) offer thumping beats and cruising crowds, while at the far north are the family-friendly sands of Platja del Llevant.

06

Palau de la Música Catalana *p98*

A fierce contender for Barcelona's prettiest building, this Modernista flight of fancy was designed by a contemporary of Gaudí's and has functioned as a concert hall ever since. The façade is really quite special, but it's also worth getting a guided tour of the auditorium if you can, or – even better – catching a concert while you're here. Failing that, wander through the lobby to the high-ceilinged café at the back.

07

La Rambla *p78*

Barcelona's golden mile is a long boulevard of street performers, card sharps, hawkers, buskers, human statues and bewildered-looking tourists. Though these days it has more in common with Oxford Street than the Champs-Élysées, it's still a must-see, and beyond the Mexican hats and flower stalls are some fine buildings and a whole host of attractions from La Boqueria food market (*see p81*) to the surprisingly tasteful Museu de l'Eròtica.

08

Park Güell *p155*

Gaudí's 'garden city' project was never completed, but instead he bequeathed the wonderful Park Güell to the city. What is termed the 'monumental' zone of the park is now fenced off and ticketed and includes the fairy-tale gatehouses, the famous 'dragon' (actually a giant lizard), and the hypostyle market, topped with the vast terrace and winding tiled benches that form the backdrop for so many holiday snaps.

09

Fundació Joan Miró *p127*

Joan Miró was born and grew up in Barcelona, where he honed his surrealist skills at the same art school that Picasso attended. His huge, colourful artworks have a universal appeal, but this stark white Le Corbusier-influenced museum building is a draw in itself, along with the view of the city that it commands from its position on Montjuïc. The Miró also hosts some of the best temporary exhibitions in the city.

10

Catedral de Barcelona *p73*

Gaudí's Sagrada Família is often wrongly described as a cathedral, but the real thing is this Gothic fantasy in the heart of the Old City. Built on the site of a Roman temple, it took centuries to complete, and its façade wasn't added until the early 20th century. This element of medieval fakery doesn't detract from its appeal, however, and it graces a thousand postcards.

11

MUHBA *p75*

The Museu d'Història de Barcelona, to give it its full name, encompasses various buildings; the 15th-century Casa Padellàs, which houses most of the displays of archeological findings, prints and so on; the Santa Àgata chapel; and the splendid Saló del Tinell, once the seat of the Catalan parliament. The *pièce de résistance*, however, is the extraordinary underground labyrinth of Roman remains, which runs from the Plaça del Rei as far as the cathedral.

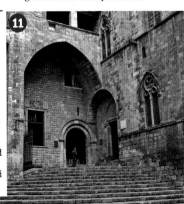

12

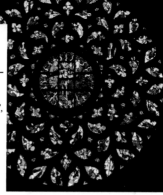

Santa Maria del Mar *p92*

Known as the 'people's cathedral', the 14th-century basilica of Santa Maria del Mar was erected by locals who volunteered their labour, and built it in record time. It's an incredible sight, deceptively large inside, with columns that rise to a dizzyingly high vaulted ceiling and a vast rose window on the front façade. It was twice gutted by anarchists, and it's to this that it owes its clean lines and simplicity.

13

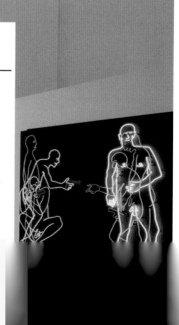

MACBA *p104*

Richard Meier's hulking white behemoth of a museum signified a grand turnaround in the fortunes of the Raval, and still shines as a beacon of modernity outside as well as in. It houses the city's main collection of contemporary art (which, in this instance, means 'post World War II'), and while its permanent holdings focus on Catalan and Spanish artists, temporary exhibitions have a more international flavour.

14

Recinte Modernista de Sant Pau *p145*

One of Barcelona's lesser-known gems, the Hospital de Sant Pau (as it was until a few years ago) was designed by Modernista architect Domènech i Montaner as a place where the sick could recover more quickly through the power of beautiful surroundings, a popular belief at the time. It comprises a series of dazzling garden 'pavilions', each of which was once a ward, while the dirty aspects of hospital life happened underground.

15

Festes de la Mercè *p57*

There is no shortage of neighbourhood festivals throughout the year, but La Mercè is where the entire city erupts in a week of music, fireworks, dancing and very, very late nights. Held around 24 September, the feast day of Barcelona's patron saint, the Virgin of Mercy, it brings together the best of all the cultural quirks of Catalan festes – papier mâché giants, fire-breathing dragons, human castles and *sardana* folk-dancing.

16

Palau Güell *p107*

From street level, it's hard to believe that Gaudí was behind this sombre medievalist townhouse, but the riot of colour on the rooftop terrace bears all the trademarks of his technique. Built on a narrow strip of land and hemmed in on both sides, its construction is a miracle of architectural cunning, the rooms facing into a graceful central hall, topped with a dome pierced with shafts of light.

17

La Boqueria *p81*

Europe's biggest food market is a feast for the senses. Despite its location on La Rambla and the fascination it holds for visitors, it's still the first choice for locals, particularly for produce hard to find anywhere else. Beat your way past the crowds at the front for a taste of local life – preferably viewed from one of the market's various tapas bars.

18

Parc de la Ciutadella *p88*

The verdant Parc de la Ciutadella is the perfect combination of elegant landscaping and spaces intended for nothing but fun. There are playgrounds for little ones (including one for children with disabilities), a boating lake, a waterfall, zoo, picnic area, giant sculptures, statues and acres of grass for romping, juggling and bongo-playing. Be sure to visit its rose garden in spring.

19

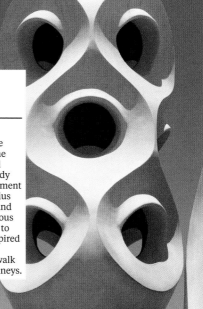

La Pedrera *p140*

'La Pedrera' means 'the stone quarry' and was originally the nickname used by a scornful public who weren't quite ready for Gaudí's undulating apartment block. More recently, its genius has been fully appreciated, and its interior given over to various exhibition spaces, the better to appreciate the maritime-inspired design. No visit is complete without a trip to the roof to walk among the warrior-like chimneys.

Casa Calvet p139

Sightseeing

The evocative beauty of Barcelona's Old City is so alluring that many visitors remain willing captives of its labyrinthine streets, entranced by the atmosphere and wealth of ancient buildings. It's a shame to miss out on the rest of the city, however, such as the Modernista glories of the Eixample, the hills of Montjuïc and Tibidabo, and the Forum district, which has arisen bright and bold from the ashes of a post-industrial wasteland. Barcelona emerged triumphantly from a crippling recession, with visitor numbers soaring, and many stalled municipal projects are finally seeing the light of day. What's more, plenty of existing museums and galleries have revamped their collections and undergone extensive overhauls, which means there's more to see than ever before.

Best for art enthusiasts
Fundació Joan Miró *p127*
MACBA *p104*
Museu Picasso *p90*

**Best for communing
with nature**
Parc de la Ciutadella *p88*
Parc del Laberint *p164*
Park Güell *p155*

Best for museum buffs
MUHBA *p75*
Museu Frederic Marès *p71*

Best for communing with God
Catedral de Barcelona *p73*
Sagrada Família *p142*
Santa Maria del Mar *p92*

Best for idle wandering
Barri Gòtic *p67*
Beaches *p116*
Montjuïc *p122*
La Rambla *p78*

Best for grown-up kids
Camp Nou Experience *p159*
Font Màgica *p122*
Tibidabo funfair *p161*

Best for little kids
CosmoCaixa *p161*
Museu de la Xocolata *p91*
Zoo *p91*

Best for escaping the crowds
Monestir de Pedralbes *p162*
Recinte Modernista de Sant Pau *p145*

Best views
Monument a Colom *p114*
Montjuïc *p122*

Gaudí and friends
Casa Batlló *p138*
Palau de la Música Catalana *p98*
Palau Güell *p107*
La Pedrera *p140*

The buildings of Barcelona

Barcelona's architectural history begins with the Roman citadel of Barcino, founded just behind the cathedral, which to this day remains the religious and civic heart of the city. Fragments of the fourth-century city wall are visible at many points around the Old City.

When the Catalan state began to form from the ninth century, its dominant architecture was Romanesque. The city's greatest Romanesque monument is the beautifully plain 12th-century church and cloister of Sant Pau del Camp (*see p103*). By the 13th century, commercial growth and political eminence set the scene for the great flowering of the Catalan Gothic style, which saw the construction of many of the city's most important civic and religious buildings. The cathedral was begun in 1298, in place of an 11th-century building, and work began on the Ajuntament (Casa de la Ciutat; *see p69*) and the Palau de la Generalitat (*see p72*). The Catalan Gothic style is clearly distinguished from classic northern Gothic by its relative simplicity. The classic example of this style is the beautiful Santa Maria del Pi in Plaça del Pi, built between 1322 and 1453. The magnificent masterpiece of Catalan Gothic, Santa Maria del Mar, was built between 1329 and 1384 in the commercial centre of the city, La Ribera.

In the 18th century, La Rambla was converted into a paved promenade. As the modern city expanded outwards, it was connected to Gràcia and other outlying towns by the Eixample (*see pp133-152*), designed by Ildefons Cerdà in the 1850s.

Between 1890 and 1914, the influence of art nouveau merged with the cultural and political movement of the Catalan Renaixença to produce what became known as Modernisme. For all Catalonia's traditions in building and the arts, no style is as synonymous with Barcelona as Modernisme, due its mix of decoration, eccentric unpredictability, dedicated craftsmanship and practicality. The Eixample is the style's display case, with the greatest concentration of art nouveau in Europe.

Casa Vicens *p22*

Gaudí and Modernisme

Meet Antoni Gaudí, devout Christian and visionary architect

Over the last century or so, the public images of architect Antoni Gaudí and the city of Barcelona have virtually blended into one. Crazy paving and splintered shards of tile, surrealist distortions marching across rooftops like injured golems, kaleidoscopic explosions of garish colour: the city has almost grown to be defined by the creations of its most famous architectural son. Gaudí's work has transformed Barcelona into a virtual pilgrimage site, with many visitors praying at the feet of the high priest of kitsch.

Although Gaudí is widely regarded as the genius of the Modernista movement, he was really an unclassifiable one-off. His work was a product of the social and cultural context of the time, but also of his individual perception of the world, together with a deep patriotic devotion to anything Catalan.

Gaudí first worked on the building of the Parc de la Ciutadella (*see p88*) under Josep Fontseré in the 1870s; the gates and fountain are attributed to him. His first major commission was for Casa Vicens in Gràcia, built between 1883 and 1888. An orientalist fantasy, Gaudí's use of surface material stands out in the neo-Moorish decoration, multicoloured tiling and superbly elaborate ironwork on the gates.

In 1878, Gaudí met Eusebi Güell, heir to one of the largest industrial fortunes in Catalonia, and Gaudí produced several buildings for Güell. Among them was Palau Güell (1886-88; *see p107*), an impressive, historicist building that established his reputation.

In 1883, Gaudí became involved in the design of the Sagrada Família (*see p142*), which had begun the previous year. From 1908 until his death in 1926, he worked on no other project. Gaudí was profoundly religious, and part of his obsession with the building came from a belief that it would help redeem Barcelona from the sins of secularism and the modern era.

In his greatest years, Gaudí combined other commissions with his cathedral. La Pedrera (*see p140*), which he began in 1905, was his most complete project. The building has an aquatic feel about it: the undulating façade is reminiscent of the sea. Casa Batlló (*see p138*) was an existing building that Gaudí remodelled in 1905-07; the roof looks like a reptilian creature perched high above the street. Gaudí's fascination with natural forms found full expression in the Park Güell (1900-14; *see p155*), for which he blurred the distinction between natural and artificial forms.

Casa Batlló

Edifici Fòrum *p165*

The most important buildings for the Universal Exhibition of 1888 were planned by Lluís Domènech i Montaner (1850-1923), and include the Castell dels Tres Dragons in the Parc de la Ciutadella. Domènech's greatest creations are the Hospital de la Santa Creu i Sant Pau (*see p145*), built as small 'pavilions' within a garden, and the Palau de la Música Catalana (*see p98*), an extraordinary display of outrageous decoration. Another leading Modernista architect was Josep Puig i Cadafalch (1867-1957), who combined traditional Catalan touches with a neo-Gothic influence in such buildings as the Casa de les Punxes ('House of Spikes') and his best-known work, the Casa Àmatller.

By the 1910s, Modernisme had become too extreme for Barcelona's middle classes; Gaudí's later buildings were met with derision. The new 'proper' style for Catalan architecture was Noucentisme, which stressed the importance of classical proportions. But it produced little of note: the main buildings that survive are those of the 1929 Exhibition, neo-Baroque Palau Nacional (now home to the MNAC).

The Franco years saw a massive influx of migrants, and the city became ringed by a chaotic mass of high-rise suburbs. When a democratic city administration took over at the end of the 1970s, there was much to be done. Limited budgets were initially concentrated not on buildings but on the gaps between them: public spaces, modern parks and squares. From this quiet beginning, Barcelona placed itself at the forefront of international urban design.

The 1992 Olympic Games were intended to be stylish and innovative, but they also provided a focus for a sweeping renovation of the city, with emblematic new buildings (such as Lord Foster's Torre de Collserola; *see p160*). Post-1992, the focus shifted to the Raval and the Port Vell ('Old Port'), then to the Diagonal Mar area in the north of the city.

Other contributions to post-Olympic Barcelona were Richard Meier's bold white MACBA (*see p104*) and Frank Gehry's Fish sculpture overlooking the beach. Many of Barcelona's most recent landmark buildings are five-star hotels, such as Ricardo Bofill's W Hotel.

Since that period, the rate of growth and the proliferation of new projects has been rapid, slowed only by the global recession. In recent years a slew of new openings has included municipal projects, such as the Born Centre de Cultura i Memòria (*see p89*) and the long-awaited Museu del Disseny (*see p166*), as well as quirky attractions such as the Hemp Museum (*see p71*) and the kitsch-but-fun Gaudí Experiència (*see p154*).

In addition to the newcomers, several of the city's most iconic buildings have opened or are about to open to the public for the first time; these include Gaudí's Bellesguard (*see p163*), and Puig i Cadafalch's Casa de les Punxes (*see p137*).

Fideuà

Eating & Drinking

Barcelona's dining scene has proved itself remarkably resilient to recession, and while most other sectors have struggled through the last decade, the city's restaurants have thrived, increased in number and expanded in scope – although it's as difficult as it ever was to bag an unreserved table at a good restaurant on a Friday night. Bars and cafés also seem to be weathering the crisis, with few closures and no perceptible slowdown in business. This is partly explained by local habits; Catalans tend not to entertain at home, so the bar is as crucial a meeting place as ever, while restaurants are kept afloat by the continuing brisk trade in lunchtime *menús del día* for the workers – the sandwich habit has never really caught on in Spain.

Best dinner dates
Bangkok Café *p159*
Gresca *p150*

Best for an afternoon tipple
Balius *p166*
Bodega Quimet *p156*

Best brunch or lunch
Caravelle *p105*
Granja Petitbó *p144*
La Panxa del Bisbe *p156*

Best snack stop
La Boqueria *p81*
Escribà *p151*
Gelateria Caffetteria Italiana *p156*

Best seafood
Can Majó *p117*
Kaiku *p118*

Best bars
Casa Almirall *p108*
Dry Martini *p150*
Garage Beer Co *p150*
Paradiso *p95*

Best cakes and pastries
Cafè de l'Opera *p77*
Federal *p130*

Best food with a view
1881 *p118*
Agua *p117*

Catalan cuisine

Catalan cooking is defined by certain characteristics, such as the *sofregit* and *picada* (*see p29*) that form the base for so many dishes. The former is the foundation for soups, stews, rice and noodle dishes, and for most traditional sauces; it's the first thing in the pot. The latter gets stirred in a few minutes before the dish in question has finished cooking, and fills in all the gaps in flavour and texture. The Catalans also mix fruit with meat or fowl: duck or goose with pears, and apples stuffed with minced pork are specialities of the Empordà region of Catalonia, and *allioli* thickened with puréed apple or quince is a common accompaniment to roast rabbit or pork in the Pyrenees. Local cooks also combine seafood and poultry and/or meat in the class of dishes called *mar i muntanya*, or 'sea and mountain'.

Drink up

After the welcome comeback of Moritz beer, brewed in Barcelona and preferred by many to the ubiquitous

Estrella, came an explosion in craft beers, now widely
available everywhere and no longer confined to tap rooms
such as **Garage** (*see p150*).

Catalan wines are becoming better known
internationally as they improve, and it's worth looking
out for the local DOs, as well as the commonplace
Penedès. Most wine drunk here is red (*negre/tinto*), apart
from the many cavas, which run from *semi-sec* ('half-
dry', but actually pretty sweet) to *brut nature* (very dry).
Freixenet is the best known, but there are better cavas,
including Parxet and Llopart.

Coffee in Barcelona is mostly strong and mostly good.
The three basic types are *solo* (also known simply as *café*),
a small strong black coffee; *cortado*, the same but with a
little milk; and *café con leche*, the same with more milk.
An *americano* is black coffee diluted with more water,
and *carajillo* is a short, black coffee with a liberal dash of
brandy. Decaffeinated coffee (*descafeinado*) is popular
and widely available, but specify *de máquina* (from the
machine) unless you want instant (*de sobre*).

Crema catalana and other sweet treats

Tea is pretty poor and generally best avoided. If you can't live without it, ask for cold milk on the side ('*leche fría aparte*') or run the risk of getting a glass of hot milk and a teabag.

Tapas tips

Tapas are not especially popular in Barcelona, though there are some excellent options, including **Tapas 24** (*see p144*) and **Quimet i Quimet** (*see p131*). The custom of giving a free tapa with a drink is almost unheard of in Catalonia.

Slightly different from the archetypal Spanish tapas bars are *pintxo* bars – their Basque origin means that the word is always given in Euskera – such as **Euskal Etxea** (*see p95*). A *pintxo* (be careful not to confuse it with the Spanish term *pincho*, which refers to a very small tapa) consists of some ingenious culinary combination on a small slice of bread. Platters of them are usually brought out at particular times, often around 1pm and again at 8pm. *Pintxos* come impaled on toothpicks, which you keep on your plate so that the barman can tally them up at the end.

> **In the know**
> **A lot of bottle**
>
> Tap water is perfectly safe but quite heavily chlorinated in Barcelona (despite recent improvements), so most people drink bottled.

Catalan Dishes

A primer of local cuisine

Here is a selection of dishes considered to be classically Catalan. It's also worth noting that many dishes apparently from other cuisines – risotto, canelloni, ravioli – are entrenched in the Catalan culinary tradition. Two names borrowed from the French are *foie* (as opposed to *fetge*/*hígado* or foie gras), which has come to mean hare, duck or goose liver *mi-cuit* with liqueur, salt and sugar; and *coulant*, like a small soufflé but melting in the centre.

a la llauna 'in the tin' – baked on a metal tray with garlic, tomato, paprika and wine

allioli garlic crushed with olive oil to form a mayonnaise-like texture, similar to *aïoli*

amanida catalana/*ensalada catalana* mixed salad with a range of cold meats

arròs negre/*arroz negro* 'black rice', seafood rice cooked in squid ink

botifarra/*butifarra* Catalan sausage; variants include *botifarra negre* (blood sausage) and *blanca* (mixed with egg)

botifarra amb mongetes/*butifarra con judías* sausage with haricot beans

calçots variety of large spring onion, only available from December to spring, and eaten chargrilled with *romesco* sauce

carn d'olla traditional Christmas dish of various meats stewed with *escudella*, then served separately

conill amb cargols/*conejo con caracoles* rabbit with snails

crema catalana cold custardy dessert with burned sugar topping, similar to crème brûlée

escalivada grilled and peeled peppers, onions and aubergine

escudella winter stew of meat and vegetables

espinacs a la catalana/*espinacas a la catalana* spinach fried in olive oil with garlic, raisins and pine nuts

esqueixada summer salad of shredded, marinated salt cod with onions, olives and tomato

fideuà/*fideuá* paella made with vermicelli instead of rice

mar i muntanya a traditional Catalan combination of meat and seafood, such as lobster and chicken in the same dish

mel i mató curd cheese with honey

pa amb tomàquet/*pan con tomate* bread with tomato, oil and salt

picada mix of nuts, garlic, parsley, bread, chocolate and little chilli peppers, often used to enrich and thicken dishes

romesco a spicy sauce from the coast south of Barcelona, made with crushed almonds and hazelnuts, tomatoes, oil and a special type of red pepper called *nyora*

samfaina a mix of onion, garlic, aubergine and red and green peppers (similar to ratatouille)

sarsuela/*zarzuela* fish and seafood stew

sofregit a base for many sauces, made with caramelised onion, tomato and olive oil, occasionally with sugar

Order, order

Kitchens usually open for lunch around 1.30pm or 2pm and go on until roughly 3.30pm or 4pm; dinner is served from about 9pm until 11.30pm or midnight. Some restaurants open earlier in the evening, but arriving before 9.30pm or 10pm generally means you'll be dining alone or in the company of other foreigners. Reserving a table is generally a good idea – not only on Friday and Saturday nights, but also on Sunday evenings and Monday lunchtimes, when few restaurants are open. Many also close for holidays, including about a week over Easter, and the month of August.

Pintxo

The price is right

For US and UK visitors particularly, eating out in Barcelona is not as cheap as it used to be, but low mark-ups on wines keep the cost relatively reasonable. The majority of restaurants serve an economical, fixed-price *menú del día* at lunchtime; this usually consists of a starter, main course, dessert, bread and something to drink.

Laws governing the issue of prices are often flouted, but, legally, menus must declare if the ten per cent IVA (VAT) is included in prices or not (it rarely is), and also if there is a cover charge (generally expressed as a charge for bread).

In the know
Tipping tips

Catalans, and the Spanish in general, tend to tip very little, often rounding up to the nearest euro, but tourists should let their conscience decide.

Shopping

As is the case in most other major cities around the world, the high-street chains grow ever more ubiquitous in Barcelona. However, although the credit crunch has picked off many small start-ups, plenty of alternatives remain. Barcelona is still known for its old specialist shops, many of which have been family-run for generations; there's nowhere better to browse for just the right votive candle or handmade soap. Fashion is another strong point: head up Passeig de Gràcia and beyond to the Avinguda Diagonal for high fashion and couture, or trawl the Born, the Raval and Gràcia for an ever-changing line-up of local designers selling from hole-in-the-wall shops.

❤ Shortlist

Best markets
La Boqueria p81
Els Encants p146

Best for kids
Arlequí Màscares p96
El Ingenio p82

Best for a new wardrobe
Holala! Plaza + Gallery p109
Med Winds p109
Santa Eulàlia p147

Best shoes & accessories
Alonso p80
La Manual Alpargatera p82

Best wine shop
Torres p110
Vila Viniteca p97

Best foodie shop
Casa Gispert p96
Escribà p151
Formatgeria La Seu p82

Survival mode

Strolling down the golden retail belts of Portal de l'Angel, Rambla de Catalunya or Passeig de Gràcia, you would never know there's been a recession, and indeed new designers regularly set up shop here. Down the side streets, however, owners of small shops have had to adapt to survive, with food and wine shops such as **Formatgeria La Seu** and **Vila Viniteca** holding regular tastings or taking part in food markets. Small designers have sought safety in numbers, forming collectives and making their clothes in workshops attached to the storefront. Vintage stores are also growing steadily in popularity, particularly in the Raval and Gràcia, with many stocking repurposed garments on the side.

Large malls continue to thrive and multiply: the latest is the Richard Rogers-designed **Las Arenas**, constructed from the former bullring on Plaça Espanya.

Small is beautiful

It is Barcelona's wealth of tiny independent shops that really makes it unique as a shopping destination. Look out for the dressmakers and one-off fashion boutiques in the Born; the indie art galleries of the upper Raval;

Las Arenas

the traditional artisans, antique shops and speciality food stores of the Barri Gòtic; and the quirky jewellery workshops and vintage clothes shops of Gràcia. These shops are also among the most photogenic in the city, often holding treasures such as the old toasting ovens at **Casa Gispert** or the medieval Jewish baths at **Caelum** (*see p80*).

Market forces

In the Ajuntament's book, a revamped local market is the first step on the road to urban regeneration. The latest is the stunning new designer home for the **Els Encants** flea market (*see p146*). In an attempt to fuse

In the know
Out-of-town outlets

Designer bargain-hunters should make the half-hour pilgrimage out the city to La Roca Village (93 842 39 39, www.larocavillage.com). More than 50 discount outlets will tempt you with designer apparel from brands such as Missoni, Versace, Diesel and Armani.

modern and traditional approaches to shopping, the new markets tend to hold far fewer actual stalls than before, with more space turned over to supermarkets and restaurants.

Good, and regular, flea markets include **Lost & Found** (www.lostfoundmarket.com), which is usually held at the beach, and **Flea Market Barcelona** (www.fleamarketbcn.com), which normally happens in the Raval – check the websites for details and dates. C/Riera Baixa in the northern part of the Raval is a short strip of vintage clothes shops, and you'll find several others in this area.

Shopping practicalities

Most shops don't open until 10am and close for lunch from 2pm; after lunch, they're usually open from 5pm until about 8pm. Many small shops also close on Saturday afternoons and all day on Monday. Note that if you're paying by credit card, you usually have to show photo ID, such as a passport or a driving licence.

The rate of sales tax (IVA) depends on the type of product: it's currently ten per cent on food and 21 per cent on most other items. In any of the 700 or so shops that display a Tax-Free Shopping sticker on their door, non-EU residents can request a Tax-Free Cheque on purchases of more than €90.15 (see www.aena-aeropuertos.es or www.global-blue.com for further information). Before leaving the EU, these must be stamped at customs and can immediately be reclaimed in cash at the airport branches of La Caixa bank or Global Blue (or from refund offices in your home country).

Bargain hunters should note that the sales (*rebaixes/rebajas*) begin after the retail orgy of Christmas and Epiphany, running from 7 January to mid February, and return during July and August.

Where to shop

Barri Gòtic

The Saturday afternoon hordes head to the big-name chain stores that line Avinguda Portal de l'Àngel and C/Portaferrissa, but there are plenty of less mainstream retail options. It's possible to spend hours browsing antiques on C/Banys Nous, where tiny shops specialise in furniture, posters or textiles. The streets around Plaça Sant Jaume house some lovely, old-fashioned stores selling hats, candles, traditional toys and stationery. For something more modern, try the independent boutiques on C/Avinyó, which offer affordable, streetwise fashion and household items with a twist.

Born and Sant Pere

The streets leading off the Passeig del Born form a warren of stylish little boutiques offering quality, rather than quantity. Nearby C/Argenteria was

In the know
Museum finds

Museum shops are some of the best places to find great presents, or books on art, design and architecture. In particular, try the MACBA (see p104), CaixaForum (see p122) and Museu d'Història de Barcelona (see p75).

named after its denizen silversmiths, and a handful of shops there follow the tradition, selling affordable, if mainstream, trinkets.

Raval

The Raval's shopping, concentrated on the streets between the Boqueria market and Plaça dels Àngels, has a youthful bent: head to C/Riera Baixa and C/Tallers for second-hand clothing and streetwear, and C/Bonsuccès for specialist record shops. C/Doctor Dou and C/Elisabets feature some trendy boutiques and shoe shops; the latter also has a couple of design stores. C/Pelai, along the Raval's top edge, has an impressive number of shoe stores.

Barceloneta and the Ports

Barcelona's seafront shopping is concentrated in the shopping centre of Maremagnum, which houses a large, if sterile, collection of high-street fashion stores that are at least open late.

Eixample

Passeig de Gràcia is home to enough high-fashion and statement jewellery to satisfy a footballer's wife. Chanel, Dior, Stella McCartney and friends are present and correct, as are many Spanish luxury brands. A stone's throw away, the tree-lined Rambla de Catalunya offers high-street fashion and cute kids' boutiques.

Gràcia and other districts

Independent shops rule in bohemian Gràcia: head to C/Verdi or the streets around Plaça Vila de Gràcia and – increasingly – the streets north of here, for quirky little boutiques selling clothing, accessories and gifts.

In the know
Bargain fashion

One of Barcelona's hotspots for bargain clothes shopping is C/Girona. In particular, the two blocks between C/Ausiàs Marc and Gran Via de les Corts Catalanes are crammed with remainder stores and factory outlets of varying quality. By far the most popular is Mango Outlet (C/Girona 37, 93 412 29 35).

Entertainment

Barcelona has a remarkable cultural heritage, and it has performance venues to match. The Gran Teatre del Liceu, and two more of the city's most venerable institutions – the Auditori concert hall and the century-old Palau de la Música Catalana – continue to attract audiences with increasingly eclectic programming.

Barcelona makes no claims to be a party capital, despite a somewhat unwarranted reputation as such. Yet its nightlife is diverse, and there's an energy and creativity to it that isn't found anywhere else. It also has a thriving gay scene to suit all tastes.

♥ Shortlist

Best places to party
Arena *p148*
Heliogabal *p158*
La Terrrazza *p132*

Best for indie flicks
Cinema Maldà *p83*
Cinemes Méliès *p152*

Best for a bit of glam
CDLC *p120*
Mirablau *p161*
La Terrrazza *p132*

Best classical music venues
L'Auditori *p148*
Gran Teatre del Liceu *p83*
Palau de la Música Catalana *p98*

Best for intimate gigs
Harlem Jazz Club *p84*
Jazz Sí Club *p110*
El Paraigua *p84*

Best dance venues
Mercat de les Flors *p132*
Teatre Nacional de Catalunya *p149*

Best for big-time bands
BARTS *p131*
City Hall *p149*
Razzmatazz *p166*

Best for a late drink
Bar Pastís *p110*
Dry Martini *p150*
Paradiso *p95*

Film

The city provides a popular backdrop for filmmakers of all stripes, most memorably, perhaps, for Woody Allen's *Vicky Cristina Barcelona*, while a rather grittier portrayal of Barcelona was on view in Alejandro González Iñárritu's *Biutiful*. The key figure in Spanish cinema continues to be Pedro Almodóvar, whose films invariably shoot to the top of the charts.

Film release dates vary widely in the city. Blockbusters are usually released more or less simultaneously worldwide, but smaller productions can take up to three years to arrive at cinemas, long after they're available to stream or out on DVD. The dubbing of films into Catalan often plays a part in delays. Subtitled (as opposed to dubbed) films are marked VO or VOSE (for '*versió original subtitulada en espanyol*'). Subtitled indie flicks are also shown at occasional

In the know
Cheap flicks

Almost all cinemas have a discount night (the *dia de l'espectador*). In most cinemas it's Monday, but occasionally it's Wednesday.

outdoor cinema events, such as the **Sala Montjuïc** (www. salamontjuic.com) or Gandules in the patio of the **CCCB** (*see p103*), in the summer.

Classical music and opera

Although the canon still reigns at the **Gran Teatre del Liceu** (*see p83*), contemporary productions, local works and some adventurous formats add a bit of risk to its classical repertoire. The Conservatori – the prestigious music school attached to the Liceu – offers its own programme of recitals and contemporary compositions in a subterranean auditorium. The Liceu also stages a different opera every three or four weeks.

The main musical season runs from September to June. During this time, the city orchestra, the Orquestra Simfònica de Barcelona (OBC), plays weekly at the **Auditori** (*see p148*), which also regularly hosts resident contemporary orchestra BCN 216.

From June to August, many concerts take place outdoors. **Música als Parcs** is a programme of some 50 evening concerts hosted in a number of parks across the city. Additionally, various museums hold occasional small outdoor concerts, including the **Fundació Joan Miró** (*see p127*) and the **CaixaForum** (*see p122*).

L'Auditori

MOZART

TEATRE DEL LICEU

Performing arts

Today, most theatre is in Catalan, although Spanish-language productions tour, and **Teatre Lliure** (*see p132*) offers surtitles in English for major productions. Other major performing art venues include the **Teatre Nacional** (*see p149*), for large-scale pieces by big names, and the **Mercat de les Flors** (*see p132*), with plenty of offbeat, kookier and experimental performances.

In the world of dance, the Compañía Nacional de Danza, directed by José Carlos Martínez (cndanza.mcu.es), fills grand venues such as the Teatre Nacional. Companies such as Sol Picó and Erre que Erre usually put on a new show every year, as do Mudances and Gelabert-Azzopardi.

Main shows start around 9 to 10pm. On Sundays, there are morning matinées aimed at families and earlier evening shows at around 5 to 6.30pm. The **Grec Festival** (*see p56*) attracts major international acts in theatre and dance.

Nightlife

In Barcelona, there's no lack of opportunities for after-dark indulgence. There are superclubs hosting superstar DJs and tiny venues playing the latest electro. There are lounge clubs and gilded ballrooms, *salsatecas* and Brazilian samba bars. The thriving gay scene may be confined to the part of the Eixample known as the 'Gaixample', but it is bolstered by clubs in other parts of the city that are friendly to every sexual and gender orientation.

> **In the know**
> **Performance information**
>
> For performance information, try *Guía del Ocio, Time Out Barcelona* magazine and the *cartelera* (listings) pages of the newspapers. Online, check www.teatral.net and www.butxaca.com; for dance, try www.dansacat.org. You can also visit Canal Cultura at www.bcn.cat/cultura.

Primavera Sound p55

Going out happens late here, with people rarely meeting for a drink much before 11pm – if they do, it's a pre-dinner thing. Bars tend to close around 2am, or 3am at weekends, and it's only after this that the clubs get going, so many offer reduced entrance fees or free drinks to those willing to be seen inside before 1am.

Traditionally, you had to head uptown to hit the posh clubs, but the Port Olímpic is putting on some serious competition with places such as **CDLC** (*see p120*) luring the *pijos* (well-groomed uptowners) downtown. There are also nightly beach parties running up and down the coast from Bogatell to Mataró through the summer. Meanwhile, you'll find smaller venues pulsating with life in the Barri Gòtic, particularly around the Plaça Reial and C/Escudellers. Across La Rambla, in the Raval, you can skulk in the grittier,

In the know
Tickets please

You can get concert information and tickets from telendrada.com, www.ticketmaster.com and www.fnac.com. Specialist record shops, such as those on C/Tallers in the Raval, are good for info and flyers.

Vermouth Sundays

And on the seventh day they danced

Leave the dirty cocktails, mead and single-origin double espresso to Hoxton and Williamsburg – the hipster tipple of choice in Barcelona is vermouth. Served with ice and a slice, along with a green olive and a quick squirt of soda, it is to brunch what the Bloody Mary once was.

Many bar owners and festival organisers have been quick to jump on the trend, but none with more aplomb than Esther and Patricia, the girls behind **Ven Tú!** (ventubcn.es; loosely translated as 'Why don't you come?'), the regular event that has made Sunday the new Saturday.

Its humble beginnings were in a modest square in the Raval a few years ago. Litres of *vermút* were aligned on a trestle table, a couple of local bands got up to play, children and dogs ran amok, and the general mood was a buoyant one. Since then, it has morphed into the hipster event par excellence, but has remained refreshingly inclusive

and unpretentious for all that. The musical programming ranges from fun to excellent, and these days you can get a plate of paella when the deceptively drinkable *vermút* begins to hit. The venue changes almost every time (see the website for details), and in the winter months the event takes place indoors. There's been a gradual shift from scruffy Raval bars to bigger, more established venues, such as **Sala Apolo** (see p132), **City Hall** (see p149) or concert hall **BARTS** (see p131). The party usually kicks off around midday. In theory, it's supposed to end at around 8pm. In reality, it carries on until the last punter drops (or leaves for work on Monday morning).

There's rarely an entry fee, and food and drink goes for bargain prices – all you'll need are your Ray-Bans, a buttoned-to-the-neck shirt, a fedora if you've got one, and some dancing shoes.

grungier places. If street beers, dogs and vintage sweaters are your thing, Gràcia is heaven.

Among Barcelona's live music venues for seeing international names (as well as hotly tipped unknowns and locals) are the multi-faceted **Razzmatazz** (*see p166*), and the old dancehall **Sala Apolo** (*see p132*). The first hosts both cutting-edge live and electronic music, while the latter specialises in feel-happy DJs and special theme nights. The city also hosts two big music festivals: **Sónar** in June for fans of electronica (*see p55*), and **Primavera Sound** in May (*see p55*).

LGBT Barcelona

The gay scene – *el ambiente* in Spanish – is mostly limited to a small and otherwise unremarkable area in the Eixample. Bordered by the streets Diputació, Villarroel, Aragó and Balmes, it's delightfully if dizzily called the **Gaixample**.

Most of the city's nightlife is pretty mixed however, and there's a lot of fun to be had off the official scene. The summer's fiestas at shacks on gay-friendly **Mar Bella** beach are a fine example of minimum advertising, maximum raving.

Check local press for the latest on gay club nights held in otherwise straight clubs, such as 'The Black Room' at **City Hall** (*see p149*) on Saturdays, which has funky house downstairs and a darkroom upstairs.

You'll find lesbians in some of the spots favoured by gay men, such as **Arena** (*see p148*) or **Metro** (*see p152*). The second *xiringuito* on Mar Bella beach functions as a lesbian meeting place – at its liveliest on Sunday evenings.

> **In the know**
> **Gay festivals**
>
> For Carnaval in February, head to Sitges, but Barcelona's gay scene takes over in summer. At the end of June, Gay Pride (www.pridebarcelona.org), with parades and concerts, usually centres on the Plaça Universitat.

Barcelona Day by Day

46   Itineraries
53   Diary

Itineraries

Whether you're here for a quick weekend break or planning a leisurely sojourn, you're spoilt for choice in Barcelona. To make the most of the time you have, whatever your budget, use these itineraries as a guide.

Don't be surprised if your carefully hatched plans go to pot, as time runs away from you while you mooch through the Gothic Quarter, laze away hours at the beach or soak in the views atop Montjuïc.

Remember to factor in refreshment stops – pop into a tapas bar or grab a quick drink at a table on the street to people-watch as you rest.

► *Budgets include transport, meals and admission prices, but not accommodation or shopping.*

ESSENTIAL WEEKEND

Budget €350 for two
Getting around Walking, metro, bus, taxi

DAY 1

Morning

Start the day with a quiet stroll down La Rambla, the city's most famous boulevard, before the crowds, the living statues and the pickpockets arrive. Halfway along, duck into **Cafè de l'Òpera** (*see p77*) for coffee and a breakfast *ensaïmada*, a spiral of flaky pastry dusted with icing sugar.

Another couple of hundred yards or so down La Rambla, heading towards the sea, you'll see the **Plaça Reial** off to your left. Turn in to admire its elaborate lamp posts, an early council commission for Gaudí; then, exiting from its northern side, head right along C/Ferran to the grand **Plaça Sant Jaume**, skirting round the back of the Generalitat to the **Cathedral** (*see p73*). Take time to mooch around its magnificent cloister and take the lift up to the roof for a great view of the city. Come out of the Cathedral and head east, crossing the Via Laietana to the **Palau de la Música** (*see p98*). Take a guided tour or simply marvel at the fantastical Modernista façade.

Afternoon

Having worked up an appetite, head down into the Born proper (with a quick look at the roof of the **Mercat de Santa Caterina** en route and tuck into some tapas outside the majestic **Santa Maria del Mar** at **La Vinya del Senyor** wine bar (*see p95*). It's a skip and a hop to the **Museu Picasso** (*see p90*), an easy place to while away a couple of hours.

After this, wander down to the **Port Vell** (*see p113*). For the best view over the harbour, go up to the rooftop café of the **Museu d'Història de Catalunya** (*see p114*), where you can sip an early-evening beer before heading up Passeig Joan de Borbó to the seafront.

Evening

In this part of town there are several excellent seafood restaurants: try **Can Majó** (*see p117*) or **Kaiku** (*see p118*). And if you can't bear to go home afterwards, you could always join the glossy crowd for a late-night cocktail at fashionable **CDLC** (*see p120*), on the fringe of the beach.

La Rambla

DAY 2

Morning

To start a day of Modernisme, Barcelona's answer to art nouveau, have coffee and a pastry at La Rambla's branch of the **Escribà** patisserie (*see p151*), with its tiled façade, delicate stucco and wrought iron. From here, walk up to **Plaça Catalunya** and continue straight ahead for the elegant **Passeig de Gràcia**, a showcase for all things Modernista. Note the Gaudí-designed hexagonal paving tiles, along with Pere Falqués' elegant wrought-iron lamp posts. Unless you get sucked into some of the street's blend of swanky boutiques and major chains, it's a five-minute walk to the contrasting masterpieces of the **Manzana de la Discòrdia** (*see p136*). This block houses three extraordinary buildings designed by the holy trinity of Modernisme: Gaudí, Domènech i Montaner and Puig i Cadafalch. Another five minutes further up is Gaudí's **La Pedrera** (*see p140*). Backtrack to the **Casa Batlló** and then take a metro to Gaudí's most famous work, the spectacular **Sagrada Família** (*see p142*). While all of these buildings are now open

to the public, entrance fees are high and queues are long, but the façades alone merit a visit.

Afternoon

Time for lunch. While the Sagrada Família area is strangely bereft of decent restaurants, the adjacent **Avda Gaudí** has several spots with outdoor terraces at which to grab a *bocadillo* and a beer. Post lunch, continue along the avenue for the extravagant **Recinte Modernista de Sant Pau** (*see p145*), an unsung Modernista tour de force by Domènech i Montaner, than take bus H6 from the northwest corner to Gaudí's unmissable **Park Güell** (*see p155*).

Evening

Sticking with the Modernista theme, the deep-of-pocket will love dinner at **Casa Calvet** (*see p139*), a great, if pricey, restaurant set in a Gaudí-designed townhouse. Otherwise, head back to the many restaurants along the **Passeig de Gràcia**. Both are a cab ride from Park Güell; and you're then well placed for other nightlife options if you're not yet ready for bed …

Casa Calvet

BUDGET BREAK

Budget €90 for two
Getting around Walking

Morning

Els Quatre Gats (*see p76*) may not have the cheapest coffee in town, but it is a great way for some sedentary sightseeing over breakfast. Set in Puig i Cadafalch's Modernista Casa Martí, it was a stamping ground for Picasso, Gaudí and other luminaries of the period. From here it's a short walk to the **Cathedral** (*see p73*), the church and cloister of which are free to enter until 12.45pm. Behind the cathedral is the **Temple d'August** (*see p72*, free to enter), where you can see four soaring Corinthian columns of the Roman temple that once stood here.

Afternoon

Back in the direction of Els Quatre Gats is **Mercè Vins** (*see p76*), a little pocket of Catalan authenticity, with a great-value set lunch for €12. After this, walk up to **Plaça Catalunya**, beyond which begins the **Passeig de Gràcia**, a long boulevard of grand designs and flagship shops. Many of the greatest Modernista buildings are along here, and although punitively expensive to enter, are almost as rewarding to look at from outside. Look out for Gaudí's **La Pedrera** (*see p140*) and **Casa Batlló** (*see p138*), as well as the **Casa Àmatller** (*see p137*) and the **Casa Lleó Morera** (*see p136*). Take any street off to the left and you'll hit the leafy Rambla de Catalunya, its pedestrian section a long line of café terraces. Try **La Bodegueta** (*see p141*) for a pick-me-up.

Evening

Wander back down to Plaça Catalunya, and **La Rambla** (*see p78*), and just down on the right is the **Palau de la Virreina** (*see p72*), which often has free exhibitions. Just beyond it is **La Boqueria** market (*see p81*). One of Barcelona's great attractions in its own right, it's a riot of colour, smells and noise. Continue down La Rambla until you meet C/ Ferran, and head left for dinner at **Can Culleretes** (*see p74*), for good food at bargain prices in an unbeatable location.

Casa Milà (La Pedrera)

49

FAMILY DAY OUT

Budget €220 for two adults, two children
Getting around Walking, bus, funicular

Morning

Those with very young kids should start the morning at **La Marelle** (C/Mendez Nuñez 4, 93 007 1295), a bright, multilingual 'kids' café' with toys and games on the edge of the Born. With older kids, head round the corner to the **Plaça Sant Pere** where there are plenty of places for breakfast in the sunshine.

From here it's a five- or ten-minute walk to the verdant **Parc de la Ciutadella**, a great place to spend a morning, with a decent-sized zoo (*see p91*), a boating lake, outdoor cafés, various playgrounds and some superb climbing trees.

Afternoon

Backtrack slightly to the **Bar del Convent** (*see p94*) for a light lunch. It's a lively café with toys for tiny tots and tables outside in the former cloister, an enclosed space big enough for a run around. The building next door houses the

Museu de la Xocolata (*see p91*), an enjoyable stroll through the history of chocolate, ending with a display of the enormous chocolate sculptures that traditionally form part of a Catalan Easter. End in the café, where you can revive flagging energy levels with steaming mugs of the brown stuff.

Evening

Back on Passeig Picasso, catch the H14 bus to its final stop on Avda Paral·lel and from there take the funicular railway up the hill of **Montjuïc**. At the top you could take a cable car to the castle (*see p129*) or wander over to the **Fundació Joan Miró** (*see p127*), always a hit with kids for the bold use of colour and surrealism. Afterwards follow the signs for the **MNAC** (*see p126*), below which sits the **Magic Fountain** (*see p122*), a fabulously kitsch display of music and colour. It's easy to get back into town from the nearby transport hub of Plaça Espanya.

Parc de la Ciutadella

IN PICASSO'S FOOTSTEPS

Budget €120 for two
Getting around Walking

Morning

Start at one of the many café terraces of the **Pla del Palau** in the Born. Picasso and his family moved here in 1895, to C/Reina Cristina 3. Just over the road is **La Llotja** (*see p90*), which then housed an art school where Picasso studied.

From here, cross Via Laietana to **C/Mercè 3**, the next Picasso family home, now destroyed. This area was an insalubrious red-light district and later inspired his masterpiece, *Les Demoiselles D'Avignon* (1907). Continue along C/Mercè and cross La Rambla to the site of Picasso's bedsit-studio at **C/Nou de la Rambla 10**, opposite Gaudí's Palau Güell. Some have suggested that the bright colours and fragmented mosaics of the terrace chimneys might have sown the seeds of Picasso's cubism.

Back on La Rambla, walk up and right on C/Cardenal Casañas and then left at C/Petritxol. The **Sala Parès** gallery (*see p82*) was a meeting point for the fin-de-siècle set of Barcelona and also exhibited the work of the young Picasso in 1901.

Afternoon

From the gallery it's a short walk to the most famous symbol of Picasso's days in Barcelona: **Els Quatre Gats** (*see p76*). It's no gastro temple but has a decent set lunch for €14. After lunch, head back down **Portal de l'Àngel**; on the corner of Plaça Nova, opposite the Cathedral, is the **Col·legi d'Arquitectes**. Its façade is decorated with a graffiti-style triptych of Catalan folk scenes, from a design drawn by Picasso while in exile in the 1950s. After this, head over to the Born for an afternoon at the **Museu Picasso** (*see p90*).

Evening

Take an early evening stroll down C/Princesa to the entrance of the **Parc de la Ciutadella** (*see p88*). Turn right before the gates and halfway along Passeig Picasso stands Antoni Tàpies' *Homage to Picasso* (1981). Turning back to the Born, you'll find a wealth of dining options on the **Plaça Comercial**.

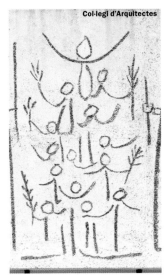

Col·legi d'Arquitectes

TimeOut

EXPLORING THE WORLD'S FAVOURITE CITIES SINCE 1968...

WHERE NEXT?

Setmana Santa

Diary

The Catalans' seemingly endless enthusiasm for festivals means that whenever you visit, there's likely to be at least a couple of events happening in the city. These range from the full-on traditional knees-up, with giants, dwarfs and dragons wheeling through fireworks, to gentle street fairs, graffiti art exhibitions and the renowned music and technology festival Sónar, which attracts some 80,000 people each year. Information and exact dates can be found nearer the time from the festivals section at lameva.barcelona.cat/culturapopular.

Spring

Barcelona's high season starts earlier and earlier, and by Easter, hotels have seen their prices rise and their rooms fill. The weather can be changeable around this time of year, and most rain will fall in March and April, although showers tend not to last too long. Watch out for the feast day of **Sant Jordi** at the end of April when red roses decorate the city's many statues and paintings of George in all his dragon-slaying glory. The increasingly popular **Primavera Sound** happens at the end of May

3 Mar Festes de Sant Medir de Gràcia

www.santmedir.org
People driving horse-drawn carts through Gràcia shower the crowds with sweets.

Late Mar Kosmopolis

kosmopolis.cccb.org
Three-day festival of literature held at the CCCB (see *p103*).

Late Mar/Apr Setmana Santa (Holy Week)

Palm fronds are blessed at the cathedral on Palm Sunday. On Good Friday, a series of small processions and blessings takes place in front of the cathedral. Children receive elaborate chocolate creations on Easter Sunday.

Mid April Fira de la Terra

Festival celebrating St Anthony's day in Sant Antoni.

23 Apr Sant Jordi

Feast day of Sant Jordi (St George), the patron saint of Catalonia. Couples exchange gifts of red roses and books.

Late Apr/early May Feria de Abril de Catalunya

Week-long satellite of Seville's famous fair, with decorated marquees, flamenco and manzanilla sherry in the Fòrum area.

1 May Dia del Treball (May Day)

A day of demonstrations and trade union-led marches takes place across the city.

11 May Fira de Sant Ponç

Street market on C/Hospital, in the Raval, of herbs, honey and candied fruit to celebrate the patron saint of beekeepers and herbalists.

Mid May Barcelona Poesia & Festival Internacional de Poesia

lameva.barcelona.cat/barcelonapoesia
Week-long city-wide poetry festival, with readings in English.

Mid May Festa Major de Nou Barris

lameva.barcelona.cat/noubarris
Nou Barris' neighbourhood festival, famous for flamenco.

Mid May Ciutat Flamenco

ciutatflamenco.com
A four-day flamenco festival at the CCCB (see pxxx), with concerts, films and activities for children.

18 May Dia Internacional dels Museus

icom.museum/activities/international-museum-day
Free entrance to the city's museums during the daytime.

Mid May Nit dels Museus

lameva.barcelona.cat/lanitdelsmuseus
Museums open late – and they're free.

Festa Major de Gràcia

❤ Late May Primavera Sound
www.primaverasound.com
Four-day big-name music festival held in the Parc del Fòrum. Tickets sell out quickly and are not cheap, but the first day is free to all, and the organisers put on free concerts around the city over the same period.

Late May Segona Pasqua (Whitsun) & Festa dels Cors de la Barceloneta
Choirs sing and parade on Saturday morning and Monday afternoon in Barceloneta over Whitsun weekend.

Summer
Barcelona does not normally get as hot as, for example, Madrid, but it is humid in summer, which can be debilitating. July and August are busy times for tourists, but the streets are notably free of traffic, since Catalans melt away to their families' second homes after **Sant Joan** to recover from several weeks of nighttime festivities.

June-Aug Música als Parcs
ajuntament.barcelona.cat/ ecologiaurbana
Free alfresco music in Barcelona's parks: jazz on Wednesday and Friday nights, and classical music on Thursdays and Sundays.

Early June L'Ou Com Balla
www.bcn.cat/icub
Corpus Christi processions through the Barri Gòtic, and the L'Ou Com Balla – hollowed-out eggs dancing on decorated fountains.

Early June La Tamborinada
www.fundaciolaroda.cat
One-day child-friendly festival fills Parc de la Ciutadella with concerts, workshops and circus performances.

❤ Mid June Sónar
www.sonar.es
This three-day festival of what they term 'advanced music' and 'multimedia art' remains a must for anyone into electronic music, urban art and media technologies.

Mid June Festa de la Música
www.bcn.cat/festadelamusica
Free international music festival
with amateur musicians from 100
countries.

♥ 23-24 June Sant Joan
The summer solstice means cava,
all-night bonfires and fireworks,
across the city, but especially at the
beach, running until dawn.

Late June Gran Trobada d'Havaneres
www.amicsdeleshavaneres.com
Sea shanties with fireworks and
cremat (flaming spiced rum) over a
few days on Passeig Joan de Borbó
in Barceloneta.

Late June-early Aug Grec Festival de Barcelona
lameva.barcelona.cat/grec
Two-month spree of dance, music
and theatre all over the city.

July-Aug Sala Montjuïc
www.salamontjuic.org
Outdoor cinema and live music in
the moat of the Montjuïc castle.

Early July Dies de Dansa
www.marato.com
Several days of dance performances
in public spaces dotted
around the city.

Mid July Festa Major del Raval
Three days of parades, workshops,
free concerts and food stalls on the
Rambla del Raval.

Mid July Cruïlla BCN
www.cruillabarcelona.com
A two-day festival of Spanish and
world music in Parc del Fòrum.

Aug Mas i Mas Festival
www.masimas.com
A wildly varied festival, with
performances ranging in style from
Latin to chamber music.

Aug Gandules
www.cccb.org
Films screened on the deckchair-
strewn patio of the CCCB every
Tue and Thur.

15 Aug L'Assumpció (Assumption Day)

16 Aug Festa de Sant Roc
A week of parades, fireworks and
fire-running in the Barri Gòtic.

Late Aug Festa Major de Gràcia
www.festamajordegracia.cat
Gràcia's best-dressed street
competition, with parades,
concerts and human castles.

Late Aug Festa Major de Sants
www.festamajordesants.net
Sants' neighbourhood festival
consisting of a series of street
parties, along with concerts and
fire-running.

Autumn
The sea stays warm enough to
swim in well into September,
and occasionally October, and
temperatures are comfortably
mild. November can be rainy,
but it is a quiet month with lower
prices. Lots of festivals take place
in September and October: one
of the best is **Festes de la Mercè**,
which marks the end of the
hot summer.

Sept Festival L'Hora del Jazz
Flags and marches affirm cultural
identity on Catalan National Day.

11 Sept Diada Nacional de Catalunya
www.amjm.org
A month-long festival showcasing
local jazz acts, with free
daytime concerts.

💙 Festes de la Mercè

24 Sept
lameva.barcelona.cat/merce

This week-long event held around 24 September in honour of the patron saint of the city, Our Lady of Mercy, marks the end of the long hot summer, and is a time when friends reconnect after the holidays and the kids are allowed a couple more late nights before the term begins in earnest. It's a dizzying affair, with more than 600 events taking place all over the city.

It kicks off with giants, dragons and *capgrosses* in the Plaça Sant Jaume, and though the schedule varies according to which day the 24th falls on, there are generally pyrotechnic displays on the beach on the Friday, Saturday and Sunday nights, and these are usually preceded by some incredible augmented-reality video projections on the buildings of the Plaça Sant Jaume. This is the Mercè's ground zero, and where you'll see the *castells* (human castles) on the Sunday.

There are also displays of *sardanes* and *correfocs* (a tamer version for children, followed by the biggest and wildest of the year on the Saturday night), and the Parc de la Ciutadella is filled with music and dance. Other highlights include a seafront air show, sporting events including a swim across the port and a regatta, and a heap of activities for children. The pressure on the centre has been eased of late: many events are now staged up at Montjuïc castle or in the former textile factory, Fabra i Coats, in Sant Andreu. Even so, around 100,000 people have been known to descend on the Barri Gòtic to watch the final parade. Alongside the Mercè, a free three-day street arts festival takes place, and includes family theatre and circus acts. Detailed information is available at lameva.barcelona.cat/merce in the lead-up to the festival.

Castellers at Festes de la Mercè p57

Festival Traditions

Castellers, correfoc and sardana

From September's spectacular Festes de la Mercè to the other 30 or so neighbourhood *festes* – some very low key – you'll find a wild variety of events in Barcelona. The city's festivals share many traditional ingredients: dwarfs, *castellers* (human castles), and *gegants* (huge papier-mâché/ fibreglass giants dressed as princesses, fishermen, sultans and even topless chorus girls). There are also two unique not-to-be-missed exercises: the *correfoc* and the *sardana*.

The *correfoc* ('fire run') is a frenzy of pyromania. Groups of horned devils dance through the streets, brandishing tridents that spout fireworks and generally flouting every safety rule in the book. Protected by cotton caps and long sleeves, the more daring onlookers try to stop the devils and touch the fire-breathing dragons being dragged along in their wake.

The orderly antidote to this pandemonium is the *sardana*, Catalonia's folk dance. Watching the dancers executing their fussy little hops and steps in a large circle, it's hard to believe that *sardanes* were once banned as a vestige of pagan witchcraft. The music is similarly restrained; a reedy noise played by an 11-piece *cobla* band. The *sardana* is much harder than it looks, and the joy lies in taking part rather than watching.

To try Catalan folk dancing for yourself, check out the *sardanes* held in front of the cathedral (Jan-Aug, Dec noon-2pm Sun; Sept-Nov 6-8pm Sat, noon-2pm Sun) and in the Plaça Sant Jaume (Oct-July 6pm Sun).

24 Sept La Mercè
See p57 Festes de la Mercè.

Late Sept/early Oct Festa Major de la Barceloneta
Festival fever fills the fishing quarter, with fireworks, acrobats, music and parades.

12 Oct Dia de la Hispanitat

Late Oct Open House BCN
www.48openhousebarcelona.org
Over 150 architecturally or historically significant buildings open to the public.

Late Oct-early Nov In-Edit Beefeater Festival
www.in-edit.beefeater.es
Music documentary festival.

31 Oct-1 Nov La Castanyada
All Saints' Day and the evening before are celebrated with piles of roast chestnuts and floral tributes at cemeteries.

Late Oct-Nov Festival Internacional de Jazz de Barcelona
www.jazz.barcelona
Jazz from bebop to big band.

Winter
December and January throw up some beautifully sunny days and can be surprisingly mild. **Christmas** is a magical time in Barcelona, but the downside is that many places close for a couple of weeks. February is a quiet month, though it can feel quite cold and overcast. The festival of **Santa Eulàlia** helps to gear up for **Carnaval**, when everything is completely over the top.

1-24 Dec Fira de Sant Eloi
www.bcn.cat/nadal
An artisanal Christmas street fair on C/Argenteria in the Born. Live music 6-8pm.

1-23 Dec Fira de Santa Llúcia
www.bcn.cat/nadal
A Christmas market around the cathedral.

6 Dec Día de la Constitución

8 Dec La Immaculada

25 Dec Nadal (Christmas Day)
Nadal begins with the *missa del gall* (cockerel's mass), held at dawn. Sant Esteve (Boxing Day, 26 Dec) is followed by El Dia dels Sants Innocents on 28 Dec, a cheerful version of April Fool's Day.

Carnaval

31 Dec-1 Jan Cap d'Any (New Year's Eve) & Any Nou (New Year's Day)
Traditions in Barcelona include: swill cava and eat a grape for every chime of the clock at midnight; wear red underwear for good luck.

❤ 5 Jan Cavalcada dels Reis (Epiphany)
lameva.barcelona.cat/ca/nadal
Epiphany is marked by the Kings' Parade. Melchior, Gaspar and Balthasar arrive aboard the Santa Eulàlia boat at the bottom of La Rambla before beginning a grand parade around town from 5pm to 9pm. The following day is a holiday.

Mid Jan Festa dels Tres Tombs
Festival celebrating St Anthony's day in Sant Antoni.

Late Jan Sant Antoni Bonfire Festival
Two days of Balearic folk festivities in Gràcia.

12 Feb Santa Eulàlia
lameva.barcelona.cat/santaeulalia
A blowout winter festival held in honour of Santa Eulàlia, the co-patron saint of the city and a particular favourite of children. Expect many kids' activities.

❤ Mid Feb Carnaval
www.bcn.cat/carnaval
The city drops everything for this last big hurrah of overeating, overdrinking and underdressing prior to Lent. The party starts on Shrove Tuesday with the appearance of pot-bellied King Carnestoltes – the masked personification of the carnival spirit. That's followed by the grand weekend parade, masked balls and food fights.

Feb-June Guitar BCN
www.theproject.es
Guitar festival with genres spanning flamenco to jazz.

Barcelona
By Area

62   Getting Started

67   Barri Gòtic & La Rambla

85   Born & Sant Pere

99   Raval

111   Barceloneta & the Ports

121   Montjuïc & Around

133   Eixample

153   Gràcia & Other Districts

Tramvia Blau

La Rambla

Getting Started

Barcelona is defined by its precise geography: sea, hills and rivers constrain its area. The city squeezes into the remaining available space, a dense and sometimes confusing tangle of streets and houses. In this guide we have divided Barcelona into a number of defined districts. The medieval **Barri Gòtic** (*see pp67-84*), with the cathedral at its heart, is the starting point for most visitors. A stroll through its narrow alleyways and secluded squares is the best possible introduction to the city. The western boundary of this ancient quarter is the pedestrian boulevard La Rambla (frenetic and commercial, but with a certain charm).

The last decade or so has been very kind to the **Born & Sant Pere** (*see pp85-98*); where moneyed Catalans once feared to tread, they now covet property.

The two areas are divided by C/Princesa, which runs from metro Jaume I to the verdant Parc de la Ciutadella. The Born's main artery, the wide, pedestrianised Passeig del Born, is a former jousting ground and one of Barcelona's prettiest thoroughfares.

Crossing La Rambla from the Barri Gòtic, the visitor plunges into the **Raval** (*see pp99-110*), once notorious and still an edgy part of town, though much changed in recent times. Richard Meier's monumental white MACBA houses the city's principal collection of modern art, and Gaudí's medievalist Palau Güell was an early, brave attempt towards gentrification.

The city's seafront was famously ignored until the 1992 Olympic Games, when the makeshift restaurants were controversially swept aside and thousands of tons of sand laid down; the city now has seven kilometres of golden beaches. Today, **Barceloneta & the Ports** (*see pp111-120*) offer a marine respite to city dwellers. The former fishermen's district of Barceloneta still retains its local feel and is home to some of the city's best seafood restaurants. To find the big blue, head downhill: Barcelona slopes gently down to the shore.

The hill of **Montjuïc** (*see pp121-132*) offers a welcome green escape and some of the city's best galleries and museums. At the bottom of the hill lie the areas of **Poble Sec** and **Sant Antoni** – a pocket of bar-strewn hipster heaven.

It's easy to tell when you've left the Old City and entered the **Eixample** (*see pp133-152*): narrow streets and alleys become broad, traffic-clogged, geometrically precise roads. The Eixample is divided into two along C/Balmes: to its right is the fashionable Dreta, while to the left is the more down-at-heel Esquerra. The Dreta is something of a Modernista showcase, with buildings that include the Sagrada Família and La Pedrera.

Casa de les Punxes *p137*

Beyond lies the area we've called **Gràcia & Other Districts** (*see pp153-166*), which includes once-independent towns swallowed up as Barcelona has spread; despite this you'll find each area retains a distinct identity. Visitors flock to the 'alternative' and upmarket *barri* of Gràcia to explore Gaudí's Park Güell. Other notable places outside the centre include the former industrial area of Poblenou, and Les Corts, home to football mecca Camp Nou.

Getting around

Barcelona is deceptively small, and a breeze to navigate. Many major sights are within walking distance of each other – the Old City can be crossed on foot in about 20 minutes. Remember that uphill is *muntanya* (mountain) and downhill is *mar* (sea) – locals often using directions with these terms.

The metro is quick and serves most areas, but it's worth checking a street map first, because you may find it's quicker to walk. Buses reach the parts of the city not covered by the metro and run through the night. For more information on public transport, *see p175*.

In the know
Keep your bags close

Bag snatchers and pickpockets are quite common. Don't carry unnecessary valuables, and beware anyone trying to clean something off your shoulder or sell you a posy. Those wanting to swap a coin for one from your country are also wont to empty out your wallet.

Time Out

EXPLORING THE
WORLD'S FAVOURITE
CITIES SINCE 1968...

WHERE NEXT?

Tourist information

The biggest and most helpful tourist office is at Plaça Catalunya, underground but clearly signposted (in the central ring, but on the same side as El Corte Inglés). For details of other tourist offices, *see p185*, and for further information see www.barcelonaturisme.com.

Discount schemes

Be aware that many attractions are cheaper if booked online (and normally this method avoids the need to queue). The **Articket** (www.articketbcn.org, €30) gives free entry to six major museums and art galleries (one visit is allowed to each venue over a period of six months): Fundació Miró, MACBA, the MNAC, Fundació Tàpies, the CCCB and the Museu Picasso. The **Barcelona Card** (www. barcelonacard.com, €20-€60) allows two to five days of unlimited public transport and gives discounts at sights, cablecars and airport buses. It's sold online and at the airport, tourist offices and El Corte Inglés.

Tours

The city council runs walking tours on various themes (from Picasso to Modernisme, gourmet to Gothic) taking 90 minutes to two hours. For more information, see www. barcelonaturisme.com.

There are two tourist buses: the orange **Barcelona City Tours** (93 317 64 54, www.barcelonacitytour.cat) and the white **Bus Turístic** (93 285 38 32, www.tmb.net). Bus Turístic ticket-holders benefit from discount vouchers for a range of attractions. Both visit many of the same sights and cost much the same. For more on tour options, including bike or scooter tours, *see p176*.

In the know
Free Sundays

Note that municipally owned museums are free from 3pm on Sundays, and many are also free one day a month. Check individual websites for details.

Barri Gòtic & La Rambla

The Barri Gòtic (Gothic Quarter) is the most well-preserved medieval quarter in Europe. Dotted with some astounding Roman remains, it's an essential port of call.

At the centre of the Gothic Quarter is the **Catedral de Barcelona**, surrounded by a knot of medieval streets and small, shady squares. Nearby, the imposing square of **Plaça Sant Jaume** hosts the city council (Ajuntament) and the Catalan regional government (Generalitat) buildings. From here, small streets wind to the well-preserved **Plaça del Rei**, which houses the Museu d'Història de Barcelona (MUHBA), the Escher-esque 16th-century watchtower (Mirador del Rei Martí) and the Capella de Santa Àgata.

BARRI GÒTIC & LA RAMBLA

Best for a stroll
The famous mile-long Rambla (*p78*), packed with shops, cafés and street performers.

Best Gothic sights
Catedral de Barcelona (*p73*) for its Disneyesque confection that stands at the medieval quarter's highest point.

Best food shopping
Formatgeria La Seu (*p82*) for cheese. La Boqueria (*p81*), for everything else.

Best for fashion
Alonso (*p80*) for gloves in a kaleidoscope of colours. La Manual Alpargatera (*p82*) for hand-made espadrilles.

Best museum
The MUHBA (*p75*) for its extensive Roman remains running underground.

Best music venue
Gran Teatre del Liceu (*p83*), an elegant opera house with a varied programme.

Best cafè
Cafè de l'Òpera (*p77*) for atmospheric grandeur. Els Quatre Gats (*p76*) to drink in Picasso's old haunt.

Best for intimate gigs
Harlem Jazz Club (*p84*) for emerging talent. El Paraigua (*p84*) for cocktails and live music.

Another notable square is the grand, arcaded **Plaça Reial**, known for its bars, cheap backpacker hostels and rather scuzzy atmosphere at night.

North of the Plaça Reial lie the attractive **Plaça del Pi** and **Plaça Sant Josep Oriol**, where you'll find great bars and artisanal markets. The squares are separated by **Santa Maria del Pi**, one of Barcelona's most distinguished Gothic churches, with a magnificent rose window and spacious single nave.

The Barri Gòtic is flanked to the west by **La Rambla**, the famed mile-long boulevard that leads from Plaça Catalunya to the sea. On its west side is the elegant **Gran Teatre del Liceu** opera house and the superb **Boqueria** market. Halfway down La Rambla is the pavement mosaic created in 1976 by Joan Miró and recently restored to its original glory. On the east side is the extraordinary Bruno Quadros building (1883); a former umbrella shop, it is decorated with roundels of open parasols and a Chinese dragon carrying a Peking lantern.

Santa Maria del Pi

Sights & museums

Ajuntament (City Hall)
*Plaça Sant Jaume (93 402 73 64,
www.bcn.cat). Metro Jaume I or
Liceu.* **Open** *Office 8.30am-2.30pm
Mon-Fri. Visits 10am-1.30pm Sun.*
Admission *free.* **Map** *p70 H9.*
Around the left-hand corner of the
City Hall's rather dull 18th-century
neoclassical façade sits the
old entrance, in a wonderfully
flamboyant 15th-century Catalan
Gothic façade. Inside, the
building's centrepiece (and oldest
part) is the famous Saló de Cent,
where the Consell de Cent (Council
of One Hundred) ruled the city
between 1372 and 1714. The Saló de
Cròniques is filled with Josep Maria
Sert's immense black-and-gold
mural (1928), depicting the early
14th-century Catalan campaign

in Byzantium and Greece under
the command of Roger de Flor.
Full of art and sculptures by the
great Catalan masters from Clarà
to Subirachs, the interior of the
City Hall is open on Sundays. The
Ajuntament is also open from 11am
to 8pm on certain holidays, such
as Santa Eulàlia (12 February) and
Sant Jordi (23 April), and Corpus
Christi (11 days after Whitsunday).

➜ **Getting around**
The streets are so narrow in the
Barri Gòtic that it's near impossible
for cars to pass, let alone public
transport. It's most easily accessed
from Jaume I metro to the east or
Liceu metro to the west.

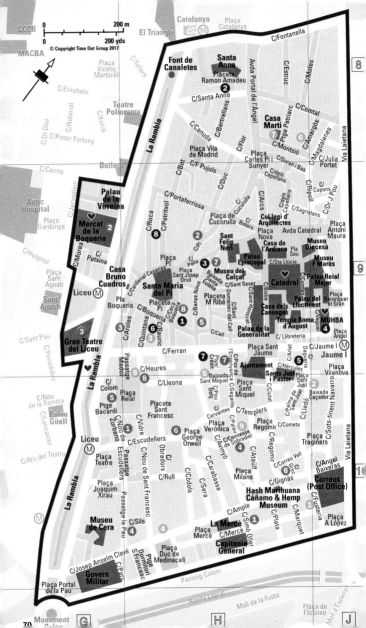

Hash Marihuana Cáñamo & Hemp Museum

C/Ample 35 (93 319 75 39, www.hempmuseumgallery.com) Metro Jaume I. **Open** *10am-10pm daily.* **Admission** *€9; free under-13s.* **Map** *p70 H10.*

An intellectual shrine to weed, set in a stunning Modernista mansion. The displays run from the botanic to the historical, with rooms devoted to prohibition, and to marijuana in art and popular culture. The Industrial Room looks at the uses of hemp through the ages, while the medicinal section contains moving testimony from those whose lives would be unbearable without it, creating, all told, an intelligent argument for decriminalisation.

Museu de Cera

Ptge de la Banca 7 (93 317 26 49, www.museocerabcn.com). Metro Drassanes. **Open** *Mid July-mid Sept 10am-10pm daily. Mid Sept-mid July 10am-1.30pm, 4-8.30pm Mon-Fri; 11am-2pm, 4.30-7.30pm Sat, Sun.* **Admission** *€15; €9 reductions; free under-5s.* **Map** *p70 G10.*

Madame Tussauds it ain't, but the Wax Museum is an enjoyable enough way to pass a rainy afternoon, particularly if you have small children, who love the 'underwater' section (a submarine and creaky old ship). Be warned that the exhibits are very dated, and a curious mix of historical and 1980s (19th-century composers alongside ET, JR from *Dallas*

and Lady Di). On Saturdays there are special 'night visits' (€20; Spanish only, at 9pm and 10pm) in the gloaming.

Museu Diocesà & Gaudí Exhibition Center

Avda de la Catedral 4 (93 315 22 13, www.cultura.arqbcn.cat). Metro Jaume I. **Open** *Apr-Oct 10am-8pm daily. Nov-Mar 10am-6pm daily.* **Admission** *€15; €12 reductions; €7.50 children; free under-7s. No cards.* **Map** *p70 H9.*

The building itself is something of a mishmash: it includes the Gothic Pia Almoina, an almshouse and soup kitchen founded in 1009, stuck on to a Renaissance canon's residence complete with Tuscan columns, which in turn was built inside an octagonal Roman defence tower. It houses both the Museu Diocesà – a hotchpotch of religious art, including 14th-century alabaster virgins, altarpieces by Bernat Martorell and wonderful Romanesque murals – and the new Gaudí Exhibition Center, an introduction to the architect's life and work that utilises the latest technology, such as virtual-reality glasses, to bring his world alive.

♥ Museu Frederic Marès

Plaça Sant Iu 5-6 (93 256 35 00, www.museumares.bcn.cat). Metro Jaume I. **Open** *10am-7pm Tue-Sat; 11am-8pm Sun.* **Admission** *€4.20; €2.40 reductions; free under-16s. Free to all 3-8pm Sun & all day 1st Sun of mth.* **Map** *p70 J9.*

Kleptomaniac and general magpie Frederic Marès (1893-1991) 'collected' everything he could lay his hands on, from hairbrushes to opera glasses and gargoyles. Unlike most private 19th-century collectors, Marès didn't come from a wealthy family, but spent every penny he earned as a sculptor and art professor on broadening his hoard. Even when the Ajuntament gave him a palazzo in which to

In the know
Civic Gaudí

An addition from the 1840s, the Plaça Reial has the Tres Gràcies fountain in the centre, and lamp-posts designed by the young Gaudí. It's the only work he ever did for the city council.

display his collection (and house himself), it wasn't enough; the overflow eventually spread to two other Marès museums in Montblanc and Arenys de Mar.

The exhibits here are divided into three main sections. The basement, ground floor and first floor are devoted to sculpture dating from the Pre-Roman era to the 19th century, including a vast array of polychromed religious carvings, tombs, capitals and entire church portals, exquisitely carved. On the second floor sits the Collector's Cabinet, with objects from everyday life; look out for the Ladies' Room, filled with fans, sewing scissors and perfume flasks, and a room dedicated to smoking paraphernalia. Also on the second floor is a room devoted to photography, and Marès' study and library. It's now filled with sculptures, many of them his own. The second floor also houses the Weapons Room, with collections from the now defunct Military Museum on Montjuïc. The Entertainment Room, with mechanical toys and puppets, is found on the third floor.

Palau de la Generalitat

Plaça Sant Jaume (www.president. cat). Metro Jaume I or Liceu. **Open** *guided tours (by appt, every 30-40mins) 2nd & 4th wknd of mth, except Aug.* **Admission** *free.* **Map** *p70 H9.*
Like the Ajuntament, the Palau de la Generalitat has a Gothic side entrance, which here opens out on to C/Bisbe, with a beautiful relief depicting St George (Sant Jordi), patron saint of Catalonia, made by Pere Johan in 1418. Inside the building, the finest features are the first-floor Pati de Tarongers (Orange Tree Patio), which was to become the model for many Barcelona patios, and the chapel of Sant Jordi (1432-34), the masterpiece of Catalan architect Marc Safont. The

Generalitat is traditionally open to the public on Sant Jordi (St George's Day, 23 April), when its patios are spectacularly decorated with red roses, but queues are long. It normally also opens on 11 September (Catalan National Day) and 24 September (La Mercè). Tours need to be booked on the website, but the page is hard to find – put 'Palau' and '*visites*' into the search bar.

Palau de la Virreina

La Rambla 99 (93 316 10 00, www.lavirreina.bcn.cat). Metro Liceu. **Open** *noon-8pm Tue-Sun.* **Admission** *free.* **Map** *p70 G9.*
This classical palazzo, with Baroque features, takes its name from the widow of an unpopular viceroy of Peru – she commissioned it and lived in it after its completion in the 1770s. The Virreina now houses the city cultural department, and has information on events and shows as well as strong programming in its two gallery spaces. On the first floor, Espai 2 is devoted to exhibitions of contemporary art, while the free downstairs gallery is focused on photography and hosts Barcelona's prestigious annual photo competition, the FotoMercè, which takes place during the Mercè festival in September.

Temple d'August

C/Paradís 10 (93 256 21 22, www. museuhistoria.bcn.cat). Metro Jaume I. **Open** *10am-2pm Mon; 10am-7pm Tue-Sat; 10am-8pm Sun.* **Admission** *free.* **Map** *p70 H9.*
Four stunning fluted Corinthian columns dating from the first century BC soar out of their podium in the most unlikely of places: a back patio of the Mountaineering Centre of Catalonia. Part of the rear corner of the temple devoted to the Roman emperor Augustus (who after his death was elevated to the pantheon), the columns were discovered and isolated from the

💜 Catedral de Barcelona

Pla de la Seu (93 342 82 62, www. catedralbcn.org). Metro Jaume I. **Open** *Church, cloister & museum 1-5.30pm Mon-Fri; 1-5pm Sat; 2-5pm Sun. Worshippers only at other times.* **Admission** *Church, cloister & museum (combined ticket) €7. Lift to roof €3. Choir €3. Free to worshippers. No cards.* **Map** *p70 H9.*

The construction of Barcelona's Gothic cathedral began in 1298. However, thanks to civil wars and plagues, building dragged on at a pace that makes the Sagrada Família project look snappy: although the architects remained faithful to the vertical Nordic lines of the 15th-century plans, the façade and central spire were not finished until 1913. Indeed, the façade continues to cause problems, and in recent years has been painstakingly rebuilt with the same Montserrat stone that was used for the original.

Inside, the cathedral is a cavernous and slightly forbidding place, but many paintings, sculptures and an intricately carved central choir (built in the 1390s) all shine through the gloom.

The cathedral is dedicated to Saint Eulàlia, an outspoken 13-year-old martyred by the Romans in AD 303. Her remains lie in the dramatically lit crypt, in an alabaster tomb carved with torture scenes from her martyrdom (being rolled in a nail-filled barrel down what is today the Baixada de Santa Eulàlia, for instance). To one side, there's a lift to the roof; take it for a magnificent view of the Old City.

The glorious, light-filled cloister is famous for its 13 fierce geese – one for each year of Eulàlia's life – and half-erased floor engravings, detailing which guild paid for which side chapel: scissors to represent the tailors, shoes for the cobblers and so on. The cathedral museum, housed in the 17th-century chapterhouse, includes paintings and sculptures by Gothic masters Jaume Huguet, Bernat Martorell and Bartolomé Bermejo.

BARRI GÒTIC & LA RAMBLA

structure of a medieval building in 1835. The current layout is actually a slight fudging of the original as the right-hand column resided separately in the Plaça del Rei until it was slotted next to the other three in 1956.

Restaurants

Belmonte €€

C/Mercè 29 (93 310 76 84). Metro Jaume I. **Open** *8-11.15pm Tue-Thur; 1-3.30pm, 8pm-midnight Sat, Sun. Closed 2wks Aug.* **Map** *p70 H10* ❶ *Catalan*
Cosy little Belmonte is one of the city's better-guarded secrets (or maybe just doesn't get the recognition it deserves). Its long and ever-changing list of daily specials is testament to the spontaneous approach in the kitchen and the freshness of the produce (much of it grown in the owners' garden). Try the quail, the pork with shallot confit, one of the ranges of home-made tortillas, or just order a bunch of tapas to share, along with a bottle of the good, cheap house red.

Cafè de l'Acadèmia €€

C/Lledó 1 (93 319 82 53). Metro Jaume I. **Open** *1-3.30pm, 8-11pm Mon-Fri. Closed 2wks Aug.* **Map** *p70 J10* ❷ *Catalan*
An assured approach to the classics of Catalan cuisine, combined with sunny tables on the pretty Plaça Sant Just, make this one of the best-value restaurants around. The brick-walled dining room gets full and the tables are close together, so it doesn't really work for a date, but it's an animated spot for a power lunch among the suits from nearby City Hall. Eat à la carte for the likes of quail stuffed with duck's liver and *botifarra* with wild mushroom sauce.

Can Culleretes €

C/Quintana 5 (93 317 30 22, www. culleretes.com). Metro Liceu. **Open** *1.30-4pm, 9-11pm Tue-Sat; 1.30-4pm Sun. Closed mid July-mid Aug.* **Map** *p70 H9* ❸ *Catalan*
The rambling dining rooms at the 'house of teaspoons' have been packing 'em in since 1786. The secret to this restaurant's longevity is a straightforward one: honest, hearty cooking and decent wine served at the lowest possible prices. Under huge oil paintings and a thousand signed black-and-white photos, diners munch sticky boar stew, tender pork with prunes and dates, goose with apples, partridge *escabeche* and superbly fresh seafood.

Chicken Shop €

Plaça del Duc de Medinaceli 2 (93 220 47 00, www.chickenshop.com/ en/barcelona). Metro Drassanes. **Open** *1pm-midnight Mon-Thur, Sun; 1pm-1am Fri, Sat.* **Map** *p70 H10* ❹ *American*
The name leaves few surprises, and the most complicated decision you'll need to make is whether to order a quarter, half or the whole beast, cooked on a spit. Sides are simple but generously portioned and the €8 cocktails make a great accompaniment. A bare-bricked space with a subtle sprinkling of Americana, the Chicken Shop attracts a fairly groovy crowd, thanks to its affiliation with the nearby Soho House Barcelona (*see p171*).

El Gran Café €€

C/Avinyó 9 (93 318 79 86, www. restaurantelgrancafe.com). Metro Liceu. **Open** *12.30-4pm, 7pm-midnight daily.* **Map** *p70 H9* ❺ *Mediterranean*
The fluted columns, bronze nymphs, suspended globe lamps and wood panelling help to replicate a classic Parisian vibe,

💗 Museu d'Història de Barcelona (MUHBA)

Plaça del Rei 1 (93 256 21 00, www. museuhistoria.bcn.cat). Metro Jaume I. **Open** *10am-7pm Tue-Sat; 10am-8pm Sun.* **Admission** *€7; €5 reductions; free under-16s. Free to all 3-8pm Sun & all day 1st Sun of mth. No cards.* **Map** *p70 J9.*

Stretching from the Plaça del Rei to the cathedral are some 4,000sq m (43,000sq ft) of subterranean Roman excavations – streets, villas and storage vats for oil and wine – all discovered by accident in the late 1920s when a whole swathe of the Gothic Quarter was dug up to make way for the central avenue of Via Laietana. The excavations continued until 1960. Today, the labyrinth can be reached via the Casa Padellàs, a merchant's palace dating from 1498, which was laboriously moved from its original location in C/Mercaders to allow the construction of Via Laietana.

Admission also allows access to the Capella de Santa Àgata, with a 15th-century altarpiece by Jaume Huguet, and the **Saló del Tinell**, at least when there's no temporary exhibition. This majestic room began life in 1370 as the seat of the Catalan parliament and was converted in the 18th century into a Baroque church, which was dismantled in 1934. The Rei Martí watchtower is closed to the public. Tickets for the museum are valid for all seven MUHBA sites.

and the cornerstones of brasserie cuisine – onion soup, duck magret, tarte tatin and even crêpe suzette – are all present and correct. The imaginative Catalan dishes spliced into the menu also work, but the distinctly non-Gallic attitude towards the hastily assembled set lunch is less convincing.

Mercè Vins €

C/Amargós 1 (93 302 60 56). Metro Urquinaona. Open 8am-5pm Mon-Fri. Closed 2wks Aug. Map p70 H8 ❻ Catalan

Set in the heart of the Barri Gòtic, this cosy, daytime-only restaurant is aimed at office workers. Dishes on the *menú del día* change daily, but might include a pumpkin soup or inventive salad, followed by *botifarra* with sautéed garlic potatoes. Dessert regulars are flat, sweet coca bread with a glass of muscatel, chocolate flan or figgy pudding. In the morning, Mercè Vins opens for breakfast, which here tends to be *pa amb tomàquet* (bread rubbed with tomato) topped with cheese or ham.

❤ Els Quatre Gats €€

C/Montsió 3 (93 302 41 40, www.4gats.com). Metro Catalunya. Restaurant noon-1am daily. Café 9am-1am daily. Map p70 H8 ❼ Catalan

Dazzling in its design, Els Quatre Gats, the 'Four Cats', is an unmissable stop for those interested in the architecture of the period. It was designed by Modernista heavyweight Puig i Cadafalch and patronised by the cultural glitterati of the era – most notably Picasso, who hung out here with Modernista painters Santiago Rusiñol and Ramon Casas. Nowadays, it chiefly caters to tourists, but makes an essential stop nonetheless. The restaurant is no crucible for Catalan gastronomy – nor is it cheap. There is, however, a more reasonably priced and generously portioned set lunch, and when it's all over you can buy the T-shirt. To appreciate the building without forking out for dinner, you can just have a drink in the café.

Les Quinze Nits €

Plaça Reial 6 (93 317 30 75, www. grupandilana.com). Metro Liceu. Open 1-3.45pm, 7.30-11.30pm Mon-Thur; 1-11.30pm Fri, Sat; 12.30-11pm Sun. Map p70 H9 ❽ Spanish

The staggering success of the Quinze Nits enterprise (there are countless branches here in Barcelona and in Madrid, and a handful of hotels) is down to one concept: style on a budget. All the restaurants have a certain Manhattan chic, yet you'll struggle to spend much more than €20 a head. The food plays second fiddle and is a bit hit-or-miss, but order simple dishes and at these prices you can't go far wrong. The queues tend to be shorter at the other branches.

Rasoterra €

C/Palau 5 (93 318 69 26, www. rasoterra.cat). Metro Liceu. Open 1-4pm, 7-11pm Tue-Sun. Map p70 H10 ❾ Spanish

Putting aside the worthy manifesto about 'eating as dialogue', Rasoterra is a light, bright and chilled place, that cherishes locavore and healthy concepts but encourages the idea that no meal is complete without a glass of wine. A sprinkling of fusion enlivens a loosely Catalan-based menu, which includes dishes such as *trinxat* (a Catalan bubble-and-squeak) with chilli and seaweed mayonnaise, and cannelloni stuffed with radicchio, blue cheese and pears.

▶ *For other eating options, visit La Boqueria (see p81).*

Cafés, tapas & bars

Bar Celta

C/Mercè 9 (93 315 00 06, www.
barcelta.com). Metro Drassanes.
Open *noon-midnight Tue-Sun.*
Map *p70 H10* ①
Celta's unapologetically '60s
interior is fiercely lit, noisy and not
recommended for anyone feeling a
bit rough. It is, however, one of the
more authentic experiences to be
had in the Barri Gòtic. A Galician
tapas bar, it specialises in food from
the region, such as *lacón con grelos*
(boiled gammon with turnip tops)
and good seafood, accompanied
by crisp Albariño wine served in
traditional white ceramic bowls.

Bar Pinotxo

La Boqueria 466-467, La Rambla
89 (mobile 647 869 821). Metro
Liceu. **Open** *6.30am-4pm Mon-*
Sat. **No cards.** **Map** *p70 G9* ②
Just inside the entrance of the
Boqueria, on the right-hand side,
is this essential market bar. It's run
by Juanito, one of the city's best-
loved figures. In the early morning
the place is popular with ravenous
night owls on their way home and,
at lunchtime, foodies in the know.
Various tapas are available, along
with excellent daily specials such
as tuna casserole or scrambled eggs
with clams.

❤ Cafè de l'Òpera

La Rambla 74 (93 317 75 85, www.
cafeoperabcn.com). Metro Liceu.
Open *8am-1am Mon-Thur, Sun;*
8am-2am Fri, Sat. **Map** *p70 G9* ③
Cast-iron pillars, etched mirrors
and bucolic murals create an air of
fading grandeur at Cafè de l'Òpera,
which now seems incongruous
among the fast-food joints and
tawdry souvenir shops on La
Rambla. Coffee, hot chocolate,
pastries and a handful of tapas
are served by attentive bow-tied
waiters to a largely tourist clientele,
but given the atmosphere (and

the competition) there's no better
place to sit and enjoy a cup of
coffee on the city's most celebrated
boulevard.

Federal

Passatge de la Pau 11 (93 280 81
71, www.federalcafe.es/barcelona-
gotic). Metro Drassanes. **Open**
9am-midnight Mon-Thur;
9am-1am Fri, Sat; 9am-5.30pm
Sun. **Map** *p70 H10* ④
One of the favoured haunts for
the MacBook crowd, this relaxed
Australian-run café is an easy
place to spend some time, with a
wide-ranging menu from fry-ups
to veggie burgers, granola to Thai
curry. Hidden down a sidestreet,
it's spitting distance from La
Rambla but you'll generally
find a table, or at least space at a
shared one.

La Granja 1872

C/Banys Nous 4 (mobile 617 370
290). Metro Liceu. **Open** *9am-9pm*
daily. **No cards.** **Map** *p70 H9* ⑤
La Granja is an old-fashioned café
filled with yellowing photos and
antiques, which has its very own
section of Roman wall. You can
stand your spoon in the tarry-thick
hot chocolate, which won't be to all
tastes, but the *xocolata amb café*,
a mocha espresso, or the *xocolata*
picant, chocolate with chilli, pack a
mid-afternoon energy punch.

Milk

C/Gignàs 21 (93 268 09 22, www.
milkbarcelona.com). Metro Jaume
I. **Open** *9am-1am Mon-Thur,*
Sun; 9am-1.30am Fri, Sat. **Map**
p70 H9 ⑥
The first place in the Old City to
provide a decent brunch, Milk's
fry-ups, pancakes and smoothies
are available every day, until 4pm.
Its candlelit, low-key baroque look,
charming service and cheap prices
make it a good bet at any time, with
home-made bistro grub ranging
from Caesar salad to fish and chips.

♥ La Rambla

Whether you catch it on a Saturday night full of sombrero-wearing stags or early in the morning when the kiosk-holders are bursting open their fresh stacks of newspapers, one thing is for sure: you won't get La Rambla to yourself. And, indeed, why would you want to? In the absence of any great buildings or museums, it's the people who provide the spectacle: from flower-sellers to living statues, operagoers to saucer-eyed clubbers, market shoppers to tango dancers, all human life is here.

However, there's no escaping the fact that, these days, it's mostly tourists who walk the golden mile from Plaça Catalunya down to the harbour. The business of extracting as much of their money as possible, whether by fair means or foul, has had an inevitable impact on the character of the boulevard, filling it with fast food outlets, short-stay apartments, identikit souvenir shops and pickpockets.

La Rambla started life as a seasonal riverbed, which explains both its snaking trajectory, broadening out at the sea end, and its name, which derives from *ramla*, an Arabic word for sand. The river ran along the western edge of the 13th-century city; after it became an open sewer, it was gradually paved over; the distinctive wave-patterned paving slabs were added after the Civil War.

La Rambla also served as the meeting ground for city and country dwellers in this era – on the far side of the church buildings, built along here from the Middle Ages to the Baroque era, lay the still scarcely built-up Raval, 'the city outside the walls', and rural Catalonia. At the fountain on the corner with C/Portaferrissa, colourful tiles depict the city gateway that once stood here (*porta ferrissa* means 'iron gate'). The space by the gates became a natural marketplace; from these humble beginnings sprang **La Boqueria** (*see p81*).

La Rambla took on its present form between approximately 1770 and 1860. The second city wall came down in 1775, and La Rambla was paved and turned into a boulevard. But the avenue only acquired its final shape after the closure of the monasteries in the 1830s, which made land available for new building. No longer on the city's edge, La Rambla became a wide path through the city's heart.

La Rambla is divided into territories. The first part – at the top, by Plaça Catalunya – was long the territory of shoeshiners and groups of men who came to play chess and hold informal debates, although the sparse new single-seat benches have made it a markedly less sociable place to sit these days. The **Font de Canaletes** drinking fountain, which gives this section its name, is beside them, and is where Barça fans converge to celebrate their triumphs.

This part segues into the **Rambla dels Ocells**; it's named after the ranks of cacophonous bird (*ocell*) stalls that stood here until they were removed by the Ajuntament in an attempt to raise the tone of the boulevard. Next comes perhaps the best-loved section, known as **Rambla de les Flors** for its line of flower stalls. A little further down is the **Pla de l'Os** (or Pla de la Boqueria), the centrepoint of La Rambla.

The lower half of La Rambla is initially a more restrained affair, flowing between the sober façade of the **Gran Teatre del Liceu** opera house (*see p83*) and the more fin-de-siècle (architecturally and atmospherically) **Café de l'Opera** (*see p77*). On the right is C/Nou de la Rambla (where you'll find Gaudí's neo-Gothic **Palau Güell** (*see p107*); the promenade then widens into the Rambla de Santa Mònica, an area that has long been a haunt of prostitutes. Clean-up efforts have reduced their visibility, and various renovations have done much to dilute the seediness of the area, but single males walking at night can still expect to be approached.

Then it's a short hop to the port and the Columbus column.

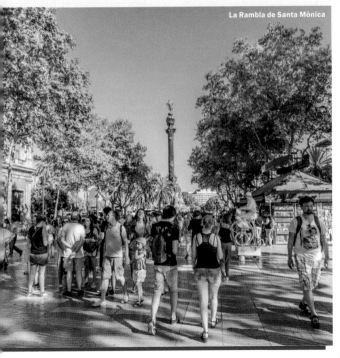

La Rambla de Santa Mònica

El Portalón

C/Banys Nous 20 (93 302 11 87). Metro Liceu. **Open** *9am-midnight Mon-Sat. Closed Jan & Aug.* **Map** *p70 H9* ❼

A rare pocket of authenticity in the touristy Barri Gòtic neighbourhood, recent renovations notwithstanding, this traditional tapas bar is located in what were once medieval stables. The tapas list is long and the *torrades* are good: toasted bread topped with juicy red peppers and anchovies, cheese, ham or whatever takes your fancy. The house wine comes in terracotta jugs.

Taller de Tapas

Plaça Sant Josep Oriol 9 (93 301 80 20, www.tallerdetapas.com). Metro Liceu. **Open** *noon-midnight Mon-Thur; noon-1am Fri-Sun.* **Map** *p70 H9* ❽

Taller de Tapas is an easy, multilingual environment, with plentiful outdoor seating and a good selection of tapas, from heavenly razor clams to local wild mushrooms, along with a well-priced wine list. At busy periods, however, the service can be a little hurried, so it pays to avoid the lunchtime and evening rush hours.

Shops & services

Almacenes del Pilar

C/Boqueria 43 (93 317 79 84, www. almacenesdelpilar.com). Metro Liceu. **Open** *10am-2pm, 4-8pm Mon-Sat. Closed 2wks Aug.* **Map** *p70 H9* ❶ *Fashion*

An array of fabrics and accessories for traditional Spanish costumes is on display in this colourful, shambolic interior, dating all the way back to 1886. Making your way through bolts of material, you'll find the richly hued brocades used for Valencian *fallera* outfits and other rudiments of folkloric dress from various parts of the country. Lace *mantillas*, and the high combs over which they are worn, are stocked, along with fringed, hand-embroidered pure silk *mantones de manila* (shawls) and colourful wooden fans.

❤ Alonso

C/Santa Anna 27 (93 317 60 85, www.tiendacenter.com). Metro Liceu. **Open** *10am-8pm Mon-Sat. Closed 1wk Sept.* **Map** *p70 H8* ❷ *Fashion*

Elegant Catalan ladies have come to Alonso for those important finishing touches for their outfits for more than a century. Behind the Modernista façade lie soft gloves in leather and lace, intricate fans, both traditional and modern, and scarves made from mohair and silk.

Caelum

C/Palla 8 (93 302 69 93, www. caelumbarcelona.com). Metro Liceu. **Open** *10.30am-8.30pm Mon-Thur; 10.30am-11pm Fri, Sat; 11.30am-9pm Sun. Closed 2wks Aug.* **Map** *p70 H9* ❸ *Food & Drink*

Spain's monks and nuns have a naughty sideline in sweets including '*pets de monja*' (little chocolate biscuits known as 'nuns' farts'), candied saints' bones, and drinkable goodies such as eucalyptus and orange liqueur, all beautifully packaged. If you'd like to sample before committing to a whole box of Santa Teresa's sugared egg yolks, there's a café downstairs on the site of the medieval Jewish thermal baths.

Cereria Subirà

Baixada de Llibreteria 7 (93 315 26 06). Metro Jaume I. **Open** *9.30am-1.30pm, 4.30-8pm Mon-Fri; 10am-2pm, 5-8pm Sat.* **Map** *p70 J9* ❹ *Gifts & Souvenirs*

With a staircase fit for a full swish from Scarlett O'Hara, this exquisite candle shop dates back to the pre-electric days of 1716, when candles were an everyday necessity at home and in church. These days, the

💜 La Boqueria

*La Rambla 89 (93 318 25 84,
www.boqueria.info). Metro
Liceu.* **Open** *8am-8pm Mon-Sat.*
Map *p70 G9.*

Thronged with tourists
searching for a little bit of
Barcelona's gastro magic,
but all too often ending up
with a pre-sliced quarter of
overpriced pineapple, Europe's
biggest food market is still
an essential stop for visitors.
Admire the orderly stacks of
ridged Montserrat tomatoes,
the wet sacks of snails and the
oozing razor clams on the fish
stalls. You can also eat at one of
the market tapas bars, such as
Bar Pinotxo (*see p77*).

If you visit in the morning,
you'll see the best produce,
including the smallholders'
fruit and vegetable stalls in the
little square attached to the
C/Carme side of the market,
where prices tend to be cheaper.
But if you come only to ogle,
remember that this is where
locals come to shop. Don't
touch what you don't want to
buy, ask before taking photos
and watch out for vicious old
ladies with ankle-destroying
wheeled shopping bags.

Try visiting earlier in the day,
as some stalls close at around
3pm. Fish-lovers should bear
in mind that the fish stalls
are closed on Mondays.

votive candles sit next to novelties such as After Eight-scented candles and candles in the shape of the Sagrada Família, alongside related goods such as garden torches and oil burners.

❤ Formatgeria La Seu

C/Dagueria 16 (93 412 65 48, www. formatgerialaseu.com). Metro Jaume I. **Open** *10am-2pm, 5-8pm Tue-Sat.* **No cards.** **Map** *p70 H9* ❺ *Food & Drink*

Spain has long neglected its cheese heritage, to the point where this is the only shop in the country to specialise in Spanish-only farmhouse cheeses. Scottish owner Katherine McLaughlin hand-picks her wares, such as a manchego that knocks the socks off anything you'll find in the market, or the truly strange Catalan *tupí*. She also stocks six varieties of cheese ice-cream and some excellent-value olive oils. Her taster plate of three cheeses and a glass of wine for just a few euros is a great way to explore what's on offer.

❤ El Ingenio

C/Rauric 6 (93 317 71 38, elingenio.cat). Metro Liceu. **Open** *10am-1.30pm, 4.30-8pm Mon-Fri; 11am-2pm, 5-8.30pm Sat.* **Map** *p70 H9* ❻ *Children*

At once enchanting and disturbing, El Ingenio's handcrafted toys, tricks and costumes are reminders of a pre-digital world where people made their own entertainment. Its cabinets are full of practical jokes and curious toys; its fascinating workshop produces the oversized heads and garish costumes used in Barcelona's traditional festivities.

❤ La Manual Alpargatera

C/Avinyó 7 (93 301 01 72, www. lamanualalpargatera.com). Metro Liceu. **Open** *9.30am-1.30pm, 4.30-8pm Mon-Fri, 10am-1.30pm, 4.30-8pm Sat.* **Map** *p70 H9* ❼ *Shoes*

La Manual Alpargatera opened in 1910, stocking handmade espadrilles. The store has shod such luminaries as Pope John Paul II and Jack Nicholson during its years of service – be warned, however, that these names are good indications of the kind of styles you'll find on sale. Prices are fairly low (around €12) for basic models.

Sala Parés

C/Petritxol 5 (93 318 70 20, www. salapares.com). Metro Liceu. **Open** *July 10.30am-2pm, 4-8pm Mon-Fri; 10.30am-2pm, 4-8.30pm Sat. Oct-June 10.30am-2pm, 4-8pm Mon-Fri; 10.30am-2pm, 4-8.30pm Sat; 11.30am-2pm Sun. Closed Aug.* **Map** *p70 H9* ❽ *Gallery*

The elegant Sala Parés, founded in 1840, is a grand, two-tier space that smells deliciously of wood varnish and oil paint. Conservative figurative and historical paintings are the mainstay. In September, Sala Parés hosts the Young Painters' Prize. A young Picasso held his very first solo show in the Sala Parés in 1905.

Entertainment

Café Royale

C/Nou de Zurbano 3 (93 318 89 56, www.royalebcn.com). Metro Liceu. **Open** *8.30pm-2.30am Tue-Sat.* **Admission** *free.* **Map** *p70 H10* ❶ *Bar*

Just off Plaça Reial, Café Royale offers a little more conversation, a little less action. Early in the evening it's a chilled place to slump on sofas, but later, when Fred Guzzo's funk, soul and jazz-driven beats are cranked up, the youngish crowd seems happier rubbing against each other at the bar than on the dancefloor. It's working on upgrading its image with tapas and a proper wine list.

La Manual Alpargatera

❤ Cinema Maldà

C/Pi 5, Barri Gòtic (93 301 93 50, www.cinemamalda.com). Metro Catalunya or Liceu. Tickets (all day) €5 Mon, Tue, Thur; €4.50 Wed; €9 Fri-Sun; (evening only) €5 Fri-Sun. **No cards.** *Map p70 H9* ❷ *Cinema*

In its latest incarnation, the well-loved Maldà shows a curious hotchpotch of indie and arthouse films, alongside mainstream fare and cult films of recent years. Tickets (except evening-only tickets) are valid for all of that day's screenings, so you could see up to seven films for one price.

❤ Gran Teatre del Liceu

La Rambla 51-59, Barri Gòtic (93 485 99 00, www.liceubarcelona. cat). Metro Liceu. **Box office** *9.30am-8pm Mon-Fri; 9.30am-6pm Sat, Sun. Closed 2wks Aug. Tickets vary.* **Map** *p70 G9* ❸ *Theatre*

Since it opened in 1847, two fires, a bombing and a financial crisis have failed to quash the spirit and splendour of the Liceu, one of the most prestigious venues in the world. A restrained façade opens into a 2,292-seat auditorium of red plush, gold leaf and ornate carvings. The latest mod cons include seat-back subtitles in various languages that complement the Catalan surtitles above the stage. Under the stewardship of artistic director Christina Scheppelmann and musical director Josep Pons, the Liceu has consolidated its programming, mixing co-productions with leading international opera houses with in-house productions. Classical, full-length opera is the staple –Wagner's *The Flying Dutchman*, Verdi's *Il Trovatore* and Mozart's *Don Giovanni*, for example – but pocket opera and even pop also feature.

A large basement bar hosts pre-performance talks and recitals, as well as children's shows (Le Petit Liceu) and other musical events. The **Espai Liceu** is a 50-seat auditorium with a regular programme of screenings of past operas, while the swish six-floor **Conservatori** (C/Nou de la Rambla 82-88, 93 327 12 00, www. conservatoriliceu.es), which is part of the Liceu, lends its 400-seater basement auditorium to classical and contemporary concerts, small-scale operas and jazz.

▶ *For more on classical music and opera in the city, see p39.*

BARRI GÒTIC & LA RAMBLA

♥ Harlem Jazz Club

*C/Comtessa de Sobradiel 8 (93 310
07 55, www.harlemjazzclub.es).
Metro Jaume I. **Open** July-Sept
8pm-4am Tue-Thur; 8pm-5am
Fri, Sat. Oct-June 8pm-4am Tue-
Thur, Sun; 8pm-5am Fri, Sat. Gigs
10pm Tue-Thur, Sun; 11pm Fri, Sat.
Closed 2wks Aug. **Admission** €7
Tue-Thur, Sun; €9 Fri, Sat. **Map** p70
H10* ❹ *Live music*

A hangout for not-so-cashed-up
musicians, buffs and students alike.
A lot of local history has gone down
at Harlem over the last quarter
century or so, and some of the city's
great talents have emerged here.
Jazz, klezmer, funk and flamenco
get a run in a venue that holds no
musical prejudices.

Jamboree/Los Tarantos

*Plaça Reial 17 (93 319 17 89, www.
masimas.com). Metro Liceu. **Open**
midnight-5am Mon-Thur, Sun;
midnight-6am Fri, Sat. Shows
Jamboree 8pm, 10pm daily. Los
Tarantos 8.30pm, 9.30pm, 10.30pm
daily. **Admission** Shows Jamboree
varies; Los Tarantos €15 daily. Club
€10. **Map** p70 G10* ❺ *Live music*

Every night, the cave-like Jamboree
hosts jazz, Latin or blues gigs
by mainly Spanish groups – on
Mondays, in particular, the popular
WTF jazz jam session is crammed
with a young local crowd. Upstairs,
slicker sister venue Los Tarantos
stages flamenco performances,
then joins forces with Jamboree to
become one fun, cheesy club later
on in the evening. You'll need to
leave the venue and pay again, but
admission serves for both spaces.

Marula Café

*C/Escudellers 49 (93 318 76 90,
www.marulacafe.com). Metro
Liceu. **Open** 11pm-5am Mon-
Thur, Sun; 11.30pm-6am Fri;
9.30pm-6am Sat. **Admission** free-
€10 (incl 1 drink). **Map** p70 H10*
❻ *Club*

Grown-up clubbers were thrilled
when the popular Marula Café in
Madrid announced it was opening
a sister club in Barcelona, and it
hasn't disappointed. The musical
policy is what is known in Spain,
somewhat uncomfortably, as
música negra – a fairly useless
label that in this case ranges
from Sly and the Family Stone to
Michael Jackson via Fela Kuti,
but is a byword for quality and
danceability. On Saturday nights
musicians play from about 9.30pm.
Admission is fairly randomly
charged, but seems not to apply if
there's no queue.

♥ El Paraigua

*C/Pas de l'Ensenyança 2 (93 302
11 31, www.elparaigua.com).
Metro Jaume I or Liceu. **Open**
noon-midnight Mon-Wed, noon-
2am Thur; noon-3am Fri, Sat.
Admission free. **Map** p70 H9*
❼ *Live music*

Upstairs is a beautifully elegant
Modernista cocktail bar, whereas
downstairs is a cosy vaulted space
framed by bare-brick walls, which
sees some of Barcelona's most
promising new bands performing
on Friday and Saturday nights. The
music programme in any given
month might include an Irish soul
singer, a British funk band and a
mixed-nationality a cappella group.

Sidecar Factory Club

*Plaça Reial 7 (93 302 15 86,
sidecarfactoryclub.com). Metro
Liceu. **Open** 7pm-5am Mon-Thur;
7pm-6am Fri, Sat. **Admission**
€5-€12. **Map** p70 H10* ❽ *Club*

The Sidecar Factory Club still has
all the ballsy attitude of the spit 'n'
sawdust rock club that it used to be.
Its programming, which includes
breakbeat, indie, electro and live
performances, has changed a bit
over recent times, but continues
to pack in the local indie kids and
Interrailers to its bare-bricked,
barrel-vaulted basement.

Born & Sant Pere

Demarcated to the east by the glorious Parc de la Ciutadella and to the west by Via Laietana, Born is the most uptown area of downtown. A curious blend of the ecclesiastical, the elegant and the edgy, it now commands some of the highest property prices in the city. Label-happy coolhunters throng the Born's pedestrian streets, where museums, restored 13th-century mansions and churches alternate with cafés, galleries and boutiques.

Regeneration has come more slowly for the neighbouring area of Sant Pere, north of C/Princesa, which maintains a slightly grungier feel despite the municipal money-pumping. Still, there have been recent large-scale improvements, such as the long Plaça Pou de la Figuera and the spectacularly reinvented **Santa Caterina** market. In the eastern corner of the market is the **Espai Santa Caterina**, which houses a portion of the

Best architectural gems
Palau de la Música Catalana (*p98*)
for its flamboyant interior. Santa
Maria del Mar (*p92*) for Catalan
Gothic at its finest.

Best museum
Museu Picasso (*p90*) for an
in-depth look at the artist's
youthful works.

Best outdoor space
Parc de la Ciutadella (*p88*) for
excellent tree climbing.

Best regional cuisine
Casa Delfín (*p93*) for Catalan
flavours. Euskal Etxea (*p95*) for
the best *pintxos* in the city.

Best night-time haunt
Guzzo (*p95*) for cocktails and rare
groove. Paradiso (*p95*) for late-
night munchies.

Best shops for gifts
Arlequí Màscares (*p96*) for masks,
trinkets and toys. Casa Gispert
(*p96*) for foodie fanatics.

archaeological remains discovered during the market's
remodelling. The area may be medieval in origin,
but its finest monument is an extraordinary piece of
Modernisme – the **Palau de la Música Catalana**.

At one end of the Passeig del Born is the old Born
market, a magnificent 1870s wrought-iron structure,
now a cultural centre. At the other end stands the
greatest of all Catalan Gothic buildings, the spectacular
basilica of **Santa Maria del Mar**. Opposite the church's
main doors is a 13th-century drinking fountain with
gargoyles of an eagle and a dragon; on the east side is
the **Fossar de les Moreres** (Mulberry Graveyard) – a
funnel-shaped red-brick square built in 1989 on the site
where, it's believed, the last defenders of the city were
executed after Barcelona fell to the Spanish army in 1714.
Leading off the Passeig del
Born is **C/Montcada**, one
of the unmissable streets of
old Barcelona, lined with a
succession of 15th-century
merchants' mansions and
home to the **Museu Picasso**.

→ Getting around
The Born is almost entirely
pedestrianised, and only a
five-minute walk from west to
east. Jaume I metro station is
the most convenient.

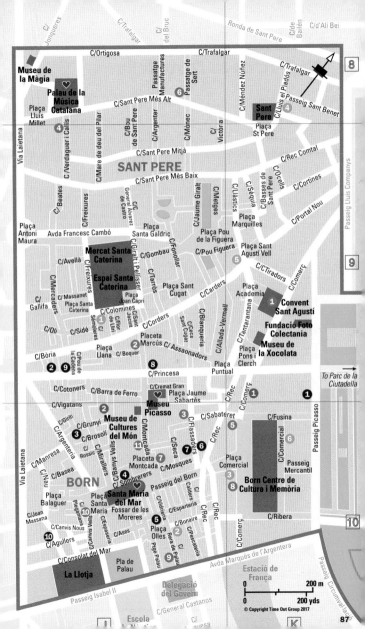

💜 Parc de la Ciutadella

Passeig Picasso (mobile 638 23 71 15). Metro Arc de Triomf or Barceloneta. **Open** *10am-sunset daily.* **Admission** *free.* **Map** *p87 K10.*

There's so much going on in this extensive park – the Zoo, Catalan parliament buildings, a school, a church, a boating lake, a bandstand – that it's sometimes hard to find a plain, old-fashioned patch of grass. On a sunny Sunday you'll have to fight with hordes of picnicking families, bongo players and dogs for a bit of the green stuff; even then it will be distinctly worn from serving as a back garden to the space-starved inhabitants of the Old City.

The park is named after the hated Bourbon citadel that occupied this site from 1716 to 1869, and came into being after the revolution of 1868, when General Prim announced the area could be reclaimed for public use. Later, pleasure gardens were built to host the 1888 Universal Exhibition.

Of interest in the park is Domènech i Montaner's red-brick-and-tile Castell de Tres Dragons. Alongside is the wide, leafy Passeig dels Til·lers. Here you'll find the iron-and-glass, Eiffel-inspired Hivernacle (Winter House) and the Umbracle (Shade House) – an elegant slatted wooden building.

Within the park you'll find La Cascada, an extravagant waterfall designed by Josep Fontseré, assisted by a young and – at the time – unknown Antoni Gaudí.

Below the pretty boating lake lie the Catalan parliament buildings, and the elegant Patio de Armes garden, full of roses in spring.

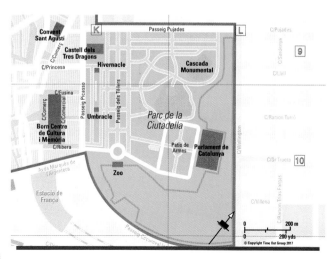

Born Centre de Cultura i Memòria

of buildings razed by Philip V's troops in 1714. These were found to contain hundreds of objects, some domestic and some, like rusty bombs, suggesting the traumas of the period. It was then that the idea for the Born Centre came about – a vast, virtually open-air space, open on four sides to the passing public, opened in time for the celebrations of the tricentenary of the Catalan defeat, in 2014.

Even the naysayers (those who wanted a library, or those who resented public money being thrown at what they perceive as nationalist endeavour) were impressed. It's a glorious, lofty space, with the archaeological remains visible from above (or close up via a guided tour). There's a Catalan restaurant, a quirky gift shop, a permanent collection displaying some of the finds uncovered in the remains, and a handful of rooms used for cultural events.

Fundació Foto Colectania

Passeig Picasso 14 (93 217 16 26, www.fotocolectania.org). Metro Jaume I. **Open** *11am-8pm Tue-Sat; 11am-3pm Sun.* **Admission** *€4; €3 reductions; free under-14s. No cards.* **Map** *p87 K9.*
This private foundation is dedicated to the promotion of the photography of major Spanish and Portuguese photographers from the 1950s to the present. It also has an extensive library of Spanish and Portuguese photography books.

Museu de Cultures del Món

C/Montcada 12 (93 256 23 00, museuculturesmon.bcn.cat). Metro Jaume I. **Open** *10am-7pm Tue-Sat; 10am-8pm Sun.* **Permanent exhibition** *€5; €3.50 reductions.* **Temporary exhibitions** *€2.20; €1.50 reductions. Free 3-8pm Sun & all day 1st Sun of mth.* **Map** *p87 J10.*

Sights & museums

Born Centre de Cultura i Memòria

Plaça Comercial 12 (93 256 68 51, www.elborncentrecultural.cat). Metro Jaume I or Barceloneta. **Open** *Mar-Oct 10am-8pm Tue-Sun. Nov-Feb 10am-7pm Tue-Sat; 10am-8pm Sun.* **Building** *free.* **Exhibitions** *€4.40; €3.08 reductions; free under-16s.* **Map** *p87 K10.*
Plans to turn the old Born market into a library were thwarted by the discovery of perfectly preserved medieval remains, the foundations

❤ Museu Picasso

C/Montcada 15-23 (93 256 30 00, www.museupicasso.bcn.cat). Metro Jaume I. **Open** *(last ticket 30mins before closing) 9am-7pm Tue, Wed, Fri-Sun; 9am-9.30pm Thur.* **Admission** *All exhibitions €11-€14; €7-€7.50 reductions. Annual pass €15. Temporary exhibition only €4.50-€6.50; €4.50 reductions; free under-18s. Free (permanent exhibition only) 3-7pm Sun & all day 1st Sun of mth.* **Map** *p87 J9.*

When it opened in 1963, the museum dedicated to Barcelona's favourite adopted son was housed in the Palau Aguilar. Five decades later, the permanent collection of some 3,500 pieces has now spread out across five adjoining palaces, two of which are devoted to temporary exhibitions.

By no means an overview of the artist's work, the Museu Picasso is a record of the vital formative years the young Picasso spent nearby at La Llotja art school (where his father taught), and later hanging out with Catalonia's fin-de-siècle avant-garde. Those looking for hits such as *Les Demoiselles d'Avignon* (1907) and the first Cubist paintings from the time (many of them done in Catalonia), as well as his collage and sculpture, will be disappointed. The founding of the museum is down to a key figure in Picasso's life, his friend and secretary Jaume Sabartés, who donated his own collection for the purpose. Tribute is paid with a room dedicated to Picasso's portraits of Sabartés (best known is the Blue Period painting of

Sabartés wearing a white ruff), and Sabartés's own doodlings. The seamless presentation of Picasso's development from 1890 to 1904 – from deft pre-adolescent portraits and sketchy landscapes to the intense innovations of his Blue Period – is unbeatable, then it leaps to a gallery of mature Cubist paintings from 1917. The *pièce de résistance* is the complete series of 58 canvases based on Velázquez's famous *Las Meninas*, donated by Picasso himself after the death of Sabartés, and now stretching through the Great Hall. The display ends with linocuts, engravings and a wonderful collection of ceramics donated by Picasso's widow.

Occupying yet another 15th-century palazzo on the C/Montcada, the Museum of World Cultures takes a look at the ancient peoples of Latin America, Asia, Oceania and sub-Saharan Africa through an impressive selection of artworks, sculpture, tools and weapons, from New Guinean fertility symbols to Ethiopian retablos. Many exhibits require background reading to be interesting, but the museum works hard on accessibility, with interactive gadgetry, a downloadable app and a series of suggested highlight tours aimed at children.

Museu de la Màgia

C/Jonqueres 15 (93 318 71 92, www.elreydelamagia.com). Metro Urquinaona. **Open** *11am-2pm, 4-8pm Tue-Sun.* **Admission** *€5; €3 reductions.* **Map** *p87 J8.*
This collector's gallery of 19th- and 20th-century tricks and posters from the magic shop El Rei de la Màgia will enchant any budding magicians. To see some live sleight of hand, book for the occasional shows (see website); places are limited. They're not in English, but they are very visual, so it doesn't matter too much.

❤ Museu de la Xocolata

C/Comerç 36 (93 268 78 78, www.museudelaxocolata.cat). Metro Arc de Triomf or Jaume I. **Open** *mid June-mid Sept 10am-8pm Mon-Sat; 10am-3pm Sun. Mid Sept-mid June 10am-7pm Mon-Sat; 10am-3pm Sun.* **Admission** *€6; €5.10 reductions; free under-7s.* **Map** *p87 K9.*
The best-smelling museum in town draws chocoholics of all ages to its collection of chocolate sculptures made by Barcelona's master *pastissers* for the Easter competition; these range from multicoloured models of Gaudí's Casa Batlló to characters from the latest Pixar film. Audio-visual shows and touch-screen computers help children make their way through what would otherwise be the rather dry history of the cocoa bean.

❤ Zoo

Parc de la Ciutadella (93 225 67 80, www.zoobarcelona.com). Metro Barceloneta or Ciutadella-Vila Olímpica. **Open** *Jan-mid Mar, Oct-Dec 10am-5pm daily. Mid Mar-mid May, mid Sept-end Oct 10am-6pm daily. Mid May-mid Sept 10am-7pm daily.* **Admission** *€19.90; €11.95 3-12s; free under-3s.* **Map** *p88 K10.*
A decently sized zoo with plenty of animals, all of which look happy enough in reasonably sized enclosures and the city's comfortable climate. The dolphin shows are no more, but other favourites include giant hippos, the prehistoric-looking rhino, sea lions, elephants, giraffes, lions and tigers. Child-friendly features include a farmyard zoo, pony rides, picnic areas and two excellent playgrounds. If all that walking is too much, there's a zoo 'train'. Bear in mind that on hot days many of the animals are sleeping and out of sight, whilst below 13°C many are kept inside.

Restaurants

Bacoa €

C/Colomines 2 (93 268 95 48). Metro Jaume I. **Open** *1-11pm Tue-Thur; 1pm-midnight Fri, Sat.* **No cards.** **Map** *p87 J9* ❶ *Burgers*
The best gourmet burger place around. Succulent chargrilled half-pounders are loaded up with manchego cheese, caramelised onions and a whole load of more outré toppings (try the Swiss, with rösti and gruyère, or the Japanese with teriyaki sauce).

💙 Santa Maria del Mar

*Plaça de Santa Maria (93 310 23 90, www.santamariadelmarbarcelona. org). Metro Jaume I. **Open** 9am-1pm, 5-8 pm Mon-Sat; 10am-2pm, 5-8pm Sun. **Admission** free. **Map** p87 J10.*

One of the most perfect surviving examples of the Catalan Gothic style, this graceful basilica stands out for its horizontal lines, plain surfaces, square buttresses and flat-topped octagonal towers. Its superb unity of style is down to the fact that it was built relatively quickly, taking just 55 years (1329-1384).

Named after Mary as patroness of sailors, it was built on the site of a small church known as Santa Maria d'Arenys (sand), for its position close to the sea. In the broad, single-nave interior, two rows of perfectly proportioned columns soar up to fan vaults,

creating an atmosphere of space around the light-flooded altar. There's also superb stained glass, especially the great 15th-century rose window above the main door. The original window fell down during an earthquake, killing 25 people. The incongruous modern window at the other end was a 1997 addition, belatedly celebrating the Olympics.

It's perhaps thanks to the group of anti-clerical anarchists who set the church ablaze for 11 days in 1936 that its superb features can be appreciated – without the wooden Baroque furniture that clutters so many Spanish churches, the simplicity of its lines can emerge.

On Saturdays, the basilica is in great demand for weddings, and it's a traditional venue for concerts: look out for a Requiem Mass at Easter and Handel's *Messiah* at Christmas.

Cal Pep €€

Plaça de les Olles 8 (93 310 79 61, www.calpep.com). Metro Barceloneta. **Open** *7.30-11.30pm Mon; 1-3.45pm, 7.30-11.30pm Tue-Fri; 1-3.45pm Sat. Closed 3wks Aug.* **Map** *p87 J10* ② *Seafood*

As much tapas bar as restaurant, Cal Pep is always packed to the hilt: get here early to bag one of the coveted seats at the front. There is a cosy dining room at the back, but it's a shame to miss the show. The affable Pep will take the order, steering neophytes towards the *trifásico* – a mélange of fried whitebait, squid rings and shrimp. Other favourites include the exquisite little *tallarines* (wedge clams), and *botifarra* sausage with beans. Then squeeze in four shot glasses of foam – coconut with rum, coffee, *crema catalana* and lemon – as a light and scrumptious pudding.

❤ Casa Delfín €€

Passeig del Born 36 (93 319 50 88, tallerdetapas.com/esp/casa-delfin). Metro Barceloneta or Jaume I. **Open** *8am-midnight Mon-Thur, Sun; 8am-1am Fri, Sat.* **Map** *p87 K10* ③ *Catalan*

Locals were heartbroken when the old, beloved Casa Delfín served its last plate of fried sardines, but it has scrubbed up very nicely indeed in its new incarnation. Meticulous attention has been paid to respecting traditional Catalan recipes, with a rich and sticky *suquet* (fish stew) and excellent 'mountain' lamb with wild mushrooms. Brit owner Kate has left her imprint, however, and you'll also find the best Eton mess this side of Windsor.

En Aparté €

C/Lluís el Piadós 2 (93 269 13 35, www.enaparte.es). Metro Arc de Triomf. **Open** *10am-1.30am Mon-Thur, Sun; 10am-2am Fri, Sat.* **Map** *p87 K8* ④ *French*

The peaceful Plaça Sant Pere has never been well served with good places to eat or drink, so this relaxed, sunny and spacious café-restaurant has been joyfully received in the neighbourhood. French cheeses and charcuterie are the mainstays of the kitchen, served for the most part on toasted bread with a well-dressed salad. The all-French wine list makes for a refreshing change, and there is a good-value set lunch.

Mundial Bar €€

Plaça Sant Agustí Vell 1 (93 319 90 56). Metro Arc de Triomf or Jaume I. **Open** *1-3.30pm, 8pm-midnight daily.* **No cards.** **Map** *p87 K9* ⑤ *Seafood*

Since 1925, this family bar has been dishing up no-frills platters of seafood, cheeseboards and the odd slice of cured meat. Colourful tiles add charm to the rather basic decoration, but it's not as cheap as it looks. People come for the steaming piles of fresh razor clams, oysters, fiddler crabs and the like, but there's also plenty of tinned produce, so check the bar displays to see exactly which is which.

La Paradeta €

C/Comercial 7 (93 268 19 39, www.laparadeta.com). Metro Arc de Triomf or Jaume I. **Open** *1-4pm, 8-11.30pm Tue-Thur; 1-4pm, 8pm-midnight Fri, Sat; 1-4pm Sun.* **No cards.** **Map** *p87 K10* ⑥ *Seafood*

Superb seafood, served in a refectory-style fashion. Choose from glistening mounds of clams, mussels, squid, spider crabs and other fresh treats, decide how you would like it cooked (grilled, steamed or *a la marinera*), pick a sauce (Marie Rose, spicy local romesco, allioli or onion), buy a drink and wait for your number to be called. A great – and cheap – experience for anyone who is not too grand to clear away their own plate.

Cafés, tapas & bars

Bar del Convent

*Plaça de l'Acàdemia (93 256 50 17,
www.bardelconvent.com). Metro
Arc de Triomf or Jaume I.* **Open**
10am-9pm Tue-Sat. **Map** *p87 K9* ❶
The 14th-century Convent
de Sant Agustí has had a new
lease of life in recent years with
James Turrell's fabulous 'light
sculpture' surrounding the C/
Comerç entrance, and a dynamic
civic centre. This secluded little
café is in the cloister. Croissants,
pastries and light dishes are
available all day, and bands, DJs,
storytellers and other performers
occasionally feature.

Bar del Pla

*C/Montcada 2 (93 268 30 03, www.
bardelpla.cat). Metro Jaume I.*
Open *noon-11pm Tue-Thur; noon-
midnight Fri, Sat.* **Map** *p87 J9* ❷
Positioned somewhere between
a French bistro and a tapas bar,
the bright Bar del Pla serves tapas
or *raciones* (divine pig's trotters
with foie gras, outstanding *pa amb
tomàquet*). Drinks include Mahou
on tap (a fine beer, often ignored
here because it's from Madrid), plus
some good wines by the glass.

La Báscula de la Cerería

*C/Flassaders 30 (93 319 98 66).
Metro Jaume I.* **Open** *1pm-11pm
Wed-Sun.* **No cards.** **Map** *p87
J10* ❸
After a sustained campaign, the
threat of demolition has been lifted
from this former chocolate factory-
turned-café. Just as well, since it's
a real find, with good vegetarian
food and a large dining room out
back. An impressive list of drinks
runs from chai to glühwein, taking
in cocktails, milkshakes, smoothies
and iced tea; and the pasta
and cakes are as good as you'll
find anywhere.

El Bitxo

*C/Verdaguer i Callis 9 (93 268 17
08). Metro Urquinaona.* **Open**
*7pm-midnight Mon; 1pm-1am Tue-
Sun.* **No cards.** **Map** *p87 J9* ❹
This small, lively tapas bar
specialises in excellent cheese and
charcuterie from the small Catalan
village of Oix, along with more
outré fare such as salmon sashimi
with a coffee reduction. The wine
list is steadily increasing and now
has around 30 suggestions, all of
them good. Being so close to the
Palau de la Música, the bar can
get packed in the early evening
before concerts.

Bormuth

*C/Rec 31 (93 310 21 86). Metro
Jaume I.* **Open** *12.30pm-1.30am
Mon-Thur, Sun; 12.30pm-2.30am
Fri, Sat.* **Map** *p87 K10* ❺
Bormuth fills a hole in the market
with good, honest tapas in an
attractive setting, at reasonable
prices. All the usual tortillas,
patatas bravas and so on are
present, along with the highly
recommended fried aubergines
drizzled with honey, tuna belly
with Raf tomatoes.

Casa Lolea

*C/Sant Pere mès Alt (93 624 10 16,
casalolea.com). Metro Urquinaona.*
Bar *9am-1am daily.* **Kitchen**
noon-midnight daily. **Map** *p87
J8* ❻
Sangría gets a bad rap in northern
Spain, but Casa Lolea is chipping
away at the stigma with its craft
version, in ceramic swing-topped
bottles with semi-ironic flamenco
polka dot patterns. The company
has now branched out with a tapas
bar, where you'll find the sangría
complemented with some top-class
sharing plates, including dry-cured
tuna with orange and almonds,
salmon blinis with truffled honey
and smoked eel with ricotta.

❤ Euskal Etxea
Placeta Montcada 1-3 (93 343 54 10, www.euskaletxetaberna. com). Metro Barceloneta or Jaume I. Bar 10am-12.30am Mon-Fri, Sun; 10am-1am Sat. Restaurant 1-4pm, 8pm-midnight daily. Map p87 J10 ❼

A Basque cultural centre and the best of the city's many *pintxo* bars. Help yourself to dainty *jamón serrano* croissants, chicken tempura with saffron mayonnaise, melted provolone with mango and crispy ham, or a mini-brochette of pork. Hang on to the toothpicks spearing each one: they'll be counted up and charged for at the end. There is also a dining room at the back.

❤ Guzzo
Plaça Comercial 10 (93 667 00 36, www.guzzoclub.es). Metro Barceloneta. Open 6pm-3am Mon-Thur; 6pm-3.30am Fri, Sat; noon-3am Sun. Map p87 K10 ❽

One of Barcelona's best-loved DJs, Fred Guzzo, finally opened his own bar, where he can give full rein to his penchant for vintage soul and funk, spiced up with some live music acts at weekends. Cocktails are the speciality, and there are snacks and light dishes available during the day.

❤ Paradiso
C/Rera Palau 4 (93 360 72 22, paradiso.cat). Metro Arc de Triomf. Open 7pm-2am daily. Map p87 J10 ❾

Speakeasy-style bars are all the rage these days, but no one does it better than Paradiso, a cavernous cocktail bar entered via the portal of an antique fridge. It's worth lingering in the antechamber, however, where a selection of smoked meats and pickles are served, with a pastrami sandwich second to none.

La Vinya del Senyor
Plaça Santa Maria 5 (93 310 33 79). Metro Barceloneta or Jaume I. Open noon-1am Mon-Thur; noon-2am Fri, Sat; noon-midnight Sun. Map p87 J10 ❿

Though many pull up a chair simply to appreciate the splendours of Santa Maria del Mar's Gothic façade, it's a sin to take up the tables of the 'Vineyard of the Lord' without sampling a few of the excellent vintages on its list, along with some top-quality tapas.

El Xampanyet
C/Montcada 22 (93 319 70 03). Metro Jaume I. Open noon-3.30pm, 7-11pm Tue-Sat; noon-3.30pm Sun. Closed Aug. Map p87 J10 ⓫

The eponymous bubbly is actually a pretty low-grade cava, but a drinkable enough accompaniment to the house tapa – a saucer of Cantabrian anchovies. Lined with coloured tiles, barrels and antique curios, the bar functions as a little slice of Barcelona history and has been run by the same family since the 1930s.

Shops & services
Aire de Barcelona
Passeig Picasso 22 (93 295 5743, airedebarcelona.com). Metro Arc de Triomf or Jaume I. Open 9am-10.30pm Mon-Thur, Sun; 9am-midnight Fri, Sat. Baths (90mins) €36/€39; (incl 15min massage) €53/€56. Map p93 K9 ❶ *Hammam*

These subterranean, bare-bricked Arab baths are superbly relaxing, and offer a range of extra massages in addition to the basic package of hot and cold pools, jacuzzi, salt-water pool, hammam and relaxation zone. Entrance is every hour from 10am (you get 90 minutes). Swimsuits can be borrowed.

💚 Arlequí Màscares

*C/Princesa 7 (93 268 27 52, www.
arlequimask.com). Metro Jaume I.
Open 10.30am-8.30pm Mon-Sat;
10.30am-7.30pm Sun.* **Map** *p87
J9* ❷ *Masks*

The walls in this lovely shop are
dripping with masks, crafted from
papier mâché and leather. Whether
gilt-laden or in feathered *commedia
dell'arte* style, simple Greek
tragicomedy styles or traditional
Japanese or Catalan varieties,
they make striking fancy dress or
decorative staples. Other trinkets
and toys include finger puppets,
mirrors and ornamental boxes.

Capricho de Muñeca

*C/Brosolí 1 (93 319 58 91, www.
caprichodemuneca.com). Metro
Jaume I.* **Open** *11.30am-3pm, 4.30-
8.30pm Mon-Sat.* **Map** *p87 J10* ❸
Luggage

Soft leather handbags in cherry
reds, parma violet and grass green
made by hand just upstairs by
designer Lisa Lempp. Sizes range
from the cute and petite to the
luxuriously large. Belts and wallets
complement the handbags.

💚 Casa Gispert

*C/Sombrerers 23 (93 319 75 35,
www.casagispert.com). Metro
Jaume I.* **Open** *10am-8.30pm Mon-
Sat.* **Map** *p87 J10* ❹ *Food & Drink*

Another Born favourite, Casa
Gispert radiates a warmth
generated by more than just its
original wood-fired nut and coffee
roaster. Like a stage-set version of
a Dickensian shoppe, its wooden
cabinets and shelves groan with
the finest and most fragrant nuts,
herbs, spices, preserves, sauces,
oils and seasonings. The kits for
making local specialities such as
panellets (Halloween bonbons)
make great gifts.

Aire de Barcelona

Custo Barcelona

*Plaça de les Olles 7 (93 268 78 93,
custo.com). Metro Jaume I.* **Open**
*10am-9pm Mon-Sat; noon-8pm
Sun.* **Map** *p87 J10* ❺ *Fashion*

The Custo look is synonymous
with Barcelona style, and the loud,
cut-and-paste print T-shirts have
spawned a thousand imitations.
Custodio Dalmau's signature prints
can now be found on everything
from coats to jeans to swimwear for
both men and women, but a T-shirt
is still the most highly prized (and
highly priced) souvenir for visiting
fashionistas. There's also a Custo
Outlet (Plaça del Pi 2, Barri Gòtic,
93 304 27 53).

Èstro

*C/Flassaders 33 (93 310 40 77).
Metro Jaume I.* **Open** *5-9pm Mon;
11.30am-3pm, 5-9pm Tue-Sat.*
Map *p87 J10* ❻ *Shoes*

This narrow street is full of original
fashion boutiques, but Èstro stands
out for its small but exquisite
collection of Italian footwear for
men and women. All beautifully
made by hand from soft, supple
leather, the range runs from high-
heeled knee boots in rich berry
shades for women to contemporary
takes on the Oxford shoe for men.
There is also a small selection of
bags, belts and clothes.

Loisada

*C/Flassaders 42 (93 295 54 92, www.loisaidabcn. com). Metro Barceloneta. **Open** 10.30am-8.30pm Mon-Sat. **Map** p87 J10* ❼ *Fashion*

Housed in the cavernous former stables of the 15th-century Royal Mint building, Loisada sells a huge range of men's and women's clothing with a distinctly 'summer in the Hamptons' feel and a touch of retro bohemian chic. You'll also find beautifully packed toiletries, chocolates and a smattering of antiques.

On Land

*C/Princesa 25 (93 310 02 11, www. on-land.com). Metro Jaume I. **Open** 1-8.30pm Mon; 11am-8.30pm Tue-Sat. **Map** p87 J9* ❽ *Fashion*

This little oasis of urban cool has all you need to hold your head up high against the Barcelona hip squad: bags and wallets by Becksöndergaard and Can't Go Naked; cute skirts by y-dress; loose cotton trousers by IKKS; covetable T-shirts by Fresh from the Lab.

El Rei de la Màgia

*C/Princesa 11 (93 319 39 20, www. elreydelamagia.com). Metro Jaume I. **Open** 10.30am-2pm, 4-7.30pm Mon-Sat. **Map** p87 J9* ❾ *Magic tricks*

Cut someone in half, make a rabbit disappear or try out any number of other professional-quality stage illusions at the beautiful old 'King of Magic'. Less ambitious tricksters can practise their sleight of hand with the huge range of whoopee cushions, squirty flowers and itching powder.

The shop operates the city's only theatre dedicated exclusively to magic shows at C/Jonqueres 15 (93 318 71 92).

❤ Vila Viniteca

*C/Agullers 7 (902 32 77 77, www. vilaviniteca.es). Metro Jaume I. **Open** Sept-June 8.30am-8.30pm Mon-Sat. July, Aug 8.30am-8.30pm Mon-Fri; 8.30am-2pm Sat. **Map** p87 J10* ❿ *Food & Drink*

Whether you want to blow €3,000 on a magnum of 2005 Clos Erasmus or just snag a €5 bottle of table wine, you'll find something to drink. The selection here is mostly Spanish and Catalan, but does cover international favourites. The food shop next door at no.9 stocks fine cheeses, cured meats and oils.

Entertainment

The Mix

*C/Comerç 21 (93 319 46 96, www. mixbcn.com). Metro Jaume I. **Open** Apr-Sept 9pm-3am Tue-Sat. Oct-Mar 9pm-3am Wed, Thur; 9pm-3.30am Fri, Sat. **Admission** free. **Map** p87 K9.* ❶ *Bar*

With an interior designed by local tastemaker Silvia Prada, a fashionable postcode and a menu of delicate finger foods, Mix attracts a professional, stylish crowd who enjoy both an after-work cocktail and an after-dinner piss-up. DJs play funk, soul and world beat on Thursdays, and safe and sophisticated rare groove the rest of the time. There's live bossa nova and jazz on Tuesdays.

Rubí

*C/Banys Vells 6 (mobile 647 737 707). Metro Jaume I. **Open** 7.30pm-2.30am Mon-Thur, Sun; 7.30pm-3am Fri, Sat. **Admission** free. **No cards**. **Map** p87 J10.* ❷ *Bar*

A long and narrow bar with stone walls, suffused with a womb-like red glow that can make it hard to leave. The speciality at Rubí is pocket-friendly (€4) mojitos, home-made gins and tasty bar snacks.

♥ Palau de la Música Catalana

C/Sant Francesc de Paula 2 (93 295 72 00, www.palaumusica.org). Metro Urquinaona. **Box office** *9.30am-9pm Mon-Sat; 10am-3pm Sun.* **Guided tours** *10am-3.30pm daily. Aug 9am-6pm daily.* **Admission** *€18; €11 reductions; free under-10s. Concert tickets vary.* **Map** *p87 J8.*

Commissioned by the Orfeó Català choral society and opened in 1908, this jaw-dropping concert hall was intended as a paean to the Catalan *renaixença* and a showcase for the most outstanding Modernista workmanship available. Domènech i Montaner's façade is a frenzy of colour and detail, including a large allegorical mosaic representing the members of the Orfeó Català, and floral tiled columns topped with the busts of Bach, Beethoven and Palestrina on the main façade and Wagner on the side. Inside, a great deal of money has been spent improving the acoustics, but visitors don't really come to feast their ears: the eyes have it.

Decoration erupts everywhere. The ceiling is an inverted bell of stained glass on which the sun bursts out of a blue sky; 18 half-mosaic, half-relief muses appear out of the back of the stage; winged horses fly over the upper balcony. The carved arch over the stage represents folk and classical music: the left side has Catalan composer/conductor Anselm Clavé sitting over young girls singing 'Flors de Maig', a traditional Catalan song, while the right has Wagnerian Valkyries riding over a bust of Beethoven.

By the 1980s, the Palau was bursting under the pressure of the musical activity going on inside it, and a church next door was demolished to make space for Òscar Tusquet's extension; a project that, combined with the extensive renovations to the old building, spanned more than 20 years. Rather than try to compete with the existing façade, the new part has subtler organic motifs in ochre brick.

Now directed by the affable Joan Oller, the Palau has welcomed some of the finest performers from around the globe over the years, including the likes of Leonard Bernstein and Daniel Barenboim. Guided tours are available in English every hour and start with a short film of the Palau's history.

Raval

The Raval was seen for a long time as the city's forbidden core, its dark 'other'. In the early 20th century, the area was notorious for its seedy theatres, brothels, anarchist groups and dosshouses. Widespread gentrification has ensued in recent times, though the Raval has not completely lost its associations with crime and sleaze. Take care, particularly after dark in the area down towards the port. That said, the Raval can make for a fascinating wander.

With an influx of non-European immigrants in the 1990s, the Raval is now one of the most ethnically diverse places in Europe, with more than 70 different nationalities calling it home. Shop signs appear in a babel of languages, plugging everything from halal meat to Bollywood films.

Best Romanesque architecture
Sant Pau del Camp (*p103*) for its façade and pretty cloister.

Best modern architecture
MACBA (*p104*) for spanking white minimalism. CCCB (*p103*) for juxtaposing old and new.

Best for a Gaudí fix
Palau Güell (*p107*) for rainbow-tiled chimneys and a deceptively grand interior.

Best for cooking with soul
Caravelle (*p105*) for a top-notch brunch. Mam i Teca (*p105*) for organic tapas.

Best for a nightcap
Casa Almirall (*p108*) for cosy Modernista decor.

Best for fashion
Holala! Plaza + Gallery (*p109*) for vintage threads. Med Winds (*p109*) for elegant tailoring.

Best for a bargain set lunch
Bar Lobo (*p106*) for fußball and tapas. Silenus (*p106*) for artistic fare.

Best authentic night out
Bar Pastís (*p110*) for a quintessentially Gallic bar experience. Jazz Sí Club (*p110*) for jazz, flamenco and Cuban music.

The area north of C/Hospital (the Upper Raval) has seen the most changes, and buzzes with art galleries and bars. Dominating the Upper Raval is the Plaça dels Àngels, where the 16th-century Convent dels Àngels houses a gigantic almshouse, the Casa de la Caritat, which has been converted into a cultural complex housing the spanking-white **MACBA** and the **CCCB**. Over the years, the square has become unofficial home to the city's skateboarders, and the surrounding streets have filled with restaurants and boutiques.

The Lower Raval's main street, C/Nou de la Rambla, is home to Gaudí's first major project: the **Palau Güell**. Nearby sits the Romanesque church of **Sant Pau del Camp**. Iberian remains dating to 200 BC have been found next to the church, marking it as one of the oldest parts of the city.

➔ Getting around
The Raval is easily traversed on foot, and the closest metro stations are on La Rambla – from top to bottom, Catalunya, Liceu and Drassanes.

RAVAL

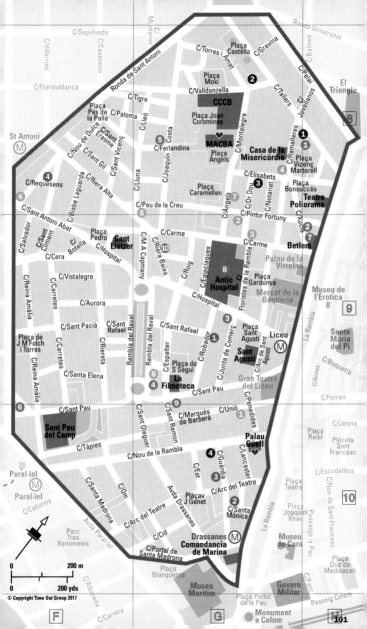

CCCB

Sights & museums

Antic Hospital de la Santa Creu & La Capella

C/Carme 47-C/Hospital 56. Metro Liceu. **Open** *9am-11pm Mon-Sat.* **Admission** *free.* **Map** *p101 G9.*

This was one of Europe's earliest medical centres. There was a hospital on the site as early as 1024, but in the 15th century it expanded to centralise all the city's hospitals and sanatoriums (with the exception of the Santa Margarida leper colony, which remained outside the city walls). By the 1920s, it was hopelessly overstretched,

and its medical facilities were moved uptown to the Hospital Sant Pau. One of the last patients was Gaudí, who died here in 1926; it was also where Picasso painted one of his first important pictures, *Dead Woman* (1903).

The buildings combine a 15th-century Gothic core with Baroque and classical additions. They are now home to the Massana Arts School and a small neighbourhood library, as well as the much larger Catalan National Library (the second largest in Spain), the headquarters of the Institute of Catalan Studies and

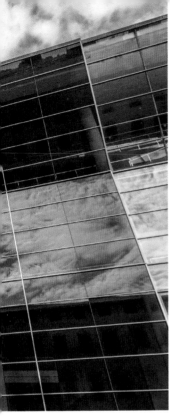

and sensitively converted into an exhibition space for contemporary art. The courtyard is a popular spot for reading or eating lunch.

💜 **CCCB** (Centre de Cultura Contemporània de Barcelona) *C/Montalegre 5 (93 306 41 00, www.cccb.org). Metro Catalunya.* **Open** *11am-8pm Tue-Sun.* **Admission** *1 exhibition €6; €4 reductions. 2 exhibitions €8; €6 reductions. Free under-12s. Free to all 3-8pm Sun.* **Map** *p101 G8.*
Spain's largest cultural centre forms part of the Casa de la Caritat, a former almshouse. The massive façade and part of the courtyard remain from the original building; the rest was rebuilt in dramatic contrast, all tilting glass and steel, by architects Piñón and Viaplana, known for the Maremagnum shopping centre (*see p120*). The CCCB's exhibitions can lean towards heavy-handed didacticism, but there are occasional gems.

💜 **Sant Pau del Camp** *C/Sant Pau 101 (93 441 00 01). Metro Paral·lel.* **Open** *10am-1.30pm, 4-7.30pm Mon-Sat. Mass 8pm Sat (Spanish); noon Sun (Catalan).* **Admission** *€3; €2 reductions; free under-14s.* **Map** *p101 F10.*
The name St Paul in the Field reflects a time when the Raval was still countryside. In fact, this little Romanesque church is over 1,000 years old; the date carved on its most prestigious headstone – that of Count Guifré II Borrell, son of Wilfred 'the Hairy' and inheritor of all Barcelona and Girona – is AD 912. The church's impressive façade includes sculptures of fantastical flora and fauna along with human grotesques. The tiny cloister is another highlight, with its extraordinary Visigoth capitals, triple-lobed arches and central fountain.

the Royal Academy of Medicine, which hosts occasional concerts. Highlights include a neoclassical lecture theatre complete with revolving marble dissection table (open 10am-2pm Mon-Fri), and the entrance hall of the Casa de Convalescència, tiled with lovely Baroque ceramic murals telling the story of St Paul; one features an artery-squirting decapitation scene.

La Capella (93 442 71 71, lacapella.bcn.cat, open noon-8pm Tue-Sat, 11am-2pm Sun, free), the hospital chapel, was rescued from a sad fate as a warehouse

♥ MACBA (Museu d'Art Contemporani de Barcelona)

Plaça dels Àngels 1 (93 412 08 10, www.macba.cat). Metro Catalunya. **Open** *24 June-24 Sept 11am-8pm Mon, Wed-Fri; 10am-9pm Sat; 10am-3pm Sun. 25 Sept-23 June 11am-7.30pm Mon, Wed-Fri; 10am-9pm Sat; 10am-3pm Sun.* **Admission** *allows unlimited entry to all exhibitions for 1 mth €10; €8 reductions; free under-14s.* **Map** *p101 G8.*

If you're used to being soft-soaped by eager-to-please art centres, you'll have to make a bit of a mental adjustment to accommodate the cryptic minimalism of the MACBA, where art is taken very seriously indeed. Yet if you can navigate the fridge-like interior of Richard Meier's enormous edifice, accept that much of the permanent collection is inaccessible to the uninitiated, tackle shows that flutter between the brilliant and the baffling, and, most importantly, are prepared to do your reading, a trip to the MACBA can be extremely rewarding.

Since its inauguration in 1995, the MACBA has become a power player on the contemporary arts scene. Its library and auditorium host an extensive programme that includes accessibly priced (or free) concerts, conferences and cinema, while two floors of exhibition rooms offer a showcase for large-scale installations and exhaustive, multidisciplinary shows. La Capella, a former medieval convent across the square, is free to enter, and provides a project space for specially commissioned works. The permanent collection sits on the ground floor of the main building, and is rooted in the second half of the 20th century. Media, sound and performance art experimentalists of the 1960s and '70s, including Bruce Nauman, Joan Jonas and John Cage, are well represented, as are Spanish and Catalan artists such as Antoni Muntadas, Antoni Tàpies and the Dau al Set group.

Restaurants

Bar Cañete €€
*C/Unió 17 (93 270 34 58, www.
barcanete.com). Metro Universitat.
Open 1-4pm, 8pm-midnight Tue-
Sat. **Map** p101 G10* ❶ *Spanish*
Superb, upmarket tapas inspired by
classic dishes from all over Spain
but often given a twist: pork cheek
with smoked herring; Santa Pau
haricot bean stew with baby squid;
beef sweetbreads with prawn and
wild mushroom. The dining room
is long but thin and it pays to book
– get a seat up at the bar if you can.

❤ Caravelle €€
*C/Pintor Fortuny 31 (93 317 98
92, www.caravelle.es). Metro
Liceu. **Open** 9.30am-5pm Mon,
Tue; 9.30pm-midnight Wed-Sat;
10am-5.30pm Sun. **Map** p101 G9* ❷
Global
A little slice of London's Shoreditch
comes to the Raval in the shape
of this bright and minimalist
restaurant with its following of
bearded and checkshirted hipsters.
Don't be misled, however, for
Caravelle's cooking is all heart and
soul, whether it's a burger with
gorgonzola and pickled cabbage or
southern fried rabbit with corn. It
also serves one of the better brunch
menus in town, from 10am to 4pm.

Dos Trece €
*C/Carme 40 (93 301 73 06,
dostrece.net). Metro Liceu.
Restaurant 10am-midnight
daily. **Bar** 10am-2am Mon-Thur,
Sun; 10am-3am Fri, Sat. **Map** p101
G9* ❸ *Global*
A relaxation of local laws governing
live music means that Dos Trece's
cosy basement space once again
jumps to DJs and jam sessions, but
also functions as another dining
room – this one with cushions and
candles for post-prandial lounging.
Apart from a little fusion confusion
(ceviche with nachos, and all

manner of things served with yucca
chips), the food is not half bad for
the price.

Elisabets €
*C/Elisabets 2-4 (93 317 58 26,
www.elisabets1962.com). Metro
Catalunya. **Open** 7.30am-11pm
Mon-Thur, Sat; 7.30am-1am Fri.
Closed Aug. **No cards**. **Map** p101
G8* ❹ *Catalan*
Open in the mornings for breakfast,
and late night for drinking at the
bar, Elisabets maintains a sociable
local feel, despite the recent
gentrification of its street. There is
only a set lunch or, in the evenings,
tapas and myriad *bocadillos*.The
lunch deal (€10.85 Monday to
Saturday) is terrific value, however,
with osso buco, vegetable and
chickpea stew, baked cod with
garlic and parsley, and roast
pork knuckle all making regular
appearances on the menu.

❤ Mam i Teca €€
*C/Lluna 4 (93 441 33 35). Metro
Sant Antoni. **Open** 1-3.30pm,
8-11.30pm Mon, Wed-Fri, Sun;
8-11.30pm Sat. **No cards**. **Map** p101
G8* ❺ *Catalan*
This bright little restaurant only
has four tables, so it pays to
reserve in advance. All the usual
tapas, from anchovies to cured
meats, are rigorously sourced, and
complemented by superb daily
specials such as organic lamb
chops, pork confit and scrambled
egg with asparagus and shrimp.
Note that the restaurant is closed
on Tuesdays.

Sésamo €€
*C/Sant Antoni Abat 52 (93 441
64 11). Metro Sant Antoni. **Open**
8pm-midnight Tue-Sun. **Map** p101
F8* ❻ *Vegetarian*
Creative vegetarian and vegan
dishes, served in a buzzing
atmosphere. Options might
include curry with dahl and wild
rice or crunchy polenta with

baked pumpkin, gorgonzola and radicchio. There is an excellent tasting menu for €25 and daily-changing specials. Leave space for the apple crumble, and try the organic wine and beer.

♥ Silenus €€

C/Àngels 8 (93 302 26 80, www. restaurantsilenus.com). Metro Liceu. **Café/Bar** *9.30am-1am Mon-Sat.* **Restaurant** *1-11.30pm.* **Map** *p101 G8* ❼ *Mediterranean*
Named after one of the drunken followers of Dionysus, Silenus is nonetheless all about restraint. Its quiet dining room has an air of scuffed elegance, with carefully chipped and stained walls whereon the ghost of a clock is projected and the faded leaves of a book float up on high. The food, too, is artistically presented. The set lunch (€14) is generally a good bet, offering dishes from Caesar salad to crunchy gnocchi with creamed spinach or spicy *botifarra* with puréed potatoes. There is also a set dinner (€18) and a tasting menu (€35).

Suculent €€

Rambla del Raval 43 (93 443 65 79, suculent.com). Metro Paral·lel. **Open** *12.30pm-1am Wed-Sun.* **Map** *p101 G9* ❽ *Mediterranean*
Another from the stable of celebrity chef Carles Abellan, less fanciful than his Michelin-starred (but now closed) Comerç 24, but still upholding the highest standards in the kitchen. The dishes are mostly based on local specialities, but look out too for the steak tartare served on marrowbone and the skate with black butter, among other things. Leave room for the brie cheesecake with muscatel *gelée*.

Cafés, tapas & bars

Bar Kasparo

Plaça Vicenç Martorell 4 (93 302 20 72, www.kasparo.es). Metro Catalunya. **Open** *9am-10.30pm Tue-Sat. Closed mid Dec-mid Jan.* **Map** *p101 H8* ❶
Still the best of the various café terraces around the edges of the quiet, traffic-free Plaça Vicenç Martorell, Kasparo serves tapas, *bocadillos*, salads and a varying selection of more substantial dishes, available all day. There is no indoor seating, so this is more of a warm weather proposition.

♥ Bar Lobo

C/Pintor Fortuny 3 (93 481 53 46, www.grupotragaluz.com). Metro Catalunya. **Open** *9am-12.30pm Mon-Wed, Sun; 9am-1.30am Thur-Sat.* **Map** *p101 H9* ❷
Bar Lobo is a friendly place, with excellent food that ranges from traditional tapas to fusion classics – guacamole, tuna tataki, decent burgers. There's a fußball table upstairs, and the terrace is a peaceful space for coffee or breakfast, despite the proximity to La Rambla, except at lunchtimes, when it can get packed.

Bar Mendizábal

C/Junta de Comerç 2 (93 566 70 52). Metro Liceu. **Open** *8am-midnight daily.* **No cards.** **Map** *p101 G9* ❸
Considered something of a classic, Bar Mendizábal has been around for decades, its jolly multicoloured tiles and serving hatch a feature in thousands of holiday snaps. Until recently, it was little more than a hole in the wall – juices, sandwiches and soup were ordered and carried across to a terrace on the other side of the road, but its huge popularity means that it has recently expanded into a (small) dining room alongside the bar.

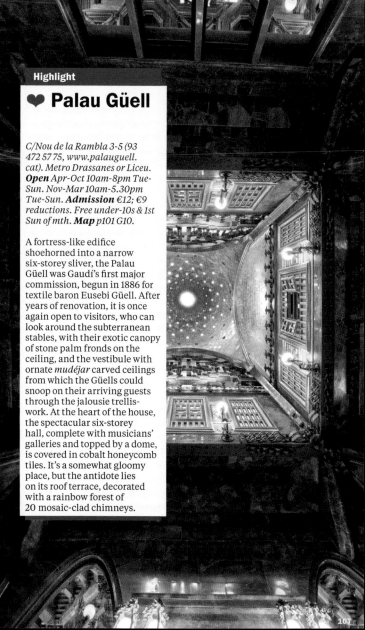

🖤 Palau Güell

C/Nou de la Rambla 3-5 (93 472 57 75, www.palauguell. cat). Metro Drassanes or Liceu. **Open** *Apr-Oct 10am-8pm Tue-Sun. Nov-Mar 10am-5.30pm Tue-Sun.* **Admission** *€12; €9 reductions. Free under-10s & 1st Sun of mth.* **Map** *p101 G10.*

A fortress-like edifice shoehorned into a narrow six-storey sliver, the Palau Güell was Gaudí's first major commission, begun in 1886 for textile baron Eusebi Güell. After years of renovation, it is once again open to visitors, who can look around the subterranean stables, with their exotic canopy of stone palm fronds on the ceiling, and the vestibule with ornate *mudéjar* carved ceilings from which the Güells could snoop on their arriving guests through the jalousie trellis-work. At the heart of the house, the spectacular six-storey hall, complete with musicians' galleries and topped by a dome, is covered in cobalt honeycomb tiles. It's a somewhat gloomy place, but the antidote lies on its roof terrace, decorated with a rainbow forest of 20 mosaic-clad chimneys.

Holalal Plaza + Gallery

Cafè de les Delicies

Rambla del Raval 47 (93 441 57 14). Metro Liceu. **Open** *9.30am-midnight Mon, Wed, Thur; 9.30am-4pm Tue; 9.30am-2am Fri; 11am-2.30am Sat, 11am-midnight Sun.* **Map** *p101 G9* ❹

The delightful Cafè de les Delicies serves breakfast, along with tapas and light dishes, in its dining room at the back. Off the corridor there's a snug with armchairs, but otherwise the buzzing front bar is the place to be, with its theatre-set mezzanine, '70s jukebox and reams of club flyers. There's occasional live music at weekends.

♥ Casa Almirall

C/Joaquín Costa 33 (93 318 99 17, www.casaalmirall.com). Metro Universitat. **Open** *4.30pm-2am Mon-Wed; noon-2.30am Thur-Sun.* **Map** *p101 G8* ❺

Opened in 1860, the Casa Almirall is the second oldest bar in the city after Marsella (*see below*). The bar for all seasons, its swooping Modernista woodwork, soft lighting and deep sofas give it a cosy feel in winter, while its glass front opens up for the summer months.

La Confitería

C/Sant Pau 128 (93 140 54 35). Metro Paral·lel. **Open** *7pm-2.30am Mon-Thur; 6pm-3am Fri, Sat; 5pm-2.30am Sun.* **No cards**. **Map** *p101 F10* ❻

This former sweetshop (*confitería*), with its etched display windows, nowadays houses an art nouveau bar, with dusty bottles, old chandeliers and extravagantly carved wooden panelling. Beyond is a cosy backroom, whose antique furniture is reproduction and only recently added under the new ownership, but tasteful and well done all the same. It's a favourite with concert-goers meeting before gigs at nearby BARTS or Sala Apolo.

Granja M Viader

C/Xuclà 4-6 (93 318 34 86, www. granjaviader.cat). Metro Liceu. **Open** *9am-1.15pm, 5-9.15pm Mon-Sat.* **Map** *p101 H9* ❼

The chocolate milk drink Cacaolat was invented in this old *granja* in 1931, and it's still on offer, along with strawberry and banana milkshakes, *orxata* (tiger nut milk) and hot chocolate. It's an evocative, charming place with century-old fittings and enamel adverts, but the waiters refuse to be hurried.

El Jardí

C/Hospital 56 (93 329 15 50, www. eljardibarcelona.es). Metro Liceu. **Open** *Mar-Nov 9pm-1am daily. Dec-Feb 9am-10pm Mon-Sat.* **Map** *p101 G9* ❽

The courtyard of the Antic Hospital is a tranquil, tree-lined spot a million miles from the hustle of C/Hospital. Terrace café El Jardí only has outdoor seating, warmed by heaters in winter. Breakfast pastries and all the usual tapas are present and correct, along with pasta dishes, quiches and salads.

Marsella

C/Sant Pau 65 (93 442 72 63). Metro Liceu. **Open** *10pm-2.30am Mon-Thur; 10pm-3am Fri, Sat.* **No cards.** *Map p101 G9* ❾

This place was opened in 1820 by a native of Marseilles – who may just have changed the course of Barcelona's artistic history by introducing absinthe, still a mainstay of the bar's delights. Untapped 100-year-old bottles of the stuff sit in glass cabinets alongside old mirrors and William Morris curtains, probably covered in the same dust kicked up by Picasso and Gaudí.

Resolis

C/Riera Baixa 22 (93 441 29 48, www.facebook.com/ barresolisbarcelona). Metro Liceu. **Open** *6pm-1am Mon-Sat.* **Map** *p101 G9* ❿

A favourite with traders from along the C/Riera Baixa, Resolis blends a trad look and run-of-the-mill tapas (tortilla, manchego cheese, prawns) with an immaculate selection of vinyl and some fanciful foodstuffs (salmon ceviche). In the summer months, its serving hatch to the alley alongside is thronged.

Shops & services

Guitar Shop

C/Tallers 27 & 46 (93 412 19 19, 93 412 66 22, www.guitarshop. barcelona). Metro Catalunya. **Open** *10am-2pm, 4.30-8pm Mon-Sat.* **Map** *p101 H8* ❶ *Music*

A mecca for fretheads, these shops have all the goodies: cedarwood Antonio Aparicio classical guitars, Prudencio Saez flamenco guitars and cheap Admiras. At no.27, there's a whole host of vintage Fenders, '80s Marshall amps and the like; bargain-hunters can browse the second-hand gear.

♥ Holala! Plaza + Gallery

Plaça Castella 2 (93 302 05 93, holala-ibiza.com). Metro Universitat. **Open** *11am-9pm Mon-Sat.* **Map** *p101 G8* ❷ *Fashion*

The upper swathe of the Raval remains the grunge-tinged stomping ground of the city's counterculture, and is dotted with quirky vintage shops. Holala! is the mothership, a vast cavern of a place that incorporates a sizeable collection of ice-cool retro furniture, a gallery and a pop-up nail bar, as well as acres and acres of preloved threads from every decade.

♥ Med Winds

C/Elisabets 7 (93 619 01 79, www. medwinds.com). Metro Catalunya. **Open** *10am-8pm Mon-Sat.* **Map** *p101 G8* ❸ *Fashion*

A small boutique that stands out for the quality and detailing of a covetable range of clothes and accessories for men and women. Richly coloured patterns stand in contrast to plain, elegant styling, and shoes and bags, in particular, have a vintage feel.

🖤 Torres
C/Nou de la Rambla 25 (93 317 32 34, www.vinosencasa.com). Metro Drassanes or Liceu. **Open** *9am-2pm, 4-9pm Mon-Sat.* **Map** *p101 G10* ❹ *Wine*
Torres's shiny shop seems a bit out of place in the rundown end of the Raval, but it's definitely worth a visit. There's a good range of Spanish wines, along with plenty of interesting beers and spirits from elsewhere, including black Mallorcan absinthe. Prices are competitive.

Entertainment

23 Robadors
C/Robador 23 (no phone, 23robadors.wordpress.com). Metro Liceu. **Open** *8pm-2.30am daily.* **Admission** *free-€4.* **No cards.** **Map** *p101 G9* ❶ *Live music & DJs*
Inside this stone-walled and smoke-filled lounge, Raval denizens dig the jazz jam on Wednesdays, jazz bands on Thursdays, the flamenco (€4) on Tuesdays, Saturdays and Sundays and, in between times, DJs playing a genre-defying range of music (Joy Division and DJ Shadow on the same night). A manga-style mural on the back wall adds to the underground appeal.

🖤 Bar Pastís
C/Santa Mònica 4 (mobile 634 938 422, www.barpastis.es). Metro Drassanes. **Open** *7.30pm-2.30am daily.* **Admission** *free.* **Map** *p101 G10* ❷ *Live music*

This quintessentially Gallic bar once served pastis to visiting sailors and denizens of the Chino underworld. It still has a louche feel, with floor-to-ceiling clippings and oil paintings, Piaf on the stereo and paper cranes swaying from the ceiling. There's live music from Wednesday to Sunday.

La Concha
C/Guàrdia 14 (93 302 41 18). Metro Drassanes. **Open** *5pm-2.30am Mon-Thur, Sun; 5pm-3am Fri, Sat.* **Admission** *free.* **No cards.** **Map** *p101 G10* ❸ *Bar*
Papered with posters of vintage Spanish sexpot Sara Montiel and filled with the sounds of Bollywood balladry, La Concha is a gem of dusty fabulousness that stands in direct contrast to all the slick and pretentious glamour of most of the newer late-night bars. The venue is under Moroccan ownership and serves mint tea in the afternoons.

🖤 Jazz Sí Club
C/Requesens 2 (93 329 00 20, tallerdemusics.com/jazzsi-club). Metro Sant Antoni. **Open** *8.30-11pm Mon, Wed-Fri; 7.45-10.30pm Tue; 7.45-11pm Sat; 6.30-10pm Sun.* **Admission** *(incl 1 drink) €5-€10.* **No cards.** **Map** *p101 F8* ❹ *Live music*
Tucked into a Raval side street, with cheap shows every night and cheap bar grub, this truly authentic place is worth seeking out. Since it functions as both a venue for known-in-the-scene locals and an auditorium for students of the music school across the street, it's packed to the brim with students, teachers, music-lovers and players. Nights vary between jazz, flamenco and Cuban, and there are jam sessions on Tuesdays and Saturdays.

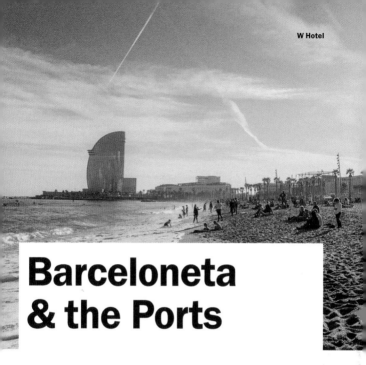

Barceloneta & the Ports

The 1992 Olympic Games were the catalyst for Barcelona's most notable transformation. The city had famously 'turned its back on the sea' until some sharp urban planners finally spotted the potential of its Mediterranean location. From industrial slum to leisure port, Barcelona's shoreline transformation is the result of two decades of development. The clean-up has extended to the whole seven kilometres of city seashore: this stretch is now a virtually continuous strip of modern construction, bristling with new docks, marinas, luxury hotels, cruise-ship terminals, ferry harbours and leisure areas.

Fishing tackle shops are moving out and cocktail bars are moving into the tight-knit seaside community

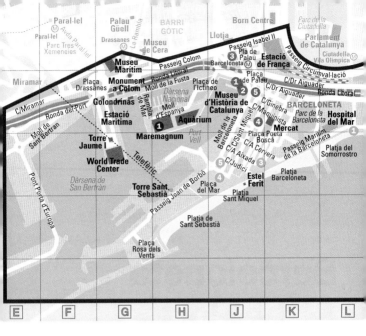

of **Barceloneta** ('Little Barcelona'). The *barri* is metamorphosing from a working-class neighbourhood dependent on fishing and heavy industry into a node of leisured bucket-and-spade tourism with an ever greater numbers of bars, restaurants and holiday rentals.

Follow the yachts moored along the Moll de la Barceloneta down to the small remaining fishing area by the clock tower (previously a beacon to guide ships into port), which is the emblem of the neighbourhood. Further down, the road leads to the Nova Bocana complex, which combines high-end leisure facilities and offices and is dominated by Ricardo Bofill's W Hotel, a towering sail-shaped building. This marks the beginning of Barcelona's beach.

If you head left where Passeig Joan de Borbó passes the beach, you'll reach Rebecca Horn's *Estel Ferit* sculpture (Wounded Shooting Star) – a tower of rusty iron boxes that pays homage to the much-missed *xiringuitos*

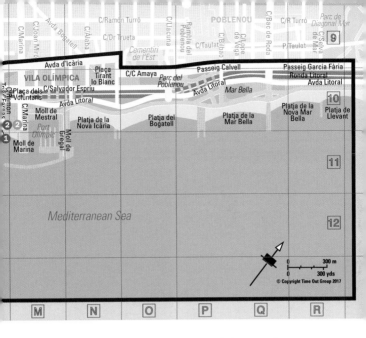

(open-air beach restaurants) that lined the Barceloneta sands in pre-Olympic days. The Passeig Marítim esplanade runs north from here and is a popular hangout for skaters and strollers.

The initial focus of the Olympic makeover was the area rechristened **Port Vell** (Old Port), sandwiched between the Barri Gòtic and the spit of land that is Barceloneta. Built on an artificial island linked to the bottom of La Rambla sits a state-of-the-art aquarium and the Maremagnum mall. The nearby **Drassanes Reials** (Royal Shipyards), now home to the **Museu Marítim**, are among the finest pieces of civilian Gothic architecture in Spain.

→ Getting around

The shoreline is better reached by buses than the metro. Useful lines from Plaça Catalunya include no.45 (as far as the Vila Olímpica) and no.59 (as far as Platja de Bogatell).

Sights & museums

💙 L'Aquàrium

*Moll d'Espanya (93 221 74 74,
www.aquariumbcn.com). Metro
Barceloneta or Drassanes. Open
(last entry 1hr before closing)
Nov-Mar 10am-7.30pm Mon-Fri;
10am-8pm Sat, Sun. Apr, May, Oct
10am-8pm Mon-Fri; 10am-8.30pm
Sat, Sun. June, Sept 10am-9pm
daily. July, Aug 10am-9.30pm
daily. Admission €20; €7-€15
reductions; free under-3s.
Map p112 H10*
The main draw here is the
Oceanari, a giant shark-infested
tank traversed via a glass tunnel
on a slow-moving conveyor belt.
Other tanks house shoals of
kaleidoscopic fish where kids can
play 'hunt Nemo'. The upstairs
section is devoted to children. For
pre-schoolers, Explora! has 50
activities, such as climbing inside
a mini-submarine. Older children
should head to Planet Aqua – an
extraordinary, split-level circular
space with Humboldt penguins.

💙 Monument a Colom

*Plaça Portal de la Pau (93 285 38
34). Metro Drassanes. Open Mar-
Sept 8.30am-8.30pm daily. Oct-Feb
8.30am-7.30pm daily. Tickets
€6, €4 reductions; free under-4s.
Map p112 G10*
Inspired by Nelson's Column in
London, and complete with eight
majestic lions, the Christopher
Columbus monument was
designed for the Universal
Exhibition of 1888. Positioned
at the base of La Rambla, the
monument allegedly marks the
spot where Columbus docked
in 1493 after his discovery of
the Americas, and the carvings
illustrate key moments in his
voyages. Take the lift to the top for
a fantastic view.

Monument a Colom

Museu d'Història de Catalunya

*Plaça Pau Vila 3 (93 225 47
00, www.mhcat.net). Metro
Barceloneta. Open 10am-7pm
Tue, Thur-Sat; 10am-8pm Wed;
10am-2.30pm Sun. Admission
All exhibitions €6.50; €4.50
reductions; free under-8s; free
to all last Tue of mth Oct-June.
Permanent exhibition €4.50; €3.50
reductions. Temporary exhibitions
€4; €3 reductions. Map p112 J10*
With exhibits spanning from the
Lower Paleolithic era up to Jordi
Pujol's proclamation as President
of the Generalitat in 1980, the
Catalan History Museum offers a
virtual chronology of the region's
past. There are two floors of
text, film, animated models and

stage-set reproductions, from a medieval shoemaker's shop to a 1960s bar. Hands-on activities, such as irrigating lettuces with a Moorish water wheel, add a little pizzazz to the rather dry early history, and to exit the exhibition, visitors walk over a huge 3D map of Catalonia. Every section has a decent introduction in English; the reception desk can offer in-depth English-language museum guides free of charge. Excellent temporary exhibitions typically examine recent aspects of regional politics and history, while the huge rooftop café terrace, dating from 1881, has unbeatable views over the city and marina.

♥ Museu Marítim

Avda Drassanes (93 342 99 20, www.mmb.cat). Metro Drassanes. **Open** *10am-8pm daily.* **Tickets** *€5, €2.50 reduction; free under-17s, free to all Sun from 3pm.* **Map** *p112 G9*
Even if you can't tell a caravel from a catamaran, the excellent Maritime Museum is worth a visit, as the soaring arches and vaults of the vast former *drassanes* (shipyards) represent one of the most perfectly preserved examples of civil Gothic architecture in Spain. In medieval times, the shipyards sat right on the water's edge and were used to dry-dock, repair and build vessels for the royal fleets. The finest of these was Don Juan de Austria's galley, from which he commanded the fleet that defeated the Ottoman navy in 1571: a full-scale replica is the mainstay of the collection. Several years of renovations end in mid 2017.

With the aid of an audio guide, the maps, mastheads, nautical instruments, multimedia displays and models show you how shipbuilding and navigation techniques have developed over the years. The admission fee also covers the beautiful 1917 *Santa Eulàlia* schooner, docked nearby in the Moll de la Fusta, and the Marítim often has some interesting temporary exhibitions.

Teleféric del Port

Torre de Sant Sebastià (93 441 48 20, www.telefericodebarcelona. com). Metro Barceloneta. **Open** *June-mid Sept 10.30am-8pm daily. Nov-Feb 11am-5.30pm daily. Mar-May, Sept, Oct 10.30am-7pm daily.* **Tickets** *€11 single; €16.50 return; free under-7s.* **Map** *p112 H11*

♥ Shortlist

Best for sunbathing
Take your pick from Barcelona's nine beaches (*p116*).

Best oceanic discoveries
L'Aquàrium (*p114*) for hands-on fun. Museu Marítim (*p115*) for nautical treasures in a medieval building.

Best panorama
Monument a Colom (*p114*) for a dizzying view. 1881 (*p118*) for breakfast looking out over the port.

Best seafood lunch
Can Majó (*p117*) for a fantastic seafood selection. Kaiku (*p118*) for delicious dishes in simple surroundings.

Best afternoon tipple
Can Paixano (*p118*) for bubbly amid the throng.

Best dinner by the sea
Agua (*p117*) for timeless classics. Bestial (*p117*) for tasty Italian puds.

♥ Beaches

Barcelona never had much of a beach culture until the 1992 Olympics opened the city's eyes to the commercial potential of its location. What little sand there was before then was grey and clogged with private swimming baths and *xiringuitos* (beach-side eateries) that served seafood on trestle tables set up on the sand; the remainder was given over to heavy industry and waste dumps, cut off from the rest of the city by a strip of rail track, warehouses and factories.

For the grand Olympic makeover, the beaches were swiftly cleared and filled with tons of golden sand, imported palm trees and landscaped promenades. Visitors flocked, but the city beaches have become a victim of their own popularity, and keeping them clean is something of a Sisyphean task for the city council. Dubbed the 'Bay of Pigs' by the papers, the most central area has been subjected to a massive clean-up campaign with more beachfront toilets, extra bins and endless posters and loudspeaker announcements reminding people to pick up their rubbish.

Of the nine city beaches, the most southerly is **Platja de Sant Sebastià**, running from the W Hotel and popular with nudists. Next is **Platja de Sant Miquel**, which gets crowded in the summer months; it's popular with a gay crowd. **Platja de la Barceloneta** and **Platja del Somorrostro** next to it provide a sandy porch for restaurants and nightclubs. The covered walkway is home to tables where old men play dominoes with all the aggressiveness of a contact sport; it also houses the beach centre, which has a small beach library (*see p117* In the know).

After the Port Olímpic and just down from the Ciutadella-Vila Olímpica metro station, **Platja de Nova Icària** is much broader, with plenty of space for volleyball and beach tennis, while **Platja de Bogatell** boasts the hippest *xiringuito,* with torches and loungers out at night from May to October. Further north, **Platja de Mar Bella** is all about sport, with the sailing club Base Nàutica, basketball nets, volleyball courts, table-tennis tables and a half-pipe for BMXers and skaters.

The most remote beaches are quiet **Platja Nova Mar Bella**, which is mostly used by local families, and the newer **Platja Llevant**, which opened to the public in 2006 when the Prim jetty was removed.

These rather battered cable cars do not appear to have been touched – except for the installation of lifts – since they were built for the 1929 Expo. They provide sky-high views over Barcelona on their grinding, squeaking path from the Sant Sebastià tower at the very far end of Passeig Joan de Borbó to the Jaume I tower in front of the World Trade Center; the final leg ends at the Miramar lookout point on Montjuïc. Make sure you go late in the day to avoid long queues.

Restaurants

♥ Agua €€

Passeig Marítim 30 (93 225 12 72, www.grupotragaluz.com). Bus 45, 59, 92. **Open** *9am-11.30pm Mon-Thur; noon-12.30am Fri, Sat.* **Map** *p112 L10* ❶ *Mediterranean*
Agua's main draw is its large terrace overlooking the beach, although the relaxed dining room is usually buzzing. The menu rarely

changes, regardless of the time of year, but regulars never tire of the competently executed monkfish tail with *sofregit*, the risotto with partridge, and the fresh pasta with juicy prawns. Scrummy puddings are worth leaving space for and include marron glacé mousse and sour apple sorbet. It's advisable to book ahead, especially during the summer months and at weekends.

♥ Bestial €€

C/Ramón Trias Fargas 2-4 (93 224 04 07, www.grupotragaluz. com). Metro Barceloneta. **Open** *11am-11.30pm daily.* **Map** *p112 M10* ❷ *Italian*
A peerless spot for alfresco seaside dining, with tiered wooden decking and ancient olive trees framing a pleasant eating area. Bestial's dining room is also a stylish affair, with black-clad waiters sashaying along sleek runways, their trays held high. The food is of a modern Italian flavour: dainty mini-pizzas, rocket salad with parma ham and a lightly poached egg, tuna with black olive risotto and all the delicious puddings that you could ever hope to find – panna cotta, tiramisu and limoncello sorbet. At weekends, a DJ takes to the decks and drinks are served until 5am.

♥ Can Majó €€

C/Almirall Aixada 23 (93 221 54 55, www.canmajo.es). Metro Barceloneta. **Open** *1-4pm, 8-11.30pm Tue-Sat; 1-4pm Sun.* **Map** *p112 J11* ❸ *Seafood*
This place is famous for its fresh-from-the-nets selection of oysters, scallops, Galician clams, whelks and just about any other mollusc that you might care to mention. Even though the menu reads much as you would expect of a Barceloneta seafood restaurant, with plates of shellfish or (exemplary) fish soup as starters, followed by rich paellas and exquisitely tasty *fideuà*, the quality

is a cut above the norm. Sit inside the dapper white and cornflower dining room, or across the road on the terrace, gazing out at the beautiful view of the sea.

💗 Kaiku €€

Plaça del Mar 1 (93 221 90 82, www.restaurantkaiku.cat). Metro Barceloneta. **Open** *mid Sep-mid May 1-4pm Tue-Sun; mid May-mid Sept 1-3.30pm, 7-10.30pm Tue-Sun.* **Map** *p112 J11* ④ *Seafood*

With its simple look, missable façade and paper tablecloths, Kaiku looks a world apart from the upmarket seafood restaurants that pepper this *barrio*, but its dishes are sophisticated takes on the seaside classics. At Kaiku, a salad starter comes with shavings of foie or red fruit vinaigrette, and paella is given a rich and earthy spin with wild mushrooms. Book ahead, particularly for any chance of reserving one of the terrace tables that look out across the lovely beach.

El Suquet de l'Almirall €€€

Passeig Joan de Borbó 65 (93 221 62 33, suquetdelalmirall.com). Metro Barceloneta. **Open** *1-4pm, 8-11pm Tue-Sat; 1-4pm Sun.* **Map** *p112 J11* ⑤ *Seafood*

One of the famous beachfront *xiringuitos* that was moved and refurbished in preparation for the 1992 Olympic Games in the city, El Suquet de l'Almirall remains a friendly and family-run concern despite the smart decor and mid-scale business lunchers. The fishy favourites on offer range from *xató* salad to *arròs negre* and include a variety of set menus, such as the 'blind' selection of tapas, a gargantuan taster menu and, most popular of all, the *pica-pica*, which includes roasted red peppers with anchovies, a bowl of steamed cockles and clams, and a heap of *fideuà* accompanied by lobster.

Cafés, tapas & bars

💗 1881

Plaça Pau Vila 3 (93 221 00 50, www.sagardi.com). Metro Barceloneta. **Open** *10am-1am daily.* **Map** *p112 J10* ①

There's no need to buy a ticket to the Museu d'Història de Catalunya to make the most of this little-known rooftop museum café with fabulous views. The set lunches don't break any ground gastronomically speaking, but are reasonable enough; or you can take coffee and a croissant to the vast terrace and watch the boats bobbing in the harbour.

Black Lab

Palau de Mar, Plaça Pau Vila (93 221 83 60, www.blacklab.es). Metro Barceloneta. **Open** *noon-1.30am daily.* **Map** *p112 J10* ②

Barcelona's first tap room is a lively place, with a huge terrace. Dozens of beers are brewed on site (tours are given on Sundays). Five of these are available year round (try El Predicador, a superb IPA), but others change with the seasons and owner James is constantly experimenting with new flavours and methods. Decent pub grub is also available.

💗 Can Paixano

C/Reina Cristina 7 (93 310 08 39, www.canpaixano.com). Metro Barceloneta. **Open** *9am-10.30pm Mon-Sat. Closed 2wks Jan.* **No cards.** **Map** *p112 J9* ③

The 'Champagne Bar', as it's invariably known, has a huge following among young Catalans and the legion of foreigners who think they discovered it first. It can be impossible to talk, get your order heard or move your elbows, yet it's always mobbed due to its age-old look and atmosphere, dirt-cheap bottles of house cava and (literally) obligatory sausage butties.

Boat Trips and Watersports

Activities for all abilities

If a boat trip is what you're after, there's a wealth of options.

Departing from the jetty just by the Monument a Colom, the 23-m (75-ft) sail **Catamaran Orsom** (93 221 82 83, www.barcelona-orsom. com) is the largest in Barcelona – it chugs up to 50 seafarers around to the Nova Bocana harbour area before unfurling its sails and peacefully gliding across the bay. There are three departures per day (noon, 3pm, 6pm) from May to October, and the trip takes about 1 hour 30 minutes in total. Tickets cost €15.50 (€13.50 reductions, free under-4s). There are also evening jazz/chill-out cruises at 6pm and 8pm on July and August weekends (€17.50, €14.50 reductions, free under-4s), and a 40-minute speedboat trip runs to the Fòrum and back (www. barcelonaspeedboat.com, €7.50, €4.50 reductions, free under-4s).

Since the 1888 World Exhibition, **Las Golondrinas** (Moll de Drassanes, 93 442 31 06, www. lasgolondrinas.com), the 'swallow boats', have chugged around the harbour, giving passengers a bosun's eye-view of Barcelona's rapidly changing seascape. The traditional double-decker pleasure boats serve the shorter port tour (approx 40mins, €7.40, €2.80 reductions), while the more powerful catamarans tour as far as the Port Fòrum (approx 1hr 30mins, €15, €5.50-€13.50 reductions, free under-4s). Sailings are hourly, from around 11.15am until sunset. Opening hours tend to be a bit erratic, so do check the website if possible.

For the willing and able, the **Base Nàutica de la Mar Bella** (93 221 04 32, www.basenautica. org) rents out kayaks, yachts, catamarans and windsurf gear to those with sufficient experience. It also offers lessons to individuals (including children aged six and above, €200/person for 8hrs) and groups of up to six participants (€50-€70/person for 2hrs). There is also a range of different options available for intensive or longer-term sailing proficiency courses. You'll find the Base Nàutica between Platja Bogatell and Platja de Mar Bella on Avda Litoral.

If you fancy a swim, the beachside **Club de Natació Atlètic Barceloneta** (Plaça del Mar, 93 221 00 10, www.cnab.cat) has an indoor pool and two outdoor pools, as well as a sauna and gym facilities. It's €12.01 for a non-member day pass, but you'll pay extra to use the sauna. There's also a *frontón* (Spanish ball-sports court) if you want to try your hand at the world's fastest sport: *jai alai*, a fierce Basque game that sits somewhere between squash and handball.

La Cova Fumada

C/Baluard 56 (93 221 40 61). Metro Barceloneta. **Open** *9am-3.15pm Mon-Wed; 9am-3.15pm, 6-8.15pm Thur, Fri; 9am-1.15pm Sat. Closed 1wk July, 3wks Aug, 1 wk Feb.* **No cards.** *Map p112 J10* ❹
An authentic family-run *bodega*, hugely popular with local workers, where you'll need to arrive early for a cramped and possibly shared table. Said to be the birthplace of the spicy potato *bomba*, La Cova Fumada also turns out a great tomato and onion salad, delicious chickpeas with *morcilla* (black pudding) and unbeatable marinated sardines.

El Vaso de Oro

C/Balboa 6 (93 319 30 98, vasodeoro.com). Metro Barceloneta. **Open** *10pm-midnight Mon-Fri; noon-midnight Sat, Sun. Closed Sept.* **No cards**. **Map** *p112 J10* ❺

The enormous popularity of this long, narrow cruise ship-style bar tells you everything you need to know about the tapas, but it also means that he who hesitates is lost when it comes to ordering. Elbow yourself a space and demand, loudly, *choricitos*, patatas bravas, *solomillo* (cubed steak) or *atún* (tuna, which here comes spicy). The beer (its storage, handling and pouring) is also a point of great pride.

Shops & services

Maremagnum

Moll d'Espanya 5 (93 225 81 00, www.maremagnum.es). Metro Drassanes. **Open** *Shops 10am-10pm daily. Food court & entertainment 11am-3am daily.* **Map** *p112 H10* ❶
Mall

When Viaplana and Piñon's black-mirrored shopping and leisure centre opened in 1995, it was the place to hang out, but after years of declining popularity, it has ditched most of the bars and nightclubs. All the high-street staples are present (Mango, H&M, Women's Secret) and the ground floor focuses on the family market, with sweets, children's clothes and a Barça shop. The upper floor is dominated by food halls, with terraces running around the outside.

Entertainment

❤ CDLC

Passeig Marítim 32 (93 224 04 70, www.cdlcbarcelona.com). Metro Ciutadella-Vila Olímpica. **Open** *noon-3.30am daily.* **Admission** *free.* **Map** *p112 L10* ❶ *Club*

Carpe Diem Lounge Club, to give the venue its full name, remains at the forefront of Barcelona's splash-the-cash, see-and-be-seen celeb circuit: the white beds flanking the dancefloor, guarded by a clipboarded hostess, are perfect for showing everyone who's the daddy. Alternatively, for those not celebrating recently signed, six-figure record deals, funky house and a busy terrace provide an opportunity for mere mortals (and models) to mingle and discuss who's going to finance their next drink and, secondly, how to get chatting to whichever member of the Barça team has just walked in.

Oplum Mar

Passeig Marítim 34 (93 414 63 62, www.opiummar.com). Metro Ciutadella-Vila Olímpica. **Open** *11.45pm-5am Mon-Thur, Sun; 11.45pm-6am Fri, Sat.* **Admission** *(incl 1 drink) €20.* **Map** *p112 L10* ❷ *Club*

It's tempting to dismiss Opium Mar as just another homogeneous upmarket beachside club, but beyond the zealous bouncers and the hefty entrance fee there is a surprisingly creative and eclectic vibe that belies the club's location. From chocolate fountains to live saxophonists, much is done to distinguish Opium Mar from the competition, but by far its most popular feature is the beach terrace, which provides a perfect spot to catch the sunrise.

Montjuïc & Around

The mists of time obscure the etymology of the name 'Montjuïc'. 'Mont' means hill, and one widely accepted theory is that 'juïc' comes from the old Catalan word meaning Jewish – it was here that the medieval Jewish community buried their dead. Today, the Cementiri de Montjuïc still stands on the sea-facing side of the hill, but Montjuïc is thought of as a huge playground, with parks, cable cars, museums and a Greek-style amphitheatre.

Poble Sec, the area that sits on the hill's northern flank, is undergoing something of a transformation from sleepy residential zone as it links up with newly cool Sant Antoni to form the latest hipster neighbourhood, bristling with new bars and cafés.

Montjuïc

In a city with as few parks as Barcelona, the hill of Montjuïc offers a precious green lung, along with some outstanding museums. The long axis from Plaça d'Espanya is still the most popular access to the park, with the climb now eased by a sequence of open-air escalators.

Scattered over the landward side of the hill are buildings from the 1929 Exhibition and the 1992 Olympic Games. They include the bombastic **Palau Nacional**, originally built as a temporary exhibition space for the Expo, and now home to the **MNAC** (Museu Nacional d'Art de Catalunya), housing Catalan art from the last millennium. At night, the scene is illuminated by a water-and-light spectacular, the **Font Màgica**, still operating with its complex original mechanisms.

Facing the sea is an enormous cemetery, while, at the top of the hill, all but invisible from below, is the heavily fortified **Castell de Montjuïc**, a dark and brooding symbol of the centuries Catalonia spent under Castilian rule.

Montjuïc's many parks and gardens include the **Jardí Botànic**, sharply designed and finally maturing into an important scientific collection.

Sights & museums

♥ CaixaForum
Casaramona, Avda Francesc Ferrer i Guàrdia 6-8 (93 476 86 00, www.obrasociallacaixa. org). Metro Espanya. **Open** *Sept-June 10am-8pm daily. July, Aug 10am-8pm Mon, Tue, Thur-Sun; 10am-11pm Wed.* **Admission** *€4.* **Map** *p124 B8*
One of the masterpieces of industrial Modernisme, this former yarn and textile factory was

designed by Puig i Cadafalch and celebrated its centenary in 2011. It spent most of the last century in a sorry state, briefly acting as a police barracks before falling into disuse. Fundació La Caixa, the charitable arm of Catalonia's largest savings bank, bought it and set about rebuilding. In addition to the permanent contemporary art collection, there are three impressive spaces for temporary exhibitions – often among the most interesting shows to be found in the city.

Castell de Montjuïc
Ctra de Montjuïc 66 (93 256 44 40, www.bcn.cat/castelldemontjuic). Metro Paral·lel then funicular & cable car. **Open** *Apr-Oct 10am-8pm daily. Nov-Mar 10am-6pm daily.* **Admission** *€5, €3 reduction; free under-16s.* **Map** *p124 C11.*
The Military Museum that was once located here closed down in 2009 and its contents were moved to Figueres, but visitors can still stroll through the castle grounds, climb the battlements for fabulous views, or picnic in the wide moat. Exhibitions explain a little about the history of the castle, but the real attraction here is the view.

♥ Font Màgica de Montjuïc
Plaça Carles Buïgas 1 (www.bcn. es/fontmagica). Metro Espanya. **Shows** *(every 30mins) Apr, May, Oct 9-10.30pm Fri, Sat. June-Sept 9.30-11pm Thur-Sun. Nov-Mar 7-8.30pm Fri, Sat.* **Map** *p124 C8.*
Still in possession of its original plumbing, the 'magic fountain' works its wonders with 3,600 pieces of tubing and more than 4,500 light bulbs. The multiple founts swell and dance to anything from the *1812 Overture* to Freddie Mercury and Montserrat Caballé's 'Barcelona', showing off a kaleidoscope of pastel colours.

Best modern art
CaixaForum (*p122*) for reliably good exhibitions in a Modernista factory. Fundació Joan Miró (*p127*) for huge splashy artworks and superb views.

Best views
Jardí Botànic (*p126*) for a panorama among plants. Martinez (*p129*) for lunch with a view.

Best Catalan art
MNAC (*p126*) for stunning collections of Romanesque and Gothic art.

Best dance venues
Sala Apolo (*p132*) for an eclectic mix of music in a 1940s dancehall. La Terrrazza (*p132*) for dancing under the stars.

Best for kids
Font Màgica (*p122*) for a gloriously kitsch celebration of light, water and music.

Best for a taste of the hipster 'hood
Federal (*p130*) for eggs over easy. Lando (*p131*) for tapas and a cool glass of wine.

➜ Getting around
The easiest way to get up the hill is the funicular railway, integrated with the city's metro system and leaving from Paral·lel station. This will take you to the upper funicular station – from there you can walk up to the castle or get on the (expensive) cable car that runs to the top (*see p129*). Alternatively, bus no.150 runs from Plaça Espanya all the way up to the castle.

A more circuitous ascent up the hill is to take the **Teleféric del Port** cable car built for the 1929 Expo. Leave from the Sant Sebastià tower at the very far end of Passeig Joan de Borbó in Barceloneta, across the harbour to Miramar, a peaceful spot with unrivalled views across the city – though the tranquillity has been somewhat disturbed by the construction of the swish Hotel Miramar.

Poble Sec is between Avda Paral·lel and the hill and is easily accessible by metro. Sant Antoni (technically in the Eixample) borders the Raval; the nearest metro stations are Poble Sec or Sant Antoni.

Font Màgica de Montjuïc

MONTJUÏC & AROUND

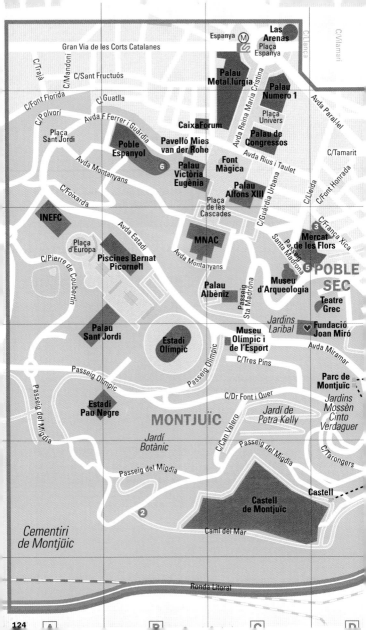

Las Arenas

Espanya Ⓜ
Plaça Espanya

Gran Via de les Corts Catalanes

C/Vilamarí
C/Llança
C/Vilamari

C/Traià
C/Mandoni
C/Sant Fructuós

Palau Metal.lúrgia

Avda Reina Maria Cristina

Palau Numero 1

C/Font Florida
C/Polvorí
C/Guatlla

Plaça Univers

Avda Paral.lel

Avda F Ferrer i Guàrdia

CaixaForum

Plaça Sant Jordi

Poble Espanyol 6

Pavelló Mies van der Rohe

Palau de Congressos

C/Tamarit

Avda Montanyans

Palau Victòria Eugènia

Font Màgica

Avda Rius i Taulet

C/Lleida
C/Font Honrada

C/Foixarda

Palau Alfons XIII

C/Guàrdia Urbana

Plaça de les Cascades

C/França Xica
Passeig Santa Madrona

3

INEFC

Avda Estadi

MNAC

Mercat de les Flors

5 POBLE SEC

Plaça d'Europa

C/Pierre de Coubertin

Piscines Bernat Picornell

Avda Montanyans

Museu d'Arqueologia

Teatre Grec

Palau Albèniz

Passeig Sta Madrona

Fundació Joan Miró

Jardins Laribal

Palau Sant Jordi

Estadi Olímpic

Museu Olímpic i de l'Esport

Avda Miramar

Passeig Olímpic

C/Tres Pins

Parc de Montjuïc

Passeig Olímpic

C/Dr Font i Quer

Estadi Pau Negre

MONTJUÏC

C/Can Valero

Jardí de Petra Kelly

Jardins Mossèn Cinto Verdaguer

Passeig del Migdia

Jardí Botànic

Passeig del Migdia

Passeig del Migdia

C/Tarongers

Castell

Castell de Montjuïc

Cementiri de Montjüic

2

Camí del Mar

Ronda Litoral

A   B   C   D

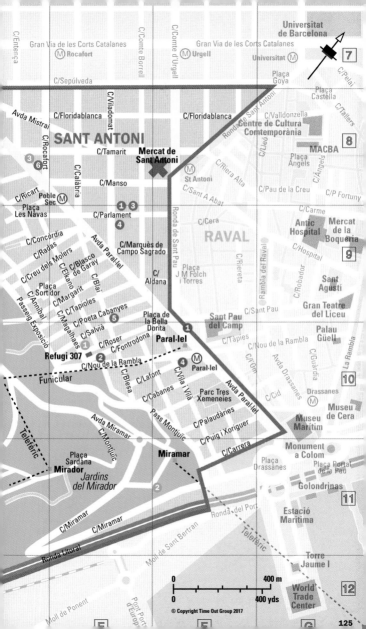

Universitat
de Barcelona

C/Enterça

Gran Via de les Corts Catalanes
Ⓜ Rocafort

C/Comte Borrell

C/Comte d'Urgell

Gran Via de les Corts Catalanes
Ⓜ Urgell

Universitat Ⓜ

C/Pelai

7

Plaça
Castella

C/Tallers

C/Sepúlveda

Plaça
Goya

Avda Mistral

C/Floridablanca

C/Viladomat

C/Floridablanca

Ronda de Sant Antoni

C/Valldonzella

Centre de Cultura
Contemporània

C/Lleó

C/Angels

MACBA

8

C/Rocafort

SANT ANTONI

C/Tamarit

Mercat de
Sant Antoni

Plaça
Angels

C/Angels

C/P Fortuny

C/Calàbria

C/Manso

Ⓜ
St Antoni

C/Riera Alta

C/Pau de la Creu

C/Carme

C/Ricart

Poble
Sec Ⓜ

Plaça
Les Navas

C/Parlament

C/Sant A Abat

Ronda de Sant Pau

C/Cera

RAVAL

Antic
Hospital

Mercat
de la
Boqueria

9

❶ ❸
❹

C/Concòrdia

C/Radas

Avda Paral·lel

C/Marquès de
Campo Sagrado

C/Riereta

C/Hospital

Rambla del Raval

C/Robador

Sant
Agustí

C/Creu dels Molers

C/Blasco
de Garay

C/Elkano

C/Blai

C/
Aldana

Plaça
J M Folch
i Torres

C/Sant Pau

Gran Teatre
del Liceu

Plaça
Sortidor

C/Anníbal

C/Margarit

C/Tapioles

Passeig Exposició

C/Magalhaes

C/Poeta Cabanyes

❺

C/Salvià

Plaça de
la Bella
Dorita

❶

Sant Pau
del Camp

C/Tàpies

Palau
Güell

La Rambla

Refugi 307

❶

C/Roser

C/Fontrodona

Paral·lel

C/Nou de la Rambla

C/Guàrdia

❷

Funicular

C/Nou de la Rambla

C/Blesa

C/Lafont

C/Vila i Vilà

❹

Paral·lel

Avda Paral·lel

C/Om

Avda Drassanes

Ⓜ
Drassanes

10

C/Cabanes

Parc Tres
Xemeneies

C/Cid

Avda Miramar

C/Montjuïc

Pass Montjuïc

C/Palaudàries

Museu
de Cera

C/Puig i Xoriguer

Museu
Marítim

Plaça
Sardana

Mirador

Jardins
del Mirador

Miramar

C/Carrera

Monument
a Colom

Plaça
Drassanes

Plaça Portal
de la Pau

Telefèric

❷

Golondrinas

11

C/Miramar

C/Miramar

Ronda del Port

Estació
Marítima

Ronda Litoral

Moll de Sant Bertran

Telefèric

Torre
Jaume I

Moll de Ponent

Port Port
d'Europa

0 ————— 400 m

0 ————— 400 yds

© Copyright Time Out Group 2017

World
Trade
Center

12

Jardí Botànic

❤ Jardí Botànic

C/Doctor Font i Quer (93 426 49 35, www.museuciencies.cat). Metro Paral·lel then Funicular de Montjuïc or 150, 13 bus. **Open** *Oct-Mar 10am-5pm daily. Apr-Sept 10.30am-7pm Tue-Sun.* **Admission** *€3.50; €1.70 reductions; free under-16s. Free after 3pm Sun & all day 1st Sun of mth.* **Map** *p124 B10.*

After the original 1930s botanical garden was disturbed by the construction for the Olympics, the only solution was to build an entirely new replacement. This opened in 1999, housing plants derived from seven global regions with a climate similar to that of the western Mediterranean. Everything about the futuristic design, from the angular concrete pathways to the raw sheet steel banking (and even the design of the bins), is the complete antithesis of the more naturalistic, Gertrude Jekyll-inspired gardens of England. It is meticulously kept, with plants tagged with Latin, Catalan, Spanish and English names, along with the date of planting, and has the added advantage of wonderful views across the city. A small space plays host to occasional exhibitions, and useful, free audio guides lead visitors through the gardens.

❤ MNAC (Museu Nacional d'Art de Catalunya)

Palau Nacional, Parc de Montjuïc (93 622 03 60, www. museunacional.cat). Metro Espanya. **Open** *May-Sept 10am-8pm Mon-Sat; 10am-3pm Sun. Oct-Apr 10am-6pm Tue-Sat; 10am-3pm Sun.* **Admission** *Permanent & temporary exhibitions (valid 2 days) €12; €8.40 reductions. Combined ticket with Poble Espanyol €19. Free under-16s & over-65s. Free to all after 3pm Sat & all day 1st Sun of mth.* **Map** *p124 B9.*

'One museum, a thousand years of art' is the slogan of the National Museum, and the collection provides a dizzying overview of Catalan art from the 12th to the 20th centuries.

The highlight is the Romanesque collection. As art historians realised that scores of

💜 Fundació Joan Miró

Parc de Montjuïc s/n (93 443 94 70, www.fmirobcn.org). Metro Paral·lel then Funicular de Montjuïc or no.150, 55 bus. **Open** *Apr-Oct 10am-8pm Tue, Wed, Fri, Sat; 10am-9pm Thur; 10am-3pm Sun. Nov-Mar 10am-6pm Tue, Wed, Fri; 10am-9pm Thur; 10am-8pm Sat; 10am-3pm Sun.* **Admission** *All exhibitions €12; €7 reductions. Temporary exhibitions €7; €5 reductions; free under-15s.* **Map** *p124 C10.*

Josep Lluís Sert, who spent the years of the Franco dictatorship as dean of the School of Design at Harvard University, designed one of the world's greatest museum buildings on his return. Approachable, light and airy, these white walls and arches house a hugely impressive collection of more than 225 paintings, 150 sculptures and all of Miró's graphic work, plus some 5,000 drawings. The permanent collection, highlighting Miró's trademark use of primary colours and simplified organic forms symbolising stars, the moon, birds and women, occupies half of the space.

In other works, Miró is shown as a cubist (*Street in Pedralbes*, 1917), naive (*Portrait of a Young Girl*, 1919) and surrealist (*Man and Woman in Front of a Pile of Excrement*, 1935). In the upper galleries, large, black-outlined paintings from Miró's final years precede a room of works with political themes.

MONTJUÏC & AROUND

Telefèric de Montjuïc

Museu Olímpic i de l'Esport

Avda Estadí 60 (93 292 53 79, www.museuolimpicbcn.cat). Metro Paral·lel then Funicular de Montjuïc or 150, 55 bus. **Open** *Apr-Sept 10am-8pm Tue-Sat; 10am-2.30pm Sun. Oct-Mar 10am-6pm Tue-Sat; 10am-2.30pm Sun.* **Admission** *€5.80; €3.60 reductions; free under-7s & over-65s.* **Map** *p124 C10.*

Opened in 2007 in a new building across from the stadium, the Olympic and Sports Museum gives an overview of the Games (and, indeed, all games), from Ancient Greece to the present day. As well as photographs and film footage of great sporting moments and heroes, there's an array of related objects (Ronaldinho's boots, Mika Häkkinen's Mercedes), along with a collection of opening ceremony costumes and Olympic torches on show.

Poble Espanyol

Avda Francesc Ferrer i Guàrdia 13 (93 508 63 00, www.poble-espanyol.com). Metro Espanya. **Village & restaurants** *9am-8pm Mon; 9am-midnight Tue-Thur, Sun; 9am-4am Fri, Sat.* **Shops** *Dec-May 10am-6pm daily. June-Aug 10am-8pm daily. Sept-Nov 10am-7pm daily.* **Admission** *€13; €7-€10 reductions; €35 family ticket; free under-4s. Night ticket €7. Combined ticket with MNAC €19.* **Map** *p124 B8.*

Built for the 1929 World Exhibition and designed by the Modernista architect Josep Puig i Cadafalch, this composite Spanish village may appear charming or kitsch, depending on your personal tastes, and features reproductions of traditional buildings and squares from every region in Spain. There are numerous bars and restaurants along the way, including a flamenco *tablao* and more than 60 shops selling Spanish crafts. Outside,

solitary tenth-century churches in the Pyrenees were falling into ruin – and with them, extraordinary Romanesque murals that had served to instruct villagers in the basics of the faith – the laborious task was begun of removing the murals from church apses.

The excellent Gothic collection starts with some late 13th-century frescoes that were discovered in 1961 and 1997, when two palaces in the city were undergoing renovation. Also unmissable is the Modernista collection, which includes Ramon Casas' mural of himself and Pere Romeu on a tandem, which decorated the famous Els Quatre Gats café.

street performers recreate snippets of Catalan and Spanish folklore.

Telefèric de Montjuïc

Estació Funicular, Avda Miramar (93 465 53 13,www. telefericdemontjuic.cat). Metro Paral·lel then Funicular de Montjuïc or 150, 55 bus. **Open** *Oct-Feb 10am-6pm daily. Mar-May 10am-7pm daily. June-Sept 10am-9pm daily.* **Tickets** *One way €8.20; €6 reductions. Return €12.50; €9 reductions; free under-4s. Map p124 D10.*

The rebuilt system features eight-person cable cars that soar from the funicular up to the castle.

Restaurants

❤ **Martinez** €€€
Ctra Miramar 38 (93 106 60 52, martinezbarcelona.com). Funicular de Montjuïc or bus 150. **Open** *1pm-1.30am daily.* **Map** *p124 E11* ❷ *Spanish*

Martinez is loosely based on a *xiringuito* (open-air beach restaurant), but sits in a stunning location high on Montjuïc, next to the Miramar hotel and the cactus gardens. The specialities are paellas and other rice dishes, along with classic tapas, but – while the food is perfectly good – know that the elevated prices are really all about the spectacular views across the port, and city. It is especially romantic at night.

Cafés, tapas & bars

La Caseta del Migdia
Mirador del Migdia, Passeig del Migdia (mobile 617 956 572, www.lacaseta.org). Funicular de Montjuïc or 150 bus, then 15min walk. Follow signs to Mirador de Montjuïc. **Open** *June-Sept 9pm-midnight Wed (only with reservation); 8pm-1am Thur;*

8pm-1.30am Fri; noon-1.30am Sat; noon-midnight Sun. Oct-May noon-sunset Sat, Sun. **No cards. Map** *p124 B11* ❷

Completely alfresco, high up in a clearing among the pines, this is a magical space, scattered with deckchairs, hammocks and candlelit tables. Rather surreally, DJs spinning funk, rare groove and lounge alternate with a faltering string quartet; food is grilled sausages and salad, plus a few rice dishes. To find it, cut through the Brossa gardens from the funicular and follow the Camí del Mar footpath south around the castle. Be aware it's a lot cooler up here than in town.

Poble Sec & Sant Antoni

Poble Sec, the name of the neighbourhood between Montjuïc and Avinguda Paral·lel, means 'dry village'; it was 1894 before the thousands of poor workers who lived on the flanks of the hill celebrated the installation of the area's first fountain (still standing in C/Margarit).

These days, Poble Sec is part of a new hub of cool, along with Sant Antoni on the other side of Avda Paral·lel. Strictly speaking, the area of Sant Antoni is part of the Eixample, but its recent promotion to desirable 'hood means it now shares more characteristics with Poble Sec than with the rest of the Eixample.

The area has taken off with breathtaking speed as a hipster enclave, with C/Parlament at the epicentre. Here you'll find cocktail and wine bars, and cutesy cupcake shops, and increasingly the overspill of cool venues has been forced around the block to C/Viladomat and C/Aldana.

Sights & museums

Refugi 307

*C/Nou de la Rambla 175 (93 256 21
22, www.museuhistoria.bcn.cat).
Metro Paral·lel.* **Open** *(guided tour
& by appt only) 10.30am (English),
11.30am (Spanish) Sun.* **Admission**
€3.40; free under-7s. No cards.
Map *p124 E10.*

Around 1,500 Barcelona civilians
were killed during the Civil War air
raids, a fact that the government
has long silenced. Poble Sec was hit
particularly hard, and a large air-
raid shelter was built partially into
the mountain at the top of C/Nou
de la Rambla; this is one of some
1,200 in the city. Now converted
into a museum, it's worth a visit;
the tour takes about 45 minutes.

Restaurants

Lascar 74 €€

*C/Roser 74 (93 017 98 72, lascar.es).
Metro Paral·lel.* **Open** *8-11.45pm
Mon-Wed, 1-4pm, 8pm-11.45pm
Thur, Fri; 1-11.45pm Sat, Sun. p124
E10* ❶ *Ceviche*

The latest vogue to hit Barcelona
is the 'cevichería', but nowhere
does it better or with a more
reasonable price than Lascar. Run
by a Scot and an Englishman, it's
a welcoming little space with good
music, great cocktails (the pisco
sours are the best in the city) and
an unpretentious vibe. As well as
classic versions of the dish, there
are 'ceviches of the world', such
as the tropical, the Japanese and
the laksa.

Tickets €€€€

*Avda Paral·lel 164 (no phone,
www.ticketsbar.es). Metro Poble
Sec.* **Open** *7-11.30pm Tue-Fri;
1-3.30pm, 7-11.30pm Sat.* **Map** *p124
D8* ❸ *Modern Spanish*

This venture comes from superchef
Ferran Adrià and his brother
Albert and, in the wake of El Bulli's

Albert Adrià at Tickets

closure, is preternaturally popular.
You'll need to book (online – there
is deliberately no phone). Expect
a parade of avant-garde and
fanciful dishes at appropriately
highfalutin prices.

Cafés, tapas & bars

Bar Calders

*C/Parlament 25 (93 329 93
49). Metro Sant Antoni.* **Open**
*5pm-1.30am Mon-Thur;
5pm-2.30am Fri; 11am-2.30am
Sat; 11am-midnight Sun.* **Map**
p124 E9 ❶

Bar Calders was one of the places
that kickstarted the regeneration
of the Sant Antoni neighbourhood
– a hybrid café, tapas and wine
bar with an adjoining terrace,
it's hugely popular among the
hip young families of the *barrio*.
Occasional events include live
music, craft-beer tastings and
guest chefs.

❤ Federal

*C/Parlament 39 (93 187 36 07,
www.federalcafe.es). Metro Sant
Antoni.* **Open** *8am-11pm Mon-
Thur; 8am-12.30am Fri; 9am-12.30
Sat; 9am-5.30pm Sun.* **Map** *p124
E9* ❸

Australian-run Federal exudes
a breezy oceanside chic and is
often credited with kickstarting
the hipsterisation of Sant Antoni

– previously a *barrio* of old-timers and market-goers. Spacious, open to the street and crowned with a pretty little roof garden, it offers own-made cupcakes, excellent brunch (try the skillet of eggs, pancetta, caramelised onion and crème fraîche) and copies of the *New Yorker* to leaf through.

♥ Lando

C/Poeta Cabanyes 25 (93 348 55 30, lando.es). Metro Paral·lel. **Open** *7pm-midnight Mon-Thur; 7pm-2am Fri; noon-2am Sat; noon-1am Sun.* **Map** *p124 E9* ❹
Lando's magpie approach to the menu means that you will find mussels with coconut, lemongrass and ginger next to smoked pastrami, taramasalata and pulled pork with gnocchis. It's a hip and spacious joint in the heart of happening Sant Antoni, with tables outside on a pedestrianised side street.

Quimet i Quimet

C/Poeta Cabanyes 25 (93 442 31 42). Metro Paral·lel. **Open** *noon-4pm, 7-10.30pm Mon-Fri; noon-4pm Sat. Closed Aug.* **Map** *p124 E6* ❺
Packed to the rafters with dusty bottles of wine, this classic but minuscule bar makes up in tapas what it lacks in space. The specialities are *conservas* (shellfish preserved in tins), which aren't always to non-Spanish tastes, but the *montaditos*, sculpted tapas served on bread, are spectacular. Try salmon sashimi with cream cheese, honey and soy, or cod, passata and black olive pâté. Get there early for any chance of a surface on which to put your drink.

Xixbar

C/Rocafort 19 (93 423 43 14, www.xixbar.com). Metro Poble Sec. **Open** *6.30pm-2.30am Mon; 6pm-2.30am Tue, Wed; 5pm-2.30am Thur; 5pm-3am Fri, Sat.* **Map** *p124 D8* ❻

Xix (pronounced 'chicks', and a play on the street number, among other things) is an unconventional cocktail bar in the candlelit surroundings of a prettily tiled former *granja* (milk bar). It's exceedingly cosy and the list of almost 300 brands of gin – the house speciality – is impressive.

Entertainment

♥ BARTS

Avda Paral·lel 62 (93 324 84 92, www.barts.cat). Metro Paral·lel. **Box office** *5pm-8pm Wed-Fri and 2hrs before shows start.* **Admission** *free-€25.* **Map** *p124 F10* ❶ *Live music*
BARTS hasn't been around long, but has rapidly become the best place in the city to see rock and pop acts from around the world, such as Lucinda Williams, Matthew Herbert, LCD Soundsystem and John McLaughlin. Its success is thanks to its great acoustics, state-of-the-art sound system, comfortable seating (for those who don't want to dance downstairs) and eclectic programming.

Maumau

C/Fontrodona 35 (93 441 80 15, www.maumaubarcelona.com). Metro Paral·lel. **Open** *9pm-2.30am Thur; 9pm-2.30am Fri, Sat. Closed Aug.* **Admission** *free.* **Map** *p124 E10* ❷ *Bar*
Ring the bell by the anonymous grey door. You no longer have to pay to get in, but the membership card gets some good discounts for cinemas and clubs (see the website). Inside, a large warehouse space is humanised with colourful projections, IKEA-style sofas and scatter cushions, and a friendly, laid-back crowd. These days, Maumau has moved upmarket and is more of a lounge bar, and its latest speciality is the G&T, with 25 different types of gin offered.

❤ Mercat de les Flors

*Plaça Margarida Xirgú, C/
Lleida 59, Poble Sec (93 256 2600,
mercatflors.cat). Metro Poble
Sec. **Box office** 2hr before show.
Advance tickets also available
from Palau de la Virreina, see p80.
Tickets vary. **No cards**. **Map** p124
C9* ❸ *Theatre*

British theatre director Peter Brook
is credited with transforming
this former flower market into
a venue for the performing arts
in 1985, when he was looking for
a place to stage his legendary
production of the Mahabharata.
After decades of fairly diffuse
programming, the Mercat has
finally focused on national and
international contemporary dance,
and offers a strong programme that
experiments with unusual formats
and mixes in new technologies and
live music.

❤ Sala Apolo

*C/Nou de la Rambla 113 (93 441 40
01, www.sala-apolo.com). Metro
Paral·lel. Club 12.30-5am Mon-
Thur; 12.30-6am Fri, Sat. Concerts
varies. **Admission** Concerts varies.
Club €10-€18. **Map** p124 F10* ❹ *Club*

This 1940s dancehall is one of
Barcelona's most popular clubs,
with all that implies for atmosphere

Sala Apolo

(good) and acoustics (bad). Live
acts range from Toots & the Maytals
to Killing Joke, but note that
buying gig tickets doesn't include
admission to the club night: you'll
need to re-enter for that, and pay
extra. On Wednesdays, the DJs
offer African and Latin rhythms; on
Thursdays, it's funk, Brazilian, hip
hop and reggae; and Fridays and
Saturdays are an extravaganza of
bleeping electronica.

Teatre Lliure

*Passeig Santa Madrona 40-46,
Poble Sec (93 289 27 70, www.
teatrelliure.com). Metro Poble Sec.
Box office 9am-8pm Mon-Fri;
2hrs before show Sat, Sun. **Map** p124
C9* ❺ *Theatre*

Under its director, Lluís Pasqual,
the Teatre Lliure's main and mini
stages host an adventurous array of
theatre and dance that occasionally
spills on to the square outside.
Bigger theatre shows are surtitled
in English on Thursdays and
Saturdays.

❤ La Terrrazza

*Poble Espanyol, Avda Francesc
Ferrer i Guàrdia 13 (93 272 49 80,
www.laterrrazza.com). Metro
Espanya. **Open** June-mid Sept
12.30-5.45am Thur; 12.30-6.45am
Fri, Sat. **Admission** €5-€20. **Map**
p124 B8* ❻ *Club*

Gorgeous, glamorous and popular
(with the young, hair-gel-and-heels
brigade), La Terrrazza is a nightclub
that Hollywood might dream of.
Wander through the night-time
silence of Poble Espanyol to the
starry patio that is the dancefloor
for one of the more surreal
experiences that it's possible to
have with a highly priced G&T
in your hand. Gazebos, lookouts
and erotic paintings add to the
magic, and if the music is mostly
crowd-pleasing house tunes (the
occasional big-name DJ, though no
one truly fabulous), so what? That's
not really what you came for.

Eixample

From an aerial perspective, it is the Eixample (pronounced esh-*am*-pluh) that gives Barcelona its distinctive appearance: the middle section of the city looks as if it has been stamped with a sizzling waffle iron. This extraordinary city plan, the 'Expansion' of Barcelona into an orthogonal grid of identical blocks, was designed as an extendable matrix for future growth. With its show-stopping architecture, elegant boutiques and cutting-edge restaurants, the Eixample forms the crucible for Barcelona's image as a city of design. The fashionable Dreta ('Right') side of C/Balmes contains the most distinguished Modernista architecture, the main sights and the shopping avenues. The Esquerra ('Left') was built slightly later; it contains some top-notch restaurants.

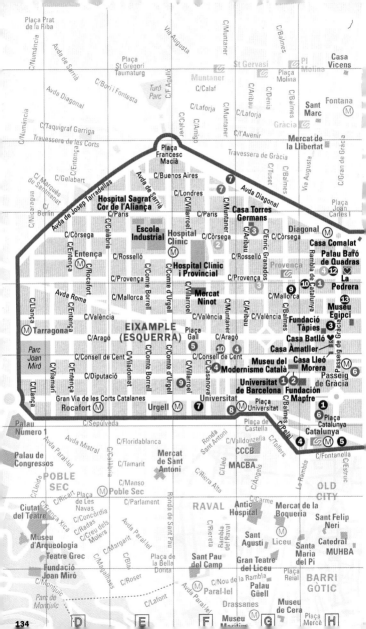

Plaça Prat de la Riba
C/Numància
Avda de Sarrià
Plaça St Gregori Taumaturg
Via Augusta
C/Muntaner
C/Balmes
St Gervasi
Pl Molina
Casa Vicens
Avda Diagonal
C/Bori i Fontesta
C/F.Agulló
Turó Parc
C/Calaf
C/Aribau
C/Dènia
C/Balmes
Plaça Molina
Fontana
C/Taquígraf Garriga
C/Numància
C/Laforja
C/Laforja
Sant Marc
Travessera de les Corts
C/Marquès de Sentmenat
C/Entença
C/Gelabert
Plaça Francesc Macià
C/Muntaner
C/l'Avenir
Gràcia
Mercat de la Llibertat
Avda de Josep Tarradellas
Avda Diagonal
C/Berlín
C/Nicaragua
C/Còrsega
Hospital Sagrat Cor de l'Aliança
C/Buenos Aires
C/Londres
Travessera de Gràcia
Via Augusta
C/Gran de Gràcia
7
7
Avda Diagonal
C/Tuset
C/Balmes
Plaça Joan Carles I
C/Paris
C/Villarroel
C/Paris
Casa Torres Germans
3
C/Enric Granados
C/Aribau
C/Còrsega
Diagonal
Escola Industrial
Hospital Clínic
C/Còrsega
2
C/Rosselló
Provença
Casa Comalat
Palau Baró de Quadras
12
C/Calàbria
C/Entença
C/Rocafort
C/Rosselló
Hospital Clínic i Provincial
C/Provença
C/Rosselló
C/Provença
9
10
Rambla de Catalunya
La Pedrera
Avda Roma
C/Comte Borrell
C/Comte d'Urgell
C/Villarroel
Mercat Ninot
C/València
C/Muntaner
C/Mallorca
C/Balmes
Museu Egipci
13
Tarragona
C/Mallorca
C/València
Fundació Tàpies
3
EIXAMPLE (ESQUERRA)
C/València
C/Aribau
Casa Batlló
1
C/Llançà
C/Entença
C/Aragó
Plaça Gall
C/Aragó
10
4
Casa Amatller
Casa Lleó Morera
C/Consell de Cent
5
C/Consell de Cent
Museu del Modernisme Català
4
Passeig de Gràcia
6
Parc Joan Miró
C/Comte Borrell
C/Viladomat
C/Casanova
Universitat de Barcelona
Fundación Mapfre
Passeig de Gràcia
C/Diputació
C/Comte d'Urgell
C/Villarroel
9
C/Balmes
1
C/Llançà
C/Entença
C/Llançà
Gran Via de les Corts Catalanes
Universitat
Plaça Universitat
6
Plaça Catalunya
Rocafort
Urgell
7
8
4
Catalunya
5
Palau Numero 1
C/Sepúlveda
Plaça de Castella
Ronda Sant Antoni
C/Valldonzella
C/Tallers
C/Fontanella
C/Estruc
Avda Mistral
C/Floridablanca
CCCB
MACBA
La Rambla
OLD CITY
Palau de Congressos
C/Calàbria
C/Tamarit
Mercat de Sant Antoni
C/Joaquín Costa
C/Àngels
POBLE SEC
Poble Sec
C/Manso
C/Parlament
Ronda de Sant Pau
C/Riera Alta
RAVAL
C/Carme
Antic Hospital
Mercat de la Boqueria
Sant Felip Neri
Plaça de Les Navas
C/Concòrdia
C/Riereta
Liceu
Catedral
MUHBA
Ciutat del Teatre
C/Ricart
C/Rabes
C/Creu dels Molers
Raval
Sant Agustí
Santa Maria del Pi
Museu d'Arqueologia
Avda Paral·lel
C/Margarit
Sant Pau del Camp
Gran Teatre del Liceu
Plaça Reial
BARRI GÒTIC
Teatre Grec
C/Blai
Plaça de la Bella Dorita
Palau Güell
Fundació Joan Miró
C/Magalhães
C/Roser
C/Nou de la Rambla
Paral·lel
Museu de Cera
C/Montjuïc
Parc de Montjuïc
C/Lafont
Avda Paral·lel
Drassanes
Plaça Mercè

D   E   F   G   H

Museu Marítim

Dreta

Most of the sites of interest for visitors are within a few blocks of the grand central boulevard of Passeig de Gràcia, which ascends directly from Plaça Catalunya. Incorporating some of Barcelona's finest Modernista gems, it is the showpiece of the Quadrat D'Or (Golden District) – a square mile between C/Muntaner and C/Roger de Flor that contains 150 protected buildings.

The three most famous sit on Passeig de Gràcia itself, on the block known as the **Manzana de la Discòrdia**. The fairest on the block is surely Gaudí's **Casa Batlló**. Runners-up are Puig i Cadafalch's Casa Àmatller and Domènech i Montaner's **Casa Lleó Morera**, a decadently melting wedding cake of a building on the corner of C/Consell de Cent. Further up is the Gaudí-designed apartment block, **La Pedrera**.

As the area surrounding Passeig de Gràcia is one of the wealthiest parts of the city, it's not surprising that it's also rich in privately owned art collections and museums; these include the **Museu Egipci de Barcelona**, and the **Fundació Antoni Tàpies**. The area is equally well provided with shops, with a mix of boutiques, international designers and high-street brands jostling for space.

For most visitors, however, the crowning glory of the Eixample experience is the darkly beautiful **Sagrada Família**. Whether you love it or hate it (George Orwell called it 'one of the most hideous buildings in the world'), it has become the city's emblem. A less famous masterpiece nearby, in the shape of Domènech i Montaner's **Hospital de la Santa Creu i Sant Pau**, has in recent years been enclosed as a tourist attraction, now known as the **Recinte Modernista de Sant Pau**.

EIXAMPLE

❤ Shortlist

Unmissable Gaudí
Sagrada Família (*p142*), the unfinished cathedral and Barna's best-loved attraction. Casa Batlló (*p138*) and La Pedrera (*p140*) for the master's unmistakable style.

Best for quiet contemplation
Recinte Modernista de Sant Pau (*p145*) for the peaceful gardens.

Best restaurant
Gresca (*p150*) for affordable haute cuisine.

Best night out
Arena (*p148*) for gay vibes. City Hall (*p149*) for hands-in-the-air action.

Best market
Els Encants (*p146*) to rummage for treasure.

Best shops
Altaïr (*p144*) for all your travel needs. Santa Eulàlia (*p147*) for designer threads.

Best snack stop
Escribà (*p151*) for a chocolate treat. Granja Petitbó (*p144*) for a sunny brunch. La Bodegueta (*p141*) for a mid-morning vermouth and tapas.

Best bars
Dry Martini (*p150*) for the perfect martini . Garage Beer Co (*p150*) for a smooth IPA.

Sights & museums

Casa Àmatller

Passeig de Gràcia 41 (93 461 7460, www.amatller.com). Metro Passeig de Gràcia. **Open** *10am-6pm daily.* **Admission** *€14; guided tour €17; free under-7s.* **Map** *p134 H6.*

Built for chocolate baron Antoni Àmatller, this playful building is one of Puig i Cadafalch's finest creations. Inspired by 17th-century Dutch townhouses, its distinctive stepped Flemish pediment is covered in shiny ceramics, while the lower façade and the doorway are decorated with lively sculptures by Eusebi Arnau. These sculptures include chocolatiers at work, almond trees and blossoms (which is a reference to the family name), and Sant Jordi slaying the dragon.

The guided tour of the house lasts around an hour and includes the ornate entrance hall, Antoni Àmatller's period photography studio and a tasting of Àmatller chocolate in the original kitchen.

Casa de les Punxes

Avda Diagonal 420 (93 018 5242, www.casadelespunxes.com). Metro Diagonal. **Open** *9am-8pm daily; last entrance 7pm.* **Admission** *€12.50; €11.25 reductions; free under-5s; audio guide included.* **Map** *p134 J5.*

Also known as the Casa Terradas, the Casa de les Punxes ('House of Spikes', named for its pointed turrets), is a magnificently medieval-looking creation designed by Puig i Cadafalch and built in 1905. Though neo-Gothic was all the rage among the architects of the time, Puig i Cadafalch was first and foremost a Modernista, and the sombre look of the façade contrasts with the colour and light of the interiors, its stained glass and tiling.

Fundació Antoni Tàpies

C/Aragó 255 (93 487 03 15, www.fundaciotapies.org). Metro Passeig de Gràcia. **Open** *10am-7pm Tue-Sun.* **Admission** *€7; €5.60 reductions; free under-16s.* **Map** *p134 H6.*

Antoni Tàpies exploded on to the art scene in the 1950s, when he began to incorporate waste paper, mud and rags into his paintings, eventually moving on to the point where his works included whole pieces of furniture, running water and girders. Today, he's Barcelona's most celebrated living artist, and his trademark scribbled and paint-daubed pieces are sought after to illustrate items from wine bottle labels to theatre posters.

The artist set up the Tàpies Foundation in this, the former Montaner i Simon publishing house, in 1984, dedicating it to the study and appreciation of contemporary art.

EIXAMPLE

→ **Getting around**

The grid-like Eixample is divided into two areas, either side of C/Balmes: the Esquerra (left) and Dreta (right). It is criss-crossed by various bus and metro lines, most of which conjoin at Plaça Catalunya. To walk from one end of Passeig de Gràcia to the other takes around 15 minutes.

It can be hard to get your bearings, but locals will often indicate directions using a handy code – 'mar' (sea) or 'muntanya' (mountain) refer to the bottom or top of the area, while 'Besos' and 'Llobregat' are the rivers to the right and left of the city, indicating which side of an Eixample street something falls on.

💙 Casa Batlló

*Passeig de Gràcia 43 (93 216 03 06, www.casabatllo.cat). Metro Passeig de Gràcia. **Open** 9am-9pm daily; last entrance 8pm. **Admission** €23.50; €20.50 reductions; free under-7s. **Map** p134 H6.*

In one of the most extreme architectural makeovers ever seen, Gaudí and his long-time collaborator Josep Maria Jujol took an ordinary apartment block and remodelled it inside and out for textile tycoon Josep Batlló between 1902 and 1906. The result was one of the most impressive and admired of all Gaudí's creations.

Opinions differ as to what the building's remarkable façade represents, particularly its polychrome shimmering walls, its sinister skeletal balconies and its humpbacked scaly roof. Some say it's the spirit of carnival, others a Costa Brava cove. However, the most popular theory, which takes into account the architect's deeply patriotic feelings, is that the façade depicts Sant Jordi and the dragon – the idea being that the cross on top is the knight's lance, the roof represents the back of the beast, and the balconies below are the skulls and bones of its hapless victims.

The chance to explore the interior (at a cost) offers the best opportunity of understanding how Gaudí, sometimes considered the lord of the bombastic and overblown, was really the master of tiny details – from the ingenious ventilation in the doors to the amazing natural light reflecting off the inner courtyard's azure walls – and the way the brass window handles are curved so as to fit the shape of a hand. An apartment is open to the public, and access has been granted to the attic and roof terrace: the whitewashed arched rooms of the top floor, originally used for laundering and hanging clothes, are among the master's most atmospheric spaces.

Fundación Mapfre

C/Diputació 250 (93 272 31 80, www.fundacionmapfre.org). *Metro Passeig de Gràcia.* **Open** 2-8pm Mon; 10am-8pm Tue-Sat; 11am-7pm Sun. **Admission** €3; €2 reductions; free under-16s; free to all Mon 2-8pm. **Map** p134 H7.

Since 2015, the Modernista masterpiece Casa Garriga i Nogués –, has housed exhibitions put on by the charitable arm of the Mapfre insurance company. The opening exhibition was a blockbuster of impressionist artworks loaned from the Musée d'Orsay in Paris, but subsequent exhibitions have focused on bringing attention to lesser known artists and photographers.

Museu del Modernisme Català

C/Balmes 48 (93 272 28 96, www.mmbcn.cat). *Metro Passeig de Gràcia.* **Open** 10.30am-8pm Tue-Sat; 10.30am-2pm Sun. **Admission** €10; €5-€8 reductions; free under-5s. **Map** p134 G7.

Inaugurated in 2010, this private collection includes work by all the heavyweights of the Modernisme movement. There is a Gaudí-designed kissing chair, some extravagant ecclesiastical pieces by Puig i Cadafalch, tiled bedheads by Gaspar Homar, marble sculptures by Josep Llimona and paintings by Santiago Rusiñol, Joaquim Mir and Ramon Casas. The furniture created by lesser-known craftsmen also includes some stunning pieces, with a collection of marquetry escritoires.

Museu Egipci de Barcelona

C/València 284 (93 488 01 88, www.museuegipci.com). *Metro Passeig de Gràcia.* **Open** Jan-mid June, mid Sept-Nov 10am-2pm, 4-8pm Mon-Fri; 10am-8pm Sat; 10am-2pm Sun. Dec, mid June-mid Sept 10am-8pm Mon-Sat; 10am-2pm Sun.

Admission €11; €8 reductions; free under-6s. **Map** p134 H6.

This is one of the finest museums of Ancient Egyptian artefacts in Europe. The collection is owned by prominent Egyptologist Jordi Clos and spans 3,000 years of Nile-drenched culture. Exhibits include religious statuary, such as the massive baboon heads used to decorate temples, everyday copper mirrors and alabaster headrests, and some rather moving infant sarcophagi.

Restaurants

Casa Calvet €€€

C/Casp 48 (93 412 40 12, www.casacalvet.es). *Metro Urquinaona.* **Open** 1-3.30pm, 8.30-11pm Mon-Sat. **Map** p134 J7 ① *Catalan*

Casa Calvet allows the time-strapped visitor to sample some excellent cooking and appreciate the master of Modernisme at the same time. One of Gaudí's more understated buildings from the outside, Casa Calvet has an interior full of glorious detail in the carpentry, stained glass and tiles. The food is up to par, with surprising combinations almost always hitting the mark: sole with pistachio sauce and sautéed aubergine; scallops with black olive tapenade and wild mushroom croquettes; and roast beef with apple sauce and truffled potatoes. The puddings are superb – try the chestnut parfait with figs in brandy and a mandarin coulis, or the mango and banana tatin.

Tragaluz €€€

Ptge de la Concepció 5 (93 487 01 96, www.grupotragaluz.com). *Metro Diagonal.* **Open** 1.30-4pm, 8-11.30pm daily. **Map** p134 H5 ④ *Mediterranean*

The stylish flagship for this extraordinarily successful restaurant group has weathered

💜 La Pedrera (Casa Milà)

*C/Provença 261-265 (93 484 59 00, www.lapedrera.com). Metro Diagonal. **Open** Nov-Feb 9am-6.30pm daily. Mar-Oct 9am-8pm daily. **Admission** €22; €11-€16.50 reductions; free under-7s. **Map** p134 H5.*

Described variously as rising dough, molten lava and a stone lung, the last secular building designed by Antoni Gaudí, the Casa Milà (popularly known as La Pedrera, 'the stone quarry') has no straight lines. It is a stupendous and daring feat of architecture, and the culmination of the architect's experimental attempts to re-create natural forms with bricks and mortar (not to mention ceramics and even smashed-up cava bottles). Now a UNESCO World Heritage Site, it appears to have been washed up on shore, with a marine feel complemented by collaborator Josep Maria Jujol's tangled balconies, doors of twisted kelp ribbon, sea-foamy ceilings and interior patios as blue as a mermaid's cave.

When it was completed in 1912, it was so far ahead of its time that the woman who financed it as her dream home, Roser Segimon, became the laughing stock of the city – hence the 'stone quarry' tag. Its rippling façade led local painter Santiago Rusiñol to quip that a snake would be a better pet than a dog for the inhabitants. But La Pedrera has become one of Barcelona's best-loved buildings, and is adored by architects for its extraordinary structure: it is supported entirely by pillars, without a single master wall, allowing the vast, asymmetrical windows of the façade to invite in great swathes of natural light.

There are three exhibition spaces at Casa Milà. The first-floor art gallery hosts free shows of work by a variety of eminent artists, while the upstairs space is dedicated to giving visitors a finer appreciation of Gaudí: accompanied by an audio guide (included in the admission price), you can visit a reconstructed Modernista flat on the fourth floor,

EIXAMPLE

with a sumptuous bedroom suite by Gaspar Homar, while the attic, framed by parabolic arches worthy of a Gothic cathedral, holds a museum offering an insightful overview of Gaudí's career. Best of all is the chance to stroll on the roof of the building amid its *trencadís*-covered ventilation shafts: their heads are shaped like the helmets of medieval knights, which led the poet Pere Gimferrer to dub the spot 'the garden of warriors'.

the city's culinary revolution exceptionally well over recent years, and is still covering fresh ground on the Mediterranean creative scene. Although the food certainly doesn't come cheap, and the wine mark-up is particularly hard to swallow, there is no faulting the tuna *tataki* served with a cardamom wafer and a dollop of ratatouille-like *pisto*; monkfish tail in a sweet tomato *sofregit* with black olive oil; or juicy braised oxtail with cabbage.

Cafés, tapas & bars

♥ La Bodegueta
Rambla de Catalunya 100 (93 215 48 94, www.labodegueta.cat). Metro Diagonal. Open 7am-1.45am Mon-Sat; 6.30pm-1.45am Sun. Map p134 H6 ①
This delightful old bodega, with a pretty tiled floor and terrace on the Rambla, is dusty and welcoming, supplying students, businessmen and pretty much everyone in between with reasonably priced wine, vermouth on tap and good-quality tapas. The emphasis is placed on locally sourced products (try Montserrat tomatoes with tuna), among old favourites such as *patatas bravas*.

Cafè del Centre
C/Girona 69 (93 488 11 10). Metro Girona. Open 9am-midnight Mon-Sat. Closed 2wks Aug. Map p134 J7 ②
The oldest café in the Eixample, and possibly the only one of its type left in the city, with a delightfully dusty air, Modernista wooden banquettes, walls stained with the nicotine of ages and marble tables sitting on a chipped chequered floor that almost certainly dates back to the bar's opening in 1873. It is still in the hands of the same family, whose youngest members' attempts to instigate change include a list of over 50 types of craft beer.

EIXAMPLE

❤ Sagrada Família

C/Mallorca 401 (93 207 30 31, www.sagradafamilia.org). Metro Sagrada Família. **Open** *Apr-Sept 9am-8pm daily. Oct, Mar 9am-7pm daily; Nov-Feb 9am-6pm daily.* **Admission** *€15; €11-€13 reductions; free under-11s. Guided tour €24, €8-€22 reductions (admission & audio guide included). Towers €29, €22-€27 reductions (admission & audio guide included).* **Map** *p134 L6.*

'Send Gaudí and the Sagrada Família to hell,' wrote Picasso – and while it is easy to see how some of the religious clichés of the building and the devotional fervour of its creator might annoy an angry young Cubist, Barcelona's iconic temple still manages to inspire delight.

Gaudí dedicated more than 40 years (the last 14 of them exclusively) to the project, and is buried beneath the nave. Many consider the crypt and the Nativity façade, which were completed in his lifetime, to be the most beautiful elements of the church. The latter, on C/Marina, looks at first glance as though some careless giant has poured candle wax over a Gothic cathedral, but closer inspection shows every protuberance to be an intricate sculpture of flora, fauna or a human figure, combining to form an astonishingly moving stone tapestry depicting scenes from Christ's early years.

Providing a grim counterpoint to the excesses of the Nativity façade is the Passion façade on C/Sardenya, where there are bone-shaped columns and haunting, angular sculptures by Josep

Maria Subirachs that show the 12 Stations of the Cross. The vast metal doors, which are set behind the sculpture of the flagellation of Jesus, are particularly arresting, covered in quotations from the Bible in various languages.

The Glory façade on C/Mallorca, the final side to be built and the eventual main entrance, is currently shooting up behind the scaffolding and is devoted to the Resurrection, a mass of stone clouds and trumpets emblazoned with quotations from the Apostles' Creed.

The most amazing thing about the Sagrada Família project, however, is that it is happening at all. Begun in 1882, setbacks have ranged from 1930s anarchists blowing up Gaudí's detailed plans and models, to lack of funds. The ongoing work is a matter of conjecture and controversy, with the finishing date expected to be somewhere within the region of 25 to 30 years; it was hoped the masterpiece would be completed in 2026 to coincide with the 100th anniversary of Gaudí's death, although this now seems unlikely. It's still something of an improvement on the prognosis in the 1900s, when construction was expected to last several hundred years; advanced computer technology is now being used to shape each intricately designed block of stone offsite to speed up the process. The latest tribulation for the architects to overcome is the municipal approval of plans to build the AVE bullet train tunnel just a few feet away from the temple's foundations.

Around five million tourists visit the Sagrada Família each year, with more than half of them entering the building. The admission fee allows you to wander through the interior of the church, a marvellous forest of columns laid out in the style of the great Gothic cathedrals, with a multi-aisled central nave crossed by a transept. The central columns are fashioned of porphyry – perhaps the only natural element capable of supporting the church's projected great dome, which is destined to rise 170m (558ft).

A ticket also gives visitors access to the museum in the basement, with displays on the history of the construction, original models for sculptural work and the chance to watch sculptors working at plaster-cast models through a large window.

Nativity façade

❤ Granja Petitbó

Passeig de Sant Joan 82 (93 265 6503, www.granjapetibo.com). Metro Tetuan or Verdaguer. **Open** *9am-11pm Mon-Wed, 9am-11.30pm Thur-Fri; 10am-11.30pm Sat, 10am-5pm Sun.* **Map** *p134 K6* ❺

Granja Petitbó was at the vanguard of the hipsterfication of the Passeig de Sant Joan, and though it has since been joined by a dozen other cafés and bars, it is still packed at peak times. It's a sunny place, amiably scruffy, with deep, battered leather sofas and a creaky wooden floor. As well as all the usual brunch dishes – eggs Benedict, pancakes, porridge – there are burgers, salads and pasta, along with huge bricks of cake.

Tapas 24

C/Diputació 269 (93 488 09 77, www.carlesabellan.com). Metro Passeig de Gràcia. **Open** *9am-midnight Mon-Sat.* **Map** *p134 H7* ❻

Another nu-trad tapas bar focusing on excellent quality produce. Among the oxtail stews, fried prawns and cod croquettes, however, fans of chef Carles Abellan will also find playful snacks more in keeping with his signature style. The McFoie Burguer is an exercise in fast-food heaven, as is the Bikini, a small version of his take on the ham and cheese toastie; his comes with truffle.

Shops & services

❤ Altaïr

Gran Via de les Corts Catalanes 616 (93 342 71 71, www.altair.es). Metro Universitat. **Open** *10am-8.30pm Mon-Sat.* **Map** *p134 H7* ❶ *Books*

Every aspect of travel is covered in this, the largest travel bookshop in Europe. You can pick up guides to free eating in Barcelona, academic tomes on geolinguistics, handbooks on successful outdoor

sex and CDs of tribal and world music. Of course, all the less arcane publications are also here: maps for hikers, travel guidebooks, multilingual dictionaries, travel diaries, atlases and equipment such as mosquito nets.

BCN Books

C/Roger de Llúria 118 (93 457 76 92, www.bcnbooks.com). Metro Diagonal. **Open** *July, Aug 9am-8pm Mon-Fri. Sept-June 9am-8pm Mon-Fri; 9am-2pm Sat.* **Map** *p134 J5* ❷ *Books*

This well-stocked English-language bookstore has a wide range of learning and teaching materials for all ages. There's also a decent selection of contemporary and classic fiction, a good kids' section, some travel guides and plenty of dictionaries.

Bulevard dels Antiquaris

Passeig de Gràcia 55 (93 215 44 99, www.bulevarddelsantiquaris.com). Metro Passeig de Gràcia. **Open** *10am-2pm, 5-8.30pm Mon-Sat.* **Map** *p134 H6* ❸ *Antiques*

This small antiques 'mall' is one of the most convenient and safest places to shop for antiques in Barcelona (experts inspect every object for authenticity). Check out the style of ethnic art that influenced the likes of Miró at Guilhem Montagut (nos.11-22), where you can pick up a Nigerian funeral urn. Collectors will love the antique pistols at Cañas (nos.35-36) and D'Art (no.70), and the vintage textiles and shawls at Antigüedades Pilar (no.65).

Camper

C/Pelai 13-37 (93 302 41 24, www.camper.com). Metro Catalunya. **Open** *10am-10pm Mon-Sat.* **Map** *p134 G8* ❹ *Shoes*

Mallorca-based eco shoe company Camper has sexed up its ladies' line in recent years. Each year, the label seems to flirt more with high heels

❤ Recinte Modernista de Sant Pau

C/Sant Antoni Maria Claret 167 (93 553 78 01, www.santpaubarcelona. org). Metro Sant Pau Dos de Maig. **Open** *Apr-Oct 10am-6.30pm Mon-Sat; 10am-2.30pm Sun. Nov-Mar 10am-4.30pm Mon-Sat; 10am-2.30pm Sun.* **Admission** *€13; €9.10 reductions; free under-12s & over-65s.* **Map** *p134 N4.*

When part of the roof of the gynaecology department collapsed in 2004, it was clear that restoration work was needed on the century-old Modernista 'garden city' hospital, a UNESCO World Heritage Site. In 2009, the last of the departments was transferred to the modern Nou Sant Pau building to the north, and the complex was fenced off and spruced up in order to turn what had been a hidden Modernista treasure into a major tourist attraction.

Given its proximity to the Sagrada Familia, it still sees relatively few visitors, and offers a peaceful way to contemplate some of the finest architecture of the period.

The former hospital is entered through a fairytale hypostyle hall of elegant pillars, polychromatic mosaics, stained glass and Gothic iron lamps. This leads out to the 20 pavilions that once served as wards. These are abundantly adorned with the colourful Byzantine, Gothic and Moorish flourishes that characterise Domènech i Montaner's style and set in peaceful gardens that spread over nine blocks in the north-east corner of the Eixample. It's set at a 45° angle from the rest of Ildefons Cerdà's grid system, so that it catches more sun: Domènech i Montaner built the hospital very much with its patients in mind, convinced that aesthetic harmony and pleasant surroundings were good for the health. Guided tours in English are held daily at 11am.

EIXAMPLE

(albeit rubbery wedgy ones) and girly straps. Of course, it still has its classic round-toed and clod-heeled classics, but Camper is definitely worth another look if you've previously dismissed it.

El Corte Inglés

*Plaça Catalunya 14 (93 306 38 00, www.elcorteingles.es). Metro Catalunya. **Open** 9.30am-9.30pm Mon-Sat. **Map** p134 H8* **5** *Department store*

This monolith sits on Plaça Catalunya and stocks all the major international brand names, along with plenty of Spanish labels. This branch is the place for toiletries, cosmetics, clothes and homewares. It also houses a well-stocked but pricey supermarket and a gourmet food store, plus services ranging from key-cutting to currency exchange. On the top floor, there's a restaurant with great views (but service station-style food). The Portal de l'Àngel branch stocks CDs, DVDs, books, electronic equipment, stationery and sports gear. There are fashion and accessories geared to a younger market on the ground floor.

❤ Els Encants

*C/Dos de Maig 177-187, Plaça de les Glòries (93 245 22 99, www. encantsbcn.com). Metro Glòries. **Open** 9am-8pm Mon, Wed, Fri, Sat. Auctions 7.30-8.30am Mon, Wed, Fri. **Map** p134 N7* **6** *Flea market*

Now in a spiffy new home on the other side of the monster intersection at Glòries, this vast and rambling flea market is still a stew of shouts, musty smells and teetering piles of everything from old horseshoes and Barça memorabilia to cheap electrical gadgets, religious relics and ancient Spanish schoolbooks.

If you want to buy furniture at a decent price, join the commercial buyers at the auctions from

7am, or arrive at noon, when unsold stuff drops in price. Avoid Saturdays, when prices shoot up and the crowds move in, and be on your guard for pickpockets and short-changing.

Flors Navarro

*C/València 320 (93 457 40 99, floristeriasnavarro.com). Metro Verdaguer. **Open** 24hrs daily. **Map** p134 J6* **8** *Flowers*

At Flors Navarro, fresh-cut blooms, pretty house plants and stunning bouquets are available to buy 24 hours a day. A dozen red roses can be delivered anywhere in town, until 10pm, for €36.

Galeria Estrany · De La Mota

*Ptge Mercader 18 (93 215 70 51, www.estranydelamota.com). FGC Provença. **Open** 10.30am-7pm Tue-Fri. Closed Aug. **No cards**. **Map** p134 G6* **9** *Gallery*

Els Encants

This cavernous basement is one of the most intriguing art spaces in the city. It hosts outstanding contemporary exhibitions, particularly in photography and film, from the likes of Finnish artist Esko Männikkö and Scottish film buff Douglas Gordon.

Du Pareil au Même

Rambla Catalunya 95 (93 487 14 49, www.dpam.com). Metro Diagonal/FGC Provença. **Open** *9.30am-8.30pm Mon-Sat.* **Map** *p134 H6* ❿ *Children*

This French chain stocks everything a pint-sized fashionista might need, though the girls do a bit better than the boys, and babies do best of all, with fabulously colourful babygros. Newborns to 14-year-olds are served with a covetable range of funky, bright and well-designed clothes.

Queviures Múrria

C/Roger de Llúria 85 (93 215 57 89). Metro Passeig de Gràcia. **Open** *9am-2pm, 5-9pm Tue-Sat. Closed Aug.* **Map** *p134 J6* ⓫ *Food*

Queviures Múrria's shopfront is a veritable art gallery, featuring original hand-painted adverts for local booze Anis del Mono by Modernista artist Ramon Casas. Head inside for a wonderful selection of cheeses, sausages and wines from Catalonia and further afield.

❤ Santa Eulàlia

Passeig de Gràcia 93 (93 215 06 74, www.santaeulalia.com). Metro Diagonal. **Open** *10am-8.30pm Mon-Sat.* **Map** *p134 H5* ⓬ *Fashion*

Barcelona's oldest design house and a pioneer in the local catwalk scene, Santa Eulàlia was founded in 1843 and remains a seriously upmarket proposition. The prêtà-porter selection at the shop is fresh and up-to-the-minute, and includes labels such as Balenciaga, Jimmy Choo, Stella McCartney and Ann Demeulemeester. Services include bespoke tailoring and wedding wear for grooms, and there is a bistro and champagne bar.

Twenty One by Esther Llongueras
Passeig de Gràcia 78 (93 215 41 75, www.twenty-one-21.com). Metro Passeig de Gràcia. **Open** *9am-6.30pm Mon-Fri; 9am-1.30pm Sat.* **Map** *p134 H6* ⑬ *Hairdresser*
A safe bet for all ages, this pricey Catalan chain has well-trained stylists who take the time to give a proper consultation, wash and massage. The cuts are up-to-the-minute but as natural as possible.

Entertainment

Aire
C/Diputació 233 (93 454 63 94, www.grupoarena.com). Metro Passeig de Gràcia. **Open** *11pm-2.30am Thur-Sat.* **Admission** *(incl 1 drink)* €5 Fri; €6 Sat.* **No cards**. **Map** *p134 G7* ❶ *Lesbian club*
The girly outpost of the Arena group is the city's largest lesbian club, and as such sees a decent

---

---

variety of girls (and their male friends, by invitation) head down to shoot pool and dance to pop, house and 1980s classics. On the first Sunday of the month, there's a women-only strip show.

❤ Arena
Classic *C/Diputació 233.* **Open** *12.30-5am Fri, Sat.* **Map** *p134 G7.* ❷ *Gay club*
Madre *C/Balmes 32.* **Open** *2.30-6am daily.* **Map** *p134 G7.*
VIP *Gran Via de les Corts Catalanes 593.* **Open** *1-6am Fri, Sat.* **Map** *p134 F7.*
All *93 487 83 42, www.grupoarena. com. Metro Universitat.* **Admission** *(incl 1 drink)* €6 Mon-Fri; Sun; €12 Sat. **No cards**
The Arena clubs are still packing in a huge variety of punters every week. The unique selling point is that you pay once, get your hand stamped and can then flit between all three gay clubs. **Madre** is the biggest and most full-on venue of the trio, with thumping house music and a darkroom. There are shows and strippers at the beginning of the week, but Wednesday's semi-riotous foam parties in July and August are where all the action takes place. **VIP** doesn't take itself too seriously and is popular with just about everyone, from mixed gangs of Erasmus students to parties of thirtysomethings in from the suburbs, all getting busy to Snoop Dogg and vintage Mariah Carey. **Classic** is similarly mixed, if even cheesier, playing mostly handbag hits.

❤ L'Auditori
C/Lepant 150 (93 247 93 00, www. auditori.cat). Metro Marina. **Box office** *5-9pm Tue-Fri; 10am-1pm, 5-9pm Sat; 1hr before performance Sun. Closed Aug. Tickets vary.* **Map** *p134 M8* ❸ *Theatre*

Designed by architect Rafael Moneo, L'Auditori tries to offer something to everyone. The 2,400-seat Pau Casals hall, dedicated to the Catalan cellist, provides a stable home for city orchestra OBC, now under the baton of conductor Kazushi Ono (although it frequently performs with guest conductors). A more intimate 600-seat chamber space, which is dedicated to choir leader Oriol Martorell, has a more diverse programme incorporating contemporary and world music. Experimental and children's work is staged in a 350-seat space named after jazz pianist Tete Montoliu.

❤ City Hall
Rambla Catalunya 2-4 (93 238 07 22, www.cityhallbarcelona.com). Metro Catalunya. Club midnight-5am Mon-Thur, Sun; midnight-6am Fri, Sat. Concerts varies. **Admission** *free before 1am; after 1am (incl 1 drink) €12-€18.* **Map** *p134 H7* ❻ *Club*

City Hall ain't big, but it is popular. The music is mixed, from deep house to electro rock, and there's an older post- (pre-?) work crowd joining the young, tanned and skinny to show the dancefloors some love. Outside, the terrace is a melting pot of tourists and locals, who rub shoulders under the watchful (and anti-pot-smoking) eye of the bouncer. Earlier in the evening it operates as an excellent mid-sized live music venue.

Sala Phenomena
C/Sant Antoni Maria Claret 168 (93 252 77 43, www.phenomena-experience.com). Metro Sant Pau or Dos de Maig. Tickets €8-€9. **Map** *p134 M4* ⓫ *Cinema*

One of Barcelona's plushest cinemas, this shows everything from cult favourites (Jaws, The Big Lebowski, Alien) to the latest Hollywood releases on an enormous screen. It also has film programmes dedicated to specific genres, directors or actors, as well as talks, kids' films and fabulous double bills. Note that some films are dubbed.

❤ Teatre Nacional de Catalunya (TNC)
Plaça de les Arts 1 (93 306 57 00, www.tnc.cat). Metro Glòries. **Box office** *5-8pm Wed-Fri; 3-8pm (9.30pm double performance days) Sat; 3-6pm Sun. Closed Aug. Tickets vary.* **Map** *p134 M8* ⓬ *Theatre*

The Generalitat-funded theatre, which was designed by Ricardo Bofill in a neo-classical style, boasts a vast airy lobby and three fabulous performance spaces. Director Xavier Albertí has opted for a good mix of contemporary and classical pieces and incorporated a fine contemporary dance programme, divided between a main stage and smaller stage.

Esquerra

When Ildefons Cerdà designed the Eixample, he consciously tried to avoid creating any upper- or lower-class side of town, imagining each of his homogeneous blocks as a cross-section of society. This vision of equality did not come to pass, however, and the left side of the tracks was immediately less fashionable than the right; eventually it was to become the repository for the sort of city services the bourgeoisie didn't want ruining the upmarket tone of their new neighbourhood.

A huge slaughterhouse was built at the western edge of the area and was only knocked down in 1979, when it was replaced by the **Parc Joan Miró**. Also here is the busy Hospital Clínic; to visit a market frequented by locals rather than tourists, try the Ninot, just below the hospital.

Sights & museums

Parc Joan Miró (Parc de l'Escorxador)

C/Tarragona & C/Aragó 2. Metro Espanya. **Open** *10am-sunset daily.* **Map** *p134 C6.*

Covering an area the size of four city blocks, the old slaughterhouse (*escorxador*) was demolished in 1979 to provide some much-needed parkland, although there's little greenery. The rows of palms and pines are dwarfed by Miró's sculpture *Dona i Ocell* (Woman and Bird) getting its feet wet in a cement lake; there's also a good playground for small kids.

Restaurants

Gaig €€€€

C/Còrsega 200 (93 453 20 20, www.restaurantgaig.com). Metro Hospital-Clínic. **Open** *1.30-3.30pm, 8.30-11pm Tue-Sat; 1.30-3.30pm Sun.* **Map** *p134 F5* ② *Catalan*

The eponymous chef Carles Gaig's cooking never fails to thrill the visitor. From his signature cannelloni with truffle cream to a shot glass holding layers of tangy lemon syrup, crema catalana mousse and caramel ice-cream, topped with burned sugar (to be eaten by plunging the spoon all the way down), every dish is as surprising and perfectly composed as the last.

❤ Gresca €€€

C/Provença 230 (93 451 61 93, www.gresca.net). Metro Diagonal or Passeig de Gràcia. **Open** *Restaurant 1.30-3.30pm, 8.30-10.30pm Mon-Fri. Bar 1.30-3.30pm, 8.30-10.30pm Mon, Tue, Thur-Sun. Restaurant closed 2wks Aug.* **Map** *p134 G6* ③ *Modern European*

After extensive remodelling and expansion into an adjacent building, Gresca's chef, Rafa Peña, has been able to slot in a wine bar and considerably expand his kitchen – perhaps this will win him a merited Michelin star, finally. There is a suitably classy wine list, but the real highlights are dishes such as foamed egg on a bed of *jamón ibérico,* fennel and courgette, or puddings like the coca bread with Roquefort, and lychee and apple sorbet.

Cafés, tapas & bars

❤ Dry Martini

C/Aribau 162-166 (93 217 50 72, www.javierdelasmuelas.com). FGC Provença. **Open** *1pm-2.30am Mon-Thur; 1pm-3am Fri; 6.30pm-3am Sat; 6.30pm-2.30am Sun.* **Map** *p134 G5* ③

A shrine to the famous cocktail, which is honoured in Martini-related artwork and served in a hundred forms. All the trappings of a traditional cocktail bar are here (bow-tied staff, leather banquettes, antiques and wooden cabinets displaying a century's worth of bottles) but there's a notable lack of stuffiness, and the musical selection owes more to trip hop than middle-aged crowd-pleasers.

❤ Garage Beer Co

C/Consell de Cent 261 (93 528 59 89, garagebeer.co). Metro Universitat. **Open** *5pm-midnight Mon-Thur; 5pm-2.30am Fri; noon-3am Sat; 2pm-midnight Sun.* **Map** *p134 G6* ④

Of the rash of tap rooms to open in recent years, Garage is the least pretentious and has some of the best beer. It started with a couple of pals making beer in a garage, and even this space has an industrial feel to it, despite the small size and the jumble of leather sofas in the back room. At any one time, they have around ten kegs of their own beer, in a range of styles, and the occasional cask of guest beer.

Eixample from above

Velódromo

C/Muntaner 213 (93 430 60 22).
Metro Hospital Clínic. **Open**
6am-2.30am Mon-Thur, Sun;
6am-3am Fri, Sat. **Map** *p134 F4* ⑦
For most of the 20th century, this
was a favoured meeting place
of the Catalan intelligentsia,
underground political groups and
– in the 1960s – an artistic group
known as La Gauche Divine. It lay
fallow during the noughties, but
its elegant art deco interior was
dusted off and gussied up thanks to
a collaboration between chef Jordi
Vilà and Moritz beer. There's a
long list of tapas and larger dishes,
along with excellent coffee and
bathrooms that pay technicolour
homage to Paul Smith.

Shops & services

♥ Escribà

Gran Via de les Corts Catalanes
546 (93 454 75 35, www.escriba.
es). Metro Urgell. **Open** *8am-3pm,*
5-8.30pm Mon-Fri; 8am-8.30pm
Sat, Sun. **Map** *p134 F7* ⑦ *Food*
Antoni Escribà, the 'Mozart of
Chocolate', died in 2004, but his
legacy lives on. His team produces
jaw-dropping creations for Easter,
from a chocolate Grand Canyon to
a life-size model of Michelangelo's
David, some of which are later
displayed in the Museu de la
Xocolata (*see p91*). The smaller
miracles include cherry liqueur
encased in red chocolate lips. The
Rambla branch is situated in a
pretty Modernista building.

Entertainment

Bacon Bear Bar

C/Casanova 64 (no phone). Metro Universitat. **Open** *6pm-2.30am Mon-Thur, Sun; 6pm-3am Fri, Sat.* **Admission** *free.* **Map** *p134 F7* ❹ *Gay bar*

It's hard to maintain an attitude in a gay bar that has teddies as a theme, and so it is with the Bacon Bear Bar, a down-to-earth bare-bricked place for bears and those who go down to the woods to find them.

❤ Cinemes Méliès

C/Villarroel 102 (93 451 00 51, www.meliescinemes.com). Metro Urgell. **Tickets** *€4 Mon; €6 Tue-Thur; €7 Fri-Sun.* **No cards.** **Map** *p134 F6* ❺ *Cinema*

This small, two-screen cinema is the nearest that Barcelona comes to an arthouse theatre, with an idiosyncratic roster of accessible classics alongside more recent films that aren't quite commercial enough for general release. This is the place to bone up on your Wilder, Antonioni, Hitchcock and others.

Luz de Gas

C/Muntaner 246 (93 209 77 11, www.luzdegas.com). FGC Muntaner. **Club** *midnight-6am Wed-Sat. Gigs daily, times vary.* **Admission** *Club (incl 1 drink) €20. Gigs varies.* **Map** *p134 F4* ❼ *Live music*

This lovingly renovated old music hall, garnished with chandeliers and classical friezes, is a mainstay on the live music scene. In between visits from international artists, you will find nightly residencies: blues on Mondays, Dixieland jazz on Tuesdays, disco on Wednesdays, pop-rock on Thursdays, soul on Fridays and vintage and Spanish rock on weekends.

Metro

C/Sepúlveda 185 (93 323 52 27, www.metrodiscobcn.com). Metro Universitat. **Open** *12.30-5am Mon-Thur, Sun; 12.30-6am Fri, Sat.* **Admission** *(incl 1 drink) €20.* **Map** *p134 G7* ❽ *Gay club*

Metro's popularity seldom wanes, whatever the time of year. This gay club is particularly packed at the weekends, which makes the smaller of the two dancefloors, specialising in Latin beats, something of a challenge for more flamboyant dancers to navigate. The larger one is a space to dance to more traditional house music. The corridor-like darkroom is where the real action takes place, though. Among other nocturnal delights there are strippers, drag queen acts and, yes, bingo.

People Lounge

C/Villarroel 71 (93 532 77 43, www. peoplebcn.com). Metro Universitat or Urgell. **Open** *8pm-3am Mon-Thur; 8pm-3.30am Fri, Sat; 7pm-3am Sun.* **Admission** *free.* **No cards.** **Map** *p134 F7* ❾ *Gay bar*

People Lounge offers a good alternative if you're tired of trekking around from gay bar to gay bar listening to non-stop Europop. Decked out as a facsimile of a posh English pub, with plush sofas and chandeliers, it attracts a mature, smartly dressed crowd.

Punto BCN

C/Muntaner 63-65 (no phone, www.grupoarena.com). Metro Universitat. **Open** *6pm-2.30am daily.* **Admission** *free.* **No cards.** **Map** *p134 F6* ❿ *Gay bar*

Punto BCN is a Gaixample staple. It's fiercely unstylish, but friendly and down to earth. It's also one of the few places where you'll find anybody early on. Tables on the mezzanine give a good view of the crowd, so you can take your pick before the object of your affections heads off into the night.

EIXAMPLE

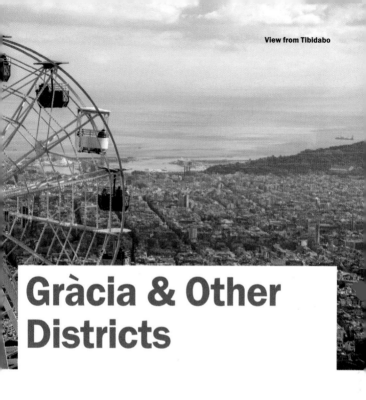

Gràcia & Other Districts

The inexorable expansion that began when Barcelona's walls were demolished in the 19th century ate away at the fields that once separated Gràcia from its neighbour. By 1897, the conurbation of Barcelona had all but swallowed up this fiercely independent town, and, amid howls of protest from its populace, Gràcia was annexed. Still, it retains its character and continues to draw visitors – as do neighbourhoods such as Les Corts (where football pilgrims head to the Camp Nou); Tibidabo, with its funfair and fantastic views; the upmarket Zona Alta, home of monster science museum CosmoCaixa; and Poblenou, scene of the most energetic attempts at urban regeneration.

Best newcomer
Museu del Disseny (*p166*) for
fashion through the ages.

Best bars
Balius (*p166*) for a sundowner
cocktail. Bodega Quimet (*p156*) for
local wines and vermut.

Hallowed turf
Camp Nou Experience (*p159*) to
walk in the footsteps of Maradona
and Messi.

Best restaurants
Bangkok Café (*p159*) for top-flight
Thai. La Panxa del Bisbe (*p156*) for
a slap-up lunch.

Best sweet treat
Gelateria Caffetteria Italiana
(*p156*) for lip-smacking dark
chocolate ice-cream.

Best retreat
Monestir de Pedralbes (*p162*) for
Gothic peace and quiet.

Best views
Park Güell (*p155*) to look out over
Barcelona from Gaudí's fairytale
garden city. Torre de Collserola
(*p160*) for vertigo-inducing views.

Best night out
Heliogàbal (*p158*) for uber-cool
arty sorts. Razzmatazz (*p166*) for
big-time bands and dancing the
night away.

Best for kids
CosmoCaixa (*p161*) to make
electricity and nearly touch a
tarantula. Tibidabo funfair (*p161*)
for a thrill a minute.

Gràcia & Park Güell

Gràcia is both alternative and
upmarket: it radiates a youthful
chic, with buzzy bars, yoga centres
and practitioners of every form
of holistic medicine, as well as
piercing and tattoo parlours,
dotted among the antique shops
and *jamonerías*. Gràcia really
comes into its own for a few days
in mid August, when its *festa
major* grips the entire city. To the
north sits Gaudí's fairytale garden
city, **Park Güell**. The climb up the

hill is worth the effort, not only
for the architecture but also for
the magnificent view of Barcelona
and the sea.

Sights & museums

Gaudí Experiència
*C/Larrard 41 (93 285 44 40, www.
gaudiexperiencia.com). Bus 24, 31,
32.* **Open** *Apr-Sept 10.30am-7pm
daily. Oct- Mar 10.30am-5pm daily.*
Admission *€9; €7.50 reductions.*
Map *p157 K1.*
The core attraction of the Gaudí
Experiència is a ten-minute film in
4D – a three-dimensional film with
a physical element. You might fly
through a rain cloud and feel damp,
for example, or zoom through a
flock of birds and feel their wings
against your legs. It's an intense
and thoroughly entertaining affair,
although best enjoyed as a fantasy
rather than something educational.

→ Getting around
Gràcia is just north of the Eixample,
accessed easily by metro, either
L3 to Fontana or L4 to Joanic. The
barrio is mostly pedestrianised,
and it's a ten-minute walk from
one side to the other.

❤ Park Güell

C/Olot (www.parkguell.cat).
Metro Lesseps or Vallcarca (for top
entrance) or bus 24, 32, 92. **Open**
10am-sunset daily. **Monumental**
zone *€8, €5.60 reduction, free*
under-7s. **Park** *free. No cards.* **Map**
p157 K1.

Gaudí's brief for the design of
what became Park Güell was to
emulate the English garden cities
so admired by his patron, Eusebi
Güell: to lay out a self-contained
suburb for the wealthy, but also
to design the public areas. (This
English influence explains the
anglicised spelling of 'Park'.) The
original plan called for the plots
to be sold and the properties
designed by other architects. But
the idea never took off – perhaps
because it was too far from the
city, or because it was too radical
– and the Güell family gave the
park to the city in 1922. It is now a
UNESCO World Heritage Site.

The fantastical exuberance
of Gaudí's imagination remains
breathtaking. Visitors were
once welcomed by two life-size
mechanical gazelles, a typically
bizarre religious reference by
Gaudí to medieval Hebrew love
poetry, although these were
unfortunately destroyed in the
Civil War. The two gatehouses
that remain were based on
designs the architect made for
the opera *Hänsel and Gretel*,
one of them featuring a red
and white mushroom for a
roof. From here you enter the
'monumental zone', and walk
up a splendid staircase flanked
by multicoloured battlements,
past the iconic mosaic lizard
sculpture, to what would have
been the main marketplace.
Here, 100 palm-shaped pillars
hold up a roof, reminiscent of
the hypostyle hall at Luxor.
On top of this structure is the
esplanade, a circular concourse
surrounded by benches in the
form of a sea-serpent decorated
with shattered tiles – a technique
called *trencadís*, perfected by
Gaudí's talented assistant Josep
Maria Jujol. Nearby, twisted
stone columns support curving
colonnades or merge with the
natural structure of the hillside.

The park surrounding the
fenced-off monumental zone
has at its peak a large cross, and
offers an amazing panorama
of Barcelona and the sea
stretching out beyond.

GRÀCIA & OTHER DISTRICTS

Check out the futuristic touchscreens in the entrance lobby. There are also screens specially designed for children, who can create their own 'Gaudí building' or simply colour in a mosaic.

Restaurants

Café Godot €€
C/Sant Domènec 19 (93 368 20 36, www.cafegodot.com). Metro Fontana. Open 10am-1am Mon-Fri; 11am-2am Sat, Sun. Map p157 J4 ❶ *Global*
Café Godot is an easygoing bistro, with a little terrace at the back and a play area for kids (along with plenty on the menu that will appeal to them, too) – the perfect spot for a lazy Sunday brunch (featuring eggs Benedict, banana pancakes, french toast and so on). The sandwich menu is particularly inspired, with roast beef, club sandwiches and Vietnamese *banh mi*, among others, while more substantial dishes include duck magret and steak frites.

♥ La Panxa del Bisbe €€
C/Torrent de les Flors 158 (93 213 70 49). Metro Joanic. Open 1.30-3.30pm, 8.30-midnight Tue-Sat. Map p157 K2 ❷ *Mediterranean*
Not long after opening, the 'Bishop's Belly' had to move to bigger premises thanks to the popularity of its exquisitely presented cooking. It's not all about looks, however, and there is real soul to beef cheeks with beetroot gnocchi, courgette flowers in tempura with sea anemones and langoustines, or a wonderful take on the Catalan favourite of bread with olive oil, salt and chocolate.

Les Tres a la Cuina €
C/Sant Lluís 35 (93 105 49 47, www.lestresalacuina.com). Metro Joanic. Open 1.30-3.30pm Mon-
Fri; 12.30-4pm Sat. Closed Aug. Map p157 K3 ❸ *Mediterranean*
If there's a better lunch deal in town (€10 Monday to Friday, €11.50 Saturday), we've yet to find it. Baffling licensing laws mean you'll be eating off a plastic plate, but who cares when it holds chicken baked with Pernod, fennel and clementine; a delicious baked garlic tart with goat's cheese; or the much-requested pork and beef lasagne? Outside lunch hours Les Tres offers coffee and home-made cakes and, on Saturday, a scrumptious brunch.

Cafés, tapas & bars

♥ Bodega Quimet
C/Vic 23 (93 218 41 89). FGC Gràcia or Metro Fontana. Open 2-11.30pm Mon-Fri; 1-11.30pm Sat, Sun. Map p157 H4 ❶
A classic of the *barrio*, Bodega Quimet has been around since 1954 and has hardly changed since, either in decor or in what's on offer. A handful of local wines are still available from the barrels (which adorn the walls), as is dirt-cheap *vermut*, and there is a list of simple but good tapas.

♥ Gelateria Caffetteria Italiana
Plaça de la Revolució 2 (93 210 23 39). Metro Fontana or Joanic. Open Apr-Oct noon-1am Mon-Thur, Sun; noon-2am Fri, Sat. Nov-Mar 9am-9pm Mon-Thur, Sun; 9am-11pm Fri, Sat. No cards. Map p157 J4 ❷
Barcelona's favourite ice-cream parlour is run by an Italian mother and daughter, and famous for its own-recipe dark chocolate ice-cream – which invariably sells out every night. Other freshly made, additive-free flavours include fig, strawberry and peach: basically, whatever fruit happens to be in season. There are tables outside

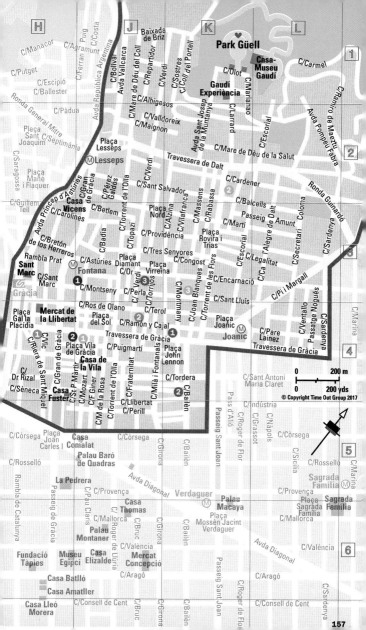

on the square, if you're lucky enough to get one – be prepared to queue, especially on balmy summer evenings.

Shops & services

Hibernian Books
C/Montseny 17 (93 217 47 96, www. hibernian-books.com). Metro Fontana. **Open** *4-8.30pm Mon; 11am-8.30pm Tue-Sat.* **No cards.** **Map** *p157 J3* ❶ *Books*

With its air of pleasantly dusty intellectualism, Hibernian feels like a proper British second-hand bookshop. There are books for all tastes, from beautifully bound early editions to classic Penguin paperbacks, biographies, cookbooks and so on, more than 30,000 titles in all. Part-exchange is possible.

Ladyloquita
C/Travessera de Gràcia 126 (93 217 82 92, www.ladyloquita.com). Metro Fontana. **Open** *5-8.30pm Mon; 11am-2pm, 5-8.30pm Tue-Sat.* **Map** *p157 H4* ❷ *Fashion*

Meeta and Laura's charming, quirky Gràcia boutique stocks a host of labels such as Pepa Loves, YUMI and Meeta's own label, Tiralahilacha, along with accessories galore, from earrings to bags. Cool interior design, a chill-out area and reasonable price tags complete the pretty picture.

Entertainment

♥ Heliogàbal
C/Ramón y Cajal 80 (www. facebook.com/heliogabal). Metro Joanic. **Open** *10pm-2am Wed-Sun.* **Admission** *free-€10.* **No cards.** **Map** *p157 K4* ❶ *Bar & arts venue*

Loved by habitués of the Gràcia arts scene, this low-key bar and performance venue is filled to bursting with neighbourhood cutie pies in cool T-shirts who just really adore live poetry. Events change nightly, running from live music to film screenings, art openings and readings, and programming focuses mostly on local talents. On concert nights arrive early for an 'at-least-I'm-not-standing' folding chair.

Texas
C/Bailén 205 (93 348 77 48, www.cinemestexas.cat). Metro Verdaguer. **Tickets** *€3.* **No cards.** **Map** *p157 K4* ❷ *Cinema*

Locals love this four-screen cinema, which shows all the biggest films from around the world in their original language with Catalan subtitles. Most films are screened some months after their main release date, which means the tickets are a bargain.

Verdi
C/Verdi 32 (93 238 79 90, www. cines-verdi.com). Metro Fontana. **Tickets** *€6 Mon; €8 Tue-Fri; €9 Sat, Sun (1st screening €6).* **Map** *p157 J3* ❸ *Cinema*

The five-screen Verdi and Verdi Park, a four-screen annexe on the next street, have transformed this corner of Gràcia with a programme of independent, mainly European and Asian cinema. At peak times, chaos reigns; arrive early and make sure you don't confuse the queue to enter for the queue to buy tickets. Non-Spanish cards are not accepted.

Sants & Les Corts

Sants, or at least the immediate environs of transport hub Estació de Sants, which is all that most visitors see of the area, stands as a monument to the worst of 1970s urban design. Another village engulfed by the expanding city in the 19th century, Les Corts ('cowsheds' or 'pigsties'), remains one of the most Catalan

💙 Camp Nou Experience

Camp Nou, Avda Arístides Maillol, access 14, Les Corts (902 189 900, www.fcbarcelona.cat). Metro Collblanc, Les Corts or Maria Cristina. **Open** *Apr-mid Oct 9.30am-7pm daily. Mid Oct-Mar 10am-6.30pm Mon-Sat; 10am-2.30pm Sun.* **Admission** *€25; €20 reductions; free under-6s.*

Camp Nou, where FC Barcelona has played since 1957, is one of football's great stadiums – a vast cauldron of a ground that holds 99,000 spectators. That's a lot of noise when the team is doing well, and an awful lot of silence when it isn't. For football fanatics, a trip to Barcelona would not be complete without visiting the hallowed turf.

Even if you can't get there on match day, it's worth visiting the club museum. The excellent audio-guided tour of the stadium takes you through the players' tunnel to the dugouts and then, on to the President's box, where there is a replica of the UEFA Champions League Cup, which the team has won five times.

The club museum makes much of the 'Dream Team' days when the likes of Kubala, Cruyff, Maradona, Koeman and Lineker trod the hallowed turf, with pictures, video clips and souvenirs spanning the century since the Swiss businessman Johan Gamper and the Englishman Arthur Witty founded the club in 1899.

of the city's *barris*, but the rows of unlovely apartment blocks have stamped out any trace of its bucolic past. The area is best known for what happens every other weekend, when tens of thousands pour in to watch FC Barcelona, whose **Camp Nou** stadium takes up much of the west of the *barri*.

Restaurants

💙 Bangkok Café €€

C/Evarist Arnús 65, Les Corts (93 339 32 69). Metro Plaça del Centre. **Open** *8-11.30pm Mon-Thur; 1-4pm, 8-11.30pm Fri-Sun.* Thai

Without a doubt, the best Thai restaurant in Barcelona, and not ridiculously expensive either. Entered via a pretty little mews street, it's a squeezed and fairly noisy little place, with an open

kitchen and a handful of tables (reserve if you can). All the Thai standards are present and beautifully executed with a good amount of heat. Leave room for mango and rice pudding.

La Parra €€

C/Joanot Martorell 3, Sants (93 332 51 34). Metro Hostafrancs. **Open** *8pm-midnight Tue-Fri; 1.30-4.30pm, 8.30pm-12.30am Sat; 1.30-4.30pm Sun. Closed Aug.* Catalan

A charming converted 19th-century coaching inn with a shady, vine-covered terrace. The open wood grill sizzles with various parts of goat, pig, rabbit and cow, as well as deer and even foal. Huge, oozing steaks are slapped on to wooden boards and accompanied by baked potatoes, *calçots* (large spring onions), grilled vegetables and *allioli*, with jugs of local wine from the giant barrels.

Entertainment

Sala BeCool
Plaça Joan Llongueras 5, Les Corts (93 362 04 13, www.salabecool. com). Metro Hospital Clínic. **Club** *midnight-6am Thur-Sat.* **Gigs** *varies.* **Admission** *Gigs varies. Club (incl 1 drink) €10-€15. Live music*

The latest from Berlin's minimal electro scene reaches Barcelona via this uptown concert hall. After the live shows by local rock stars or international indie success stories, a packed and music-loving crowd throbs to sophisticated electronica and its bizarre attendant visuals. Upstairs, in the Red Room, DJs playing indie pop rock provide an alternative to the pounding beats of the main room.

Universal
C/Marià Cubí 182 bis, Les Corts (93 201 35 96, www.grupocostaeste. com). FGC Muntaner. **Open** *11pm-5.30am Mon-Sat.* **Admission** *free Mon-Thur; free before 1am, (incl 1 drink) €12 after 1am Fri, Sat. Club*

One of the few clubs in Barcelona that caters to an older, well-dressed crowd, Universal doesn't charge admission until 1am, but the drink prices are pretty steep. Upstairs is a chill-out area, complete with aquatic slide projections, while downstairs sports a sharper look.

In the know
The view from the top

For the best view of the city from the top of Tibidabo, either take a lift up Norman Foster's tower, the **Torre de Collserola**, or walk up to the *mirador* (viewpoint) at the feet of Christ atop the Sagrat Cor.

Tibidabo & Collserola

Tibidabo is the dominant peak of the Collserola massif, with sweeping views of the whole of Barcelona. The neo-Gothic Sagrat Cor church crowning the peak has become one of the city's most recognisable landmarks. At weekends, thousands of people head to the top of the hill in order to whoop and scream at the **funfair**. Getting there on the **Tramvia Blau** (Blue Tram, *see p163*) and then the **funicular railway** is part of the fun.

The vast Parc de Collserola is more a series of forested hills than a park, its shady paths through holm oak and pine opening out to spectacular views. It's most easily reached by FGC train on the Terrassa-Sabadell line from Plaça Catalunya or Passeig de Gràcia, getting off at Baixador de Vallvidrera station.

Sights & museums

Funicular de Tibidabo
Plaça Doctor Andreu to Plaça Tibidabo (93 211 79 42). FGC Avda Tibidabo then Tramvia Blau. **Open** *as funfair, but from 15mins earlier, until 15mins later.* **Tickets** *€7.70; €2-€4.10 reductions; free under-3s.*

This art deco vehicle offers occasional glimpses of the city below as it winds through the pine forests up to the summit. The service has been operating since 1901, but only according to a complicated timetable. Holders of tickets for the funfair are entitled to a discount.

❤ Torre de Collserola
Ctra de Vallvidrera al Tibidabo (93 211 79 42, www.torredecollserola. com). FGC Peu del Funicular then funicular. **Open** *as funfair.* **Admission** *€5.60; €3.30 reductions; free under-4s.*

Just five minutes' walk from the Sagrat Cor is its main rival, and Barcelona's most visible landmark. Norman Foster's communications tower was built in 1992 to transmit images of the Olympics around the world. Those who don't suffer from vertigo attest to the wonderful views of Barcelona and the Mediterranean from the top.

❤ Tibidabo Funfair

Plaça del Tibidabo 3-4 (93 211 79 42, www.tibidabo.cat). FGC Avda Tibidabo & funicular. Open check website. Closed Jan, Feb. **Tickets** *Camí del Cel Mar-Dec €12.70; €7.80 under 120cm; free under 90cm. Parc d'Atraccions (unlimited rides) €28.50; €10.30 under 120cm; free under 90cm.*

This hilltop fairground, dating from 1889, is investing millions in getting itself bang up to date, with the freefall Pendulum and a hot-air balloon-style ride for smaller children. Adrenalin freaks are delighted with the new 80km/h rollercoaster, and the many other attractions include a house of horrors, bumper cars and the emblematic Avió, the world's first popular flight simulator when it was built in 1928.

Entertainment

Mirablau

Plaça Doctor Andreu, Tibidabo (93 418 58 79). FGC Avda Tibidabo then Tramvia Blau. Open 11am-4.30am Mon-Wed, Sun; 11am-6am Thur-Sat. **Admission** *free. Bar*

It doesn't get any more uptown than this, geographically and socially. Located at the top of Tibidabo, this small bar is packed with the high rollers of Barcelona, from local footballers living on the hill to international businessmen on the company card. They're drawn here for the view and the artificial wind that sweeps through

the tropical shrubbery outside on hot summer nights.

Zona Alta

Zona Alta (the 'upper zone', or 'uptown') is the name given collectively to a series of smart neighbourhoods – including Sant Gervasi, Sarrià and Pedralbes – that stretch out across the lower reaches of the Collserola hills. Attractions up here include the **CosmoCaixa** science museum and the **Monestir de Pedralbes** convent. The centre of Sarrià and the streets of old Pedralbes around the monastery retain a flavour of the sleepy country towns these once were.

Gaudí fans are rewarded by a trip up to the **Pavellons de la Finca Güell**; its extraordinary and rather frightening wrought-iron gate features a dragon into whose gaping mouth the foolhardy can fit their heads.

Sights & museums

❤ CosmoCaixa

C/Isaac Newton 26, Sant Gervasi (93 212 60 50, www.cosmocaixa. com). FGC Avda Tibidabo. Open 10am-8pm Tue-Sun. **Admission** *€3; €2 reductions; free under-6s & over-65s. Free to all 1st Sun of mth. Planetarium €4; €3 reductions. Toca Toca! €2; €1.50 reductions; free under-3s.*

Said to be the biggest science museum in Europe, CosmoCaixa doesn't, perhaps, make the best use of its space. A glass-enclosed spiral ramp runs down an impressive six floors, but represents a long walk to reach the main collection five floors down. Here you'll find the Flooded Forest, a reproduction of a flora- and fauna-filled corner of Amazonia, and the Geological Wall, along with temporary exhibitions.

CosmoCaixa p161

From here, it's on to the Matter Room, which covers 'inert', 'living', 'intelligent' and then 'civilised' matter: in other words, natural history.

The installations for children are excellent: the Bubble Planetarium (a digital 3D simulation of the universe); the Toca Toca! space, where mini explorers can get up close and personal with tarantulas and snakes; and the candy-bright Javier Mariscal-designed spaces of Clik (for three- to six-year-olds) and Flash (for seven- to nine-year-olds), where children learn how to generate electricity and how a kaleidoscope works.

One of the real highlights, for both young and old, is the hugely entertaining sound telescope outside on the Plaça de la Ciència.

❤ Monestir de Pedralbes

Baixada del Monestir 9, Pedralbes (93 256 3434). FGC Reina Elisenda. **Open** *Apr-Sept 10am-5pm Tue-Fri; 10am-7pm Sat; 10am-8pm Sun. Oct-Mar 10am-2pm Mon-Fri; 10am-5pm Sat, Sun.* **Admission** *€5; €3.50 reductions; free under-16s. Free 1st Sun of mth and Sun 3-8pm. No cards.*

In 1326, the widowed Queen Elisenda of Montcada used her inheritance to buy this land and construct a convent for the Poor Clare order of nuns, which she soon joined. The result is a jewel of Gothic architecture; an understated single-nave church with fine stained-glass windows and a beautiful three-storey 14th-century cloister. The place remained out of bounds to the general public until 1983, when the nuns, a closed order, opened it up as a museum (they moved to a nearby annexe). The site offers a fascinating insight into life in a medieval convent, taking you through the kitchens, pharmacy and refectory, with its huge vaulted ceiling.

Pavellons de la Finca Güell

Avda Pedralbes 7, Pedralbes (93 317 76 52, www.rutadelmodernisme. com). Metro Palau Reial. **Open** *10am-4pm daily. Tours in English 10.15am, 11.15am, 3pm.* **Admission** *€5; €2.50 reductions; free under-11s. No cards.*

Industrial textile businessman Eusebi Güell bought what is now Palau Reial in 1882 as a summer home, contracting Gaudí to remodel the entrance lodges and gardens for the estate. In 1883, they began to build what would be one of Gaudí's first projects in

Barcelona for the Güell family. This was also the first project on which Gaudí used his signature *trencadís* (mosaic motif).

The huge gardens were accessed by three entrances, of which only two remain. The Porta del Drac (Dragon's Gate), the most impressive, used to be the private entrance for the Güell family. Nowadays, the gatehouses belong to the University of Barcelona. same small house on the site. The Pavellons must be visited with a guide, and tours are offered in Spanish and English.

Torre Bellesguard

C/Bellesguard 16 (93 250 4093, www.bellesguardgaudi.com) FGC Avda Tibidabo. **Open** *10am-3pm daily.* **Admission** *€9, €7.20 reduction, free under-8s.*
The medievalist lines of this privately owned house are Gaudí's reference to the castle that stood here in the Middle Ages, and acted as country home for King Martí 'the Humane'. It is unmistakeably the work of the master, however, with his trademark sinuous forms, four-sided cross, colourful stained glass and *trencadís* (smashed-tile) benches.

Owned since the 1940s by the Guilera family, members of whom still live here, it has recently been opened to the public. Guided tours (€16) are given in English on Saturdays and Sundays at 11am.

Tramvia Blau

Avda Tibidabo (Plaça Kennedy) to Plaça del Funicular (902 075 027, www.tmb.cat). FGC Avda Tibidabo. **Open** *Nov-Mar 10am-6.15pm Sat, Sun. Apr, Aug, Sept 10am-7.30pm daily. May, June, Oct 10am-7.30pm Sat, Sun. Every 20mins.* **Tickets** *€5.50 single. No cards.*
Barcelonins and tourists have been clanking 1,225m (4,000ft) up Avda Tibidabo in the 'blue trams' since 1902. When the tram isn't running,

a rather more prosaic bus (no.195) takes you up – or you can walk it in 15 minutes.

Restaurants

18 Octubre €€

C/Julián Romea 18, Sant Gervasi (93 218 25 18). Metro Diagonal/FGC Gràcia. **Open** *1.30-4pm, 8.30-11.30pm Mon-Thur; 9pm-midnight Sat. Catalan*
Time stands still in this quiet little spot, with its quaint old-fashioned decor, swathes of lace and brown table linen. Time often stands still, in fact, between placing an order and receiving any food, but this is all part of 18 Octubre's sleepy charm. Also contributing to its appeal is a roll-call of reasonably priced, mainly Catalan dishes: squid stuffed with meatballs on a bed of *samfaina*; pig's trotter with fried cabbage and potato; and cod with a nut crust and pumpkin purée.

Hisop €€€€

Passatge Marimon 9, Sant Gervasi (93 241 32 33, www.hisop.com). Metro Diagonal or Hospital Clínic. **Open** *1.30-3.30pm, 8.30-11pm Mon-Fri; 8.30-11pm Sat. Mediterranean*
Run by two young, enthusiastic and talented chefs, Hisop aims to bring serious dining to the non-expense-account masses by keeping its prices low and its service approachable – here's hoping its shiny new Michelin star doesn't change all that. The €63 tasting menu (€92 with wine pairing) is a popular choice; dishes vary according to the season, but often include rich 'monkfish royale' (which is served with its liver, a cocoa-based sauce and tiny pearls of saffron) and a pistachio soufflé with kaffir lime ice-cream and rocket 'soup'.

Horta & around

Horta was once a picturesque little village and still remains aloof from the city that swallowed it in 1904. Originally a collection of farms (its name means 'market garden'), the barri is still peppered with old farmhouses, such as Can Mariner on C/Horta, dating back to 1050, and the medieval Can Cortada at the end of C/Campoamor.

Bagutti to design scenic gardens set around a cypress maze, with a romantic stream and a waterfall. The mansion may be gone (replaced with a 19th-century Arabic-influenced building), but the gardens are remarkably intact, shaded in the summer by oaks, laurels and an ancient sequoia. Best of all, the maze, an ingenious puzzle that intrigues those brave enough to try it, is also still in use.

Sights & museums

❤ Parc del Laberint

Passeig dels Castanyers 1, Horta (010, ajuntament.barcelona. cat/ecologiaurbana). Metro Mundet. Open 10am-sunset daily. Admission €2.23; €1.42 reductions; free under-5s, over-65s; free Wed, Sun. No cards.

In 1791, the Desvalls family, owners of this marvellously leafy estate, hired Italian architect Domenico

Restaurants

Can Travi Nou €€€

C/Jorge Manrique s/n, Parc de la Vall de Hebron, Horta (93 428 03 01, www.gruptravi.com). Metro Horta or Montbau. Open 1-4pm, 8-11pm daily. Catalan

An ancient rambling farmhouse clad in bougainvillea, perched high above the city, Can Travi Nou offers wonderfully rustic dining rooms with roaring log fires in the winter,

Museu del Disseny *p166*

whereas in the summer the action moves out to a covered terrace in a candlelit garden.

Cafés, tapas & bars
L'Esquinica
Passeig Fabra i Puig 296, Horta (93 358 25 19). Metro Virrei Amat or Vilapicina. **Open** *8am-midnight Tue-Fri; 8am-4pm, 6.30pm-midnight Sat; 8am-5pm Sun.*
Think of it not as a trek, but as a quest; queues outside are testament to the great value of the tapas. On especially busy nights you'll be asked to take a number, supermarket-style. Waiters will advise first-timers to start with *chocos* (creamy squid rings), *patatas bravas* with allioli, *llonganissa* sausage and *tigres* (stuffed mussels). After which the world is your oyster, cockle or clam.

Poblenou, Diagonal Mar & the Fòrum

In its industrial heyday, Poblenou was known as 'little Manchester' due to its concentration of cotton mills. Now, the old mills and other factories are being bulldozed or remodelled as the district is rebranded as a technology and business hub.

At the edge of the Eixample, Plaça de les Glòries finally seems ready to fulfil its destiny. After years of being little more than a glorified roundabout on the way out of town, the plaça is now home to the long-awaited design museum, the **Museu del Disseny**.

The catalyst for the development of the Diagonal Mar was the Fòrum, a six-month cultural symposium held in 2004. Its tangible legacy is the enormous conference halls and hotels that draw many wealthy business clients into the city. The Edifici Fòrum, a striking blue triangular construction, now houses the **Museu Blau** (Blue Museum), which comprises the main collections of the Natural History Museum, transplanted here from the Born. More recently, the **Parc del Fòrum** has benefited the city's youth, providing an excellent venue for one of Barcelona's biggest music festivals, **Primavera Sound** (*see p55*).

Sights & museums
Museu Blau
Plaça Leonardo da Vinci 4-5, Parc del Fòrum (93 256 60 02, www.museuciencies.cat). Metro El Maresme-Forum. **Open** *Oct-Feb 10am-6pm Tue-Fri; 10am-7pm Sat; 10am-8pm Sun. Mar-Sept 10am-7pm Tue-Sat; 10am-8pm Sun.* **Admission** *€6; €2.70 reductions; free under-16s. Free to all 1st Sun of mth.*
The Universal Forum of Cultures in 2004 was a vastly ambitious, wildly expensive attempt to put Barcelona back on the world map after years basking in the afterglow of the 1992 Olympic Games. It was pretty much an unmitigated flop, but it did leave one positive legacy in the form of some architecturally striking buildings.One such building was Herzog and de Meuron's Edifici Fòrum, a glittering creation, painted deep blue and crisscrossed with mirrored strips that give it a marine effect. Since 2011 it has been the new home of the Museum of Natural History, now also known as the Museu Blau (Blue Museum), after the building that houses it.

The museum combines the two collections of the former zoology and geology museums in Parc de la Ciutadella, whose buildings will now be given over to archiving and studying the materials.

It begins with the geology section, which includes meteorites, gems, crystals, radioactive minerals and rocks from the earth's lithosphere. There's an extensive collection of fossils and funghi, and the zoology section features dozens of stuffed animals, preserved insects and molluscs, though not much attempt is made to contextualise them.

💜 Museu del Disseny
Plaça de les Glòries 37 (93 256 68 00, www.ajuntament.barcelona. cat/museudeldisseny) Metro Glòries. Open 10am-8pm Tue-Sun. Admission Permanent exhibition €6, €4 reduction. Temporary exhibition €4.40, €3 reduction. Combined ticket €8, €5.50 reduction.

This huge monolith, squatting at the side of Plaça de les Glòries, houses the collections from the former museums of clothing, decorative arts and ceramics. The collection from the old Textile and Clothing Museum provides a chronological tour of fashion, from a man's Coptic tunic from a seventh-century tomb through to Karl Lagerfeld's creations. There are many curiosities, such as an 18th-century bridal gown in black figured silk and the world's largest collection of kidskin gloves, but the real highlight is the haute couture collection.

Cafés, tapas & bars
💜 Balius
C/Pujades 196 (93 315 86 50, www. baliusbar.com). Metro Poblenou. Open 5pm-1am Tue-Thur; 4pm-3am Fri, Sat; 4pm-1am Sun.
Until a couple of years ago, Balius was an old-time drugstore, its windows stacked high with shampoo and bleach. The name and fabulously retro façade have stayed intact, but its interior has been transformed into a glamorous cocktail bar, filled with sunlight by day and romantically lit by night.

Entertainment
💜 Razzmatazz
C/Almogàvers 122 (93 320 82 00, www.salarazzmatazz.com). Metro Bogatell or Marina. Club midnight-5am Wed, Thur; 1-6am Fri, Sat. Concerts varies. Admission Concerts varies. Club (incl 1 drink) €15-€17. Club & live music venue
This monstrous club's five distinct spaces form the night-time playground of seemingly all young Barcelona. There's indie rock in Razz Club, tech-house in the Loft, techno pop in Lolita, electro pop in the Pop Bar and electro rock in the Rex Room. Live acts run from Arctic Monkeys to Bananarama, and concerts can get rammed, with queues so long that it's worth arriving early so that you don't miss the beginning of the show. The price of admission will get you into all five rooms, though the gigs are normally ticketed separately.

Sala Beckett
C/Pere IV 228-232 (93 284 53 12, www.salabeckett.cat). Metro Poblenou. Box office 2 hrs before start of show. Theatre
This small but important theatre was founded by the Samuel Beckett-inspired Teatro Fronterizo group, which is run by playwright José Sanchís Sinisterra. Although he is no longer based at the theatre, his influence continues to prevail. Check the website for updates.

Barcelona Essentials

168   **Accommodation**

174   **Getting Around**

178   **Resources A-Z**

186   **Spanish Vocabulary**

187   **Catalan Vocabulary**

188   **Index**

Accommodation

The accommodation scene has come on in leaps and bounds over the last few years, with style and innovation appearing at every level. The glut of top-end accommodation in Barcelona means that hotels are continually revising their rates, and bargains are there for the taking. At the budget end of the market, many *hostales* are situated in fabulous old buildings with elaborate doorways and grand staircases. There's also been a rise in boutique B&Bs – bright places with en-suite bathrooms, internet access and other modern essentials.

Booking a room

High season runs year round and finding somewhere to lay your head at short notice can be tough. Hotels generally require you to guarantee your booking with card details or a deposit; it's always worth calling a few days before arrival to reconfirm the booking (get it in writing if you can; many readers have reported problems) and check the cancellation policy. Often you will lose at least the first night. *Hostales* are more laid-back and don't always ask for a deposit.

To be sure of a room with natural light or a view, ask for an outside room (*habitació/ habitación exterior*), which will usually face the street. Many of Barcelona's buildings are built around a central patio or airshaft, and the inside rooms (*habitació/habitación*

> **In the know**
> **Price categories**
>
> We have included a selection of the best hotels in the city in each pricing category. Categories are based on the cost for a double room in spring:
>
> **Luxury** over €300
>
> **Expensive** €200-€300
>
> **Moderate** €100-€200
>
> **Budget** up to €100

interior) around them can be quite gloomy, albeit quieter. However, in some cases (especially in the Eixample), these inward-facing rooms look on to large, open-air patios or gardens, which benefit from being quiet and having a view.

Hotels listed under the expensive and moderate brackets all have air-conditioning as standard and around half the *hostales* in the budget listings are equipped with it. Most hotels have banned smoking altogether, and the others will have the majority of floors/rooms as non-smoking.

Theft can be a problem, especially in lower-end establishments. Check to see if youth hostel rooms have lockers if you're sharing.

Star ratings and prices

Accommodation in Catalonia is divided into two official categories: hotels (H) and *pensiones* (P). To be a hotel (star-rated one to five), a place must feature en-suite bathrooms in every room. Ratings are based on physical attributes rather than levels of service; often the only difference between a three- and a four-star hotel is the presence of a meeting room. *Pensiones*, usually cheaper and often family-run, are star-rated one or two, and are not required to have en-suite bathrooms (though many do). *Pensiones* are also known as *hostales*, but, confusingly, are not youth hostels; those are known as *albergues*.

For a double room, expect to pay €50-€75 for a budget *pensión*, €80-€180 for a mid-range spot and €200 upwards for a top-of-the-range hotel. However, prices vary depending on the time of year; always check for special deals. All bills are subject to seven per cent IVA (value added tax) on top of the basic price; this is not normally included in the advertised rate, but we've factored it into the price categories here. Breakfast is not included as standard, but Wi-Fi is almost always free.

Where to stay

La Rambla is flanked by hotels ranging from no-frills to luxury, but the overwhelmingly touristy environment – not to mention the noise – may prove a bit too much for some people. The medieval labyrinth of the Barri Gòtic conceals some cheaper alternatives, but bear in mind that old buildings can often be grotty rather than charming. The well-to-do Born is home to plenty of restaurants, bars and boutiques and has an increasing number of hotels, while the Raval is usefully central and well served for bars and restaurants.

The broad avenues forming the vast grid of streets of the Eixample district contain some of Barcelona's most expensive and fashionable hotels, along with some great budget options hidden away in Modernista buildings.

Hotels are springing up along the waterfront, particularly in the stretch between the Hotel Arts and the Fòrum that lies north of the city centre, and slightly inland in Poblenou. These are mostly aimed at business travellers, so rates tend to fall at weekends and during holiday periods.

Poble Sec is a fast-changing neighbourhood between Montjuïc hill and the Avda Paral·lel, close to the hipster enclave of Sant Antoni, while Gràcia is off the beaten tourist track, which only adds to its allure.

Luxury
Casa Fuster

Passeig de Gràcia 132, Gràcia (93 255 30 00, www.hotelcasafuster.com). Metro Diagonal. **Map** *p157 H4.*

There was a great deal of talk about the Fuster when it first opened. Many complained that this historic Modernista building should have been preserved as a public space. What is so appealing for the luxury end of the market, however, is the air of exclusivity that envelops you on arrival. Service is spot on; rooms – while rather small – feel regal in their dove greys and purples.

Cotton House Hotel

Gran Via de les Corts Catalanes 670, Eixample (93 450 50 45, www. hotelcottonhouse.com), Metro Girona. **Map** *p134 J7.*

After a stunning renovation, the former headquarters of the cotton guild is now a plush five-star, with snowy-white rooms that contrast with the deco splendour of the common areas. There is a plunge pool lined with day beds on the roof, but in winter the library bar is the place to be.

Hotel Claris

*C/Pau Claris 150, Eixample (93 487
62 62, www.derbyhotels.com). Metro
Passeig de Gràcia. Map p134 J6.*
Antiques and contemporary design
merge behind the neoclassical exterior
of the Claris, which contains the largest
private collection of Ancient Egyptian
art in Spain. Some bedrooms are on the
small side, while others are duplex, but
all have Chesterfield sofas and plenty
of art.

Hotel Neri

*C/Sant Sever 5, Barri Gòtic (93 304 06
55, www.hotelneri.com). Metro Jaume I.
Map p70 H9.*
One of the sexiest boutiques in
town, this is the perfect treat for a
naughty weekend, located in a former
18th-century palace. Neutral tones,
natural materials and rustic finishes
stand in stylish contrast to lavish satins,
sharp-edged design and high-tech
perks. The lush rooftop garden features
plenty of private nooks for dangerous
liaisons.

Mandarin Oriental Barcelona

*Passeig de Gràcia 38-40, Eixample (93
151 88 88, www.mandarinoriental.com/
barcelona). Metro Passeig de Gràcia.
Map p134 H7.*
Top Spanish designer Patricia Urquiola's
high-design Mandarin Oriental oozes
old-style glamour with a contemporary
twist. It was originally a bank, and life
in the hotel centres on the old trading
floor – now a seafood bistro – and the
slick Bankers Bar, peopled by Catalan
TV celebs downing designer cocktails.
Rooms are as plush as you could hope
for, big on bespoke Urquiola pieces like
'Fat' sofas, cylindrical bathtubs and
'Caboche' chandeliers.

Soho House Barcelona

*Plaça del Duc de Medinaceli 4,
Barri Gòtic (93 220 46 00, www.
sohousebarcelona.com) Metro
Drassanes. Map p70 H10.*
The latest outpost of the London
members' club for creative types, this is
a blissfully comfortable place that feels
fun and unpretentious for all its cool
credentials. The style is 'English country
house', and facilities include a rooftop
pool and terrace with views second to
none, a plush Italian restaurant, the
Cowshed spa, a small cinema, sunny
gym and, of course, the relaxed but
elegant members' bar (also open to
guests).

Expensive

Casa Camper

*C/Elisabets 11, Raval (93 342 62
80, www.casacamper.com). Metro
Catalunya. Map p101 G8.*
Devised by the Mallorcan footwear
giant, this is a wonderfully quirky
concept-fest of a hotel. One of its unique
selling points is a bedroom-living room
arrangement, giving two spaces for the
price of one. Less cleverly, the living
rooms are across the corridor from
the bedrooms, so in order to enjoy the
cinema-sized TV screen, hammock and
balcony you'll need to pack respectable
pyjamas or risk the dash of shame.

Grand Hotel Central

*Via Laietana 30, Born (93 295 79 00,
www.grandhotelcentral.com). Metro
Jaume I. Map p87 J9.*
Another of the recent wave of Barcelona
hotels to adhere to the unwritten
design protocol that grey is the new
black. The Central's shadowy, almost
Hitchcockian corridors open up on to
sleekly appointed, understated rooms
with interiors that feature flat-screen
televisions, a media hub and Gilchrist &
Soames toiletries. But the real charm of
this establishment lies on the roof. Here
you can sip a cocktail and admire the
wonderful views while floating in the
vertiginous infinity pool.

Hotel Duquesa de Cardona

*Passeig Colom 12, Barri Gòtic (93 268
90 90, www.hduquesadecardona.
com). Metro Drassanes or Jaume I. Map
p70 H10.*
This elegantly restored 16th-century
palace retains many original features

and is furnished with natural materials – wood, leather, silk and stone – that are complemented by a soft colour scheme reflecting the paintwork. The cosy bedrooms make it ideal for a romantic stay, particularly the deluxe rooms and junior suites on the higher floors, with views out across the harbour.

Hotel Granados 83
*C/Enric Granados 83, Eixample (93 492 96 70, www.derbyhotels.com). Metro Diagonal. **Map** p134 G5.*
The original ironwork structure of this former hospital contrives to lend an unexpectedly industrial feel to the Granados 83. The hotel's variety of bare-bricked rooms includes details of African zebrawood and Italian leather sofas.

Hotel Petit Palace Boquería
*C/Boquería 10, Barri Gòtic (93 302 07 53, www.petitpalace.com). Metro Liceu. **Map** p70 H9.*
A private mansion was completely gutted to create this minimalist hotel on a busy street just off La Rambla. The rooms are white and futuristic, and lamps and chairs lend a 1960s air. There's a little-known public garden at the back: a delightful luxury in this densely packed area of town. The hotel offers free bike rental for residents.

Hotel Pulitzer
*C/Bergara 8, Eixample (93 481 67 67, www.hotelpulitzer.es). Metro Catalunya. **Map** p134 G8.*
Situated just off Plaça de Catalunya, the Hotel Pulitzer has become a popular place to meet before going on a night out. A discreet façade reveals an impressive lobby that's stuffed with comfortable white leather sofas, a reading area overflowing with glossy picture books and a swanky bar and restaurant. The rooftop terrace is a fabulous spot for a cocktail, with spectacular views across the heights of the city. The rooms themselves are not big, but they are sumptuously decorated.

Moderate
Ciutat de Barcelona
*C/Princesa 33, Born (93 269 74 75, www.ciutathotels.com). Metro Jaume I. **Map** p87 J9.*
The Ciutat de Barcelona is a jolly, primary-coloured affair, which offers a refreshing contrast to the chocolate and charcoal shades of most of Barna's smart hotels. The big draw, however, is a wood-decked roof terrace that is complete with shaded tables and a decent-sized plunge pool.

Hotel Constanza
*C/Bruc 33, Eixample (93 270 19 10, www.hotelconstanza.com). Metro Urquinaona. **Map** p134 J7.*
This quiet and pleasant boutique hotel has been around for a few years now and continues to please. Rooms are contemporary and simple, with warm, earthy colour palette.

Hotel España
*C/Sant Pau 9-11, Raval (93 550 00 00, www.hotelespanya.com). Metro Liceu. **Map** p101 G9.*
First opened in 1859, the España has a chequered history but has now been sympathetically restored, in keeping with its status as a Modernista gem. Ask for a room on the fourth floor – far enough up to give some distance from the occasional street noise and with slightly higher ceilings.

Hotel Mesón Castilla
*C/Valldonzella 5, Raval (93 318 21 82, www.mesoncastilla.com). Metro Universitat. **Map** p101 G8.*
If you want a change from modern design, check into this chocolate-box hotel, which opened in 1952. The best rooms have terraces, and there is also a delightful plant-filled terrace off the breakfast room.

Market Hotel

C/Comte Borrell 68, Sant Antoni (93 325 12 05, www.andilanahotels.com). Metro Sant Antoni. Map p124 E8.

The people who brought us the wildly successful Quinze Nits chain of restaurants (*see p76*) have gone on to apply their low-budget, high-design approach to this hotel. The monochrome rooms with pops of colour, though not huge, are comfortable and stylish for the price, and downstairs is a handsome and keenly priced restaurant, typical of the group.

Room Mate Emma

C/Rosselló 205, Eixample (93 238 56 06, www.room-matehotels.com). Metro Diagonal. Map p134 G5.

The arrival of 'Emma' was a boon for the design-conscious and cash-strapped. The hotel reflects a fictional personality, as do all in the chain, in this case a graphic designer with aspirations to create the next space hotel. Rooms are small – if you value space, check into the penthouse suite with a private terrace and hot tub – but the pay-off is soft, bouncy beds, power showers and a proper breakfast served until noon.

Budget
Bonic Guesthouse

C/Josep Anselm Clavé 9, 1º-4ª, Barri Gòtic (mobile 626 053 434, www.bonic-barcelona.com). Metro Drassanes. Map p70 G10.

Bonic is painted in daisy-fresh colours and sunlight streams through the windows onto meticulously restored original features. Attention to detail is exceptional for the price.

Casa Gràcia

Passeig de Gràcia 116, Gràcia (93 174 05 28 www.casagraciabcn.com). Metro Diagonal. Map p157 H5.

A cut above the regular youth hostel experience, Casa Gràcia is located in a lovely Modernista building, where natural light abounds through high windows and antiques dot the corridors.

There are numerous common areas, including a library, bar, terrace and buzzy restaurant (that serves a rather rare unpasteurised beer).

Chic&Basic Born

C/Princesa 50, Born (93 295 46 52, www.chicandbasic.com). Metro Arc de Triomf or Jaume I. Map p87 K9.

Set in a building that's over a hundred years old, this hotel takes the white-on-white theme to extremes (until you choose from the array of coloured lighting options, that is). Rooms come with white cotton sheets, white floors, white walls, mirrored cornicing and glassed-in wet rooms in the centre for hosing yourself down.

Hostal Girona

C/Girona 24, 1º-1ª, Eixample (93 265 02 59, www.hostalgirona.com). Metro Urquinaona. Map p134 J8.

A gem of a *hostal*, filled with antiques, chandeliers and oriental rugs. The rooms may be on the simple side, but all have charm to spare, with tall windows, pretty paintwork (gilt detail on the ceiling roses) and tiled floors.

Hostal Grau Barcelona

C/Ramelleres 27, Raval (93 301 81 35, www.hostalgrau.com). Metro Catalunya. Map p101 G8.

This charming, family-run eco-hostal oozes character, with a tiled spiral staircase and fabulous rustic communal areas, including a comfortable lounge and lively café. Rooms are stylish and fairly quiet. Guests can enjoy complimentary tea, coffee and homemade cake every morning, as well as a glass of wine in the early evening.

Hostal Sol y K

C/Cervantes 2, 2º-1ª, Barri Gòtic (93 318 81 48, www.solyk.es). Metro Jaume I or Liceu. Map p70 H10.

Bright and cheerful with some nice aesthetic touches (slate bathrooms and arty, bold bedheads), this *hostal* is a bargain for those who don't need any frills.

Getting Around

Barcelona's centre is compact and easily explored on foot. Bicycles are good for the Old City and port; there is a decent network of bike lanes across the city. The metro and bus systems are best for longer journeys.

ARRIVING & LEAVING

By air
Aeroport de Barcelona
902 40 47 04, 91 321 10 00, www.aena.es.
Barcelona's airport is at El Prat, south-west of the city. There are 2 main terminals: Terminal 1 (known as T1), and Terminal 2 (T2). The latter comprises the old terminals formerly called A, B and C, and now called T2A, T2B and T2C. Tourist information desks can be found in T1 and T2B, and currency exchanges are in both terminals. The map (download it from www.emt-amb.com) details all bus and train routes to and from the airport.

Aerobús 010 *www.aerobusbcn.com.*
The airport bus runs 2 routes to and from Plaça Catalunya: bus A1 from T1, and bus A2 from T2 (which makes 2 stops: at T2B and T2C; it's a 5-10min walk to T2A). From the airport, both services stop at Plaça Espanya, Gran Via Urgell, Plaça Universitat and Plaça Catalunya. On your return to the airport, both services depart from Plaça Catalunya (in front of El Corte Inglés), with stops at C/Sepúlveda and Plaça Espanya. The A1 bus runs every 5-10mins, departing the airport 5.35am-1.05am daily; and departing Plaça Catalunya 5am-12.30am daily. The A2 bus runs every 10mins, departing the airport 5.35am-1am daily; and departing Plaça Catalunya 5am-1am daily. Journey time (A1 and A2) is 35-45mins. Single €5.90; return (valid 15 days) €10.20.

Airport trains The Cercanías train (R2 Nord) leaves the airport at 08 and 38 mins past the hr until 11.38pm, stopping at Barcelona Sants and Passeig de Gràcia. Trains to the airport leave Barcelona Sants at 09 and 39 mins past the hr, until 11.14pm daily. Journey time 17-25mins and costs €2.15 one way (no return tickets). The T-10 Zone 1 metro pass (*see p175*) is also valid.

City buses Bus 46 runs between Plaça Espanya and the airport every 30mins. The service leaves from Plaça Espanya 4.50am-11.50pm daily. From the airport the first is at 5.30am and the last at 11.50pm. Journey time 45mins.

At night, the N17 runs every 20mins between both airport terminals (from 9.55pm T1, from 10.01pm T2) and Plaça Catalunya (from 11pm). Last departures are 4.45am from T1, 5am from T2. Journey time 50mins from T2, 1hr from T1.

Metro A new metro line, the orange L9, runs from T1 and T2 to Zona Universitària, in the west of the city, where it hooks up with the green L3, which will take you into the heart of the city. Tickets cost €4.50, which includes the ongoing leg, by metro, bus or FGC train. The T-10 (*see p175*) is not valid on this service. The journey takes 32mins and trains run every 7mins.

Taxis The basic taxi fare to town should be €25-€30, including a €3.10 airport supplement. Fares are about 15% higher after 8pm and at weekends. All licensed cab drivers use the ranks outside the terminals.

By bus
Most long-distance coaches (national and international) stop or terminate at **Estació d'Autobusos Barcelona-Nord** (C/Alí Bei 80, 902 26 06 06,

www.barcelonanord.com, *map p134*).
Some international Eurolines services
(93 367 44 00, www.eurolines.es) both
begin and end at Sants station.

By rail

Most long-distance services run by the
Spanish state railway company RENFE
leave from **Barcelona-Sants** station.
Many trains stop at **Passeig de Gràcia**.

RENFE *902 32 03 20, www.renfe.com.*
Open 24hrs daily.
Some English-speaking operators.
RENFE tickets can be bought online, at
stations and travel agents, or reserved
over the phone, and either collected
from machines at the train station or
delivered for a small fee.

PUBLIC TRANSPORT

Barcelona's public transport is now
highly integrated, with units on multi-
journey tickets valid for up to 3 changes
of transport (within 75mins) on bus,
tram, local train and metro lines. The
metro is generally the quickest way of
getting around the city. All metro lines
operate 5am-midnight Mon-Thur, Sun
and public holidays; 5am-2am Fri; and
nonstop on Sat. Buses run all night to
areas not covered by the metro system.
Local buses and the metro are run by
the city transport authority (TMB).
Various underground lines connect with
the metro, run by the FGC. There are 6
tramlines following 2 main routes (www.
trambcn.com), though they're of limited
use to visitors.

FGC information *Vestibule, Plaça*
Catalunya FGC station (93 205 15 15,
www.fgc.net). Open 8am-8pm Mon-Fri.
Map p134 H8.

TMB information *Main vestibule,*
Metro Universitat, Eixample (902 07 50
27, www.tmb.cat). Open 8am-8pm Mon-
Fri. Map p134 G7.

Fares & tickets

Journeys in the Barcelona urban area
have a flat fare of €2.15, but multi-
journey tickets (*targetes/tarjetas*) are
better value. The basic 10-trip *targeta*
is the **T-10** (*Te-Deu* in Catalan, *Te-Diez*
in Spanish), which can be shared
by any number of people travelling
simultaneously; the ticket is validated
in the machines on the metro, train or
bus once per person per journey. The
T-10 offers access to all 5 of the city's
main transport systems. To change
transport type using the same unit,
insert your card into a machine a second
time; unless 75mins have elapsed since
your last journey, no other unit will be
deducted. Single tickets do not allow free
transfers.

Buses

Many bus routes originate in or
pass through Plaça Catalunya, Plaça
Universitat and Plaça Urquinaona.
Most routes run 5.30am-11pm daily
except Sun. There's usually a bus every
10-15mins, but they're less frequent
before 8am, after 9pm and on Sat. On
Sun, buses are less frequent still; a few
do not run at all. Only single tickets can
be bought from the driver; if you have
a *targeta*, insert it into the machine
behind the driver as you board.

Night buses There are 17 urban night
bus (*Nitbus*) routes (010, or EMT), most
running from around 10.15-11.30pm
to 4.30-6am nightly, with buses every
20-30mins, plus an hourly bus to the
airport.

Local trains

Regional trains to Sabadell, Terrassa and
other towns beyond Tibidabo depart
from FGC Plaça Catalunya, those for
Montserrat from FGC Plaça d'Espanya.
    All trains on the RENFE local network
stop at Sants.

TAXIS

It's usually easy to find a taxi. There are ranks at railway and bus stations, in main squares and throughout the city, but taxis can also be hailed on the street when they show a green light on the roof and a sign saying *lliure/libre* ('free') behind the windscreen. Information on taxi fares, ranks and regulations can be found at www.taxi.ambcat.

Fares

Current rates and supplements are shown inside cabs on a sticker on the rear side window (in English). The basic fare for a taxi hailed in the street is €2.10. The basic rates (€1.10/km) apply 8am-8pm Mon-Fri; at other times, including public holidays, the rate is €1.30/km. Supplements and waiting charges apply.

Radio cabs

Phone cabs start the meter when a call is answered but, by the time it picks you up, it should not display more than €3.40 (€4.20 at night, weekends or public holidays).
Fono-Taxi *93 300 11 00.*
Ràdio Taxi *'033' or 93 303 30 33.*
Servi-Taxi *93 330 03 00.*
Taxi Miramar *93 433 10 20.*

DRIVING

For information on driving in Catalonia, call the local government's information line (012), which has English speakers; or see www.gen cat.net/transit.

Car & motorbike hire

Car hire is relatively pricey, but it's a competitive market, so shop around. You'll need a credit card as a guarantee.

Europcar *Plaça dels Països Catalans, Sants (902 10 50 55, www.europcar. com). Metro Sants Estació.* **Open** *6am-midnight Mon-Fri; 7am-11.30pm Sat, Sun.*

Parking

Parking is fiendishly complicated and municipal police are quick to hand out tickets or tow cars.

Pay & display areas The Àrea Verda contains zones only for use of residents (most of the Old City and centre of Gràcia – look out for *Àrea residents* signs). Elsewhere in central Barcelona, non-residents pay €2.50 or €2.25/hr with a 1- or 2hr maximum stay.

Car parks Car parks (*parkings*) are signalled by a white 'P' on a blue sign. **SABA** (902 28 30 80, www.saba.es) cost around €3.05/hr. **B:SM** has 40 car parks in the city, costing €3.07/hr (www.bsmsa. cat/activitats/mobilitat).

Towed vehicles If police tow your car, they should leave a triangular sticker on the pavement where it was. The sticker should let you know to which pound it's been taken. If not, call 901 513 151; staff generally don't speak English. Recovering your vehicle within 4 hrs costs €147.69, after which it's €1.99/ hr, or €19.86/day. You'll also have to pay a fine. You'll need your passport and documentation, or rental contract, to prove ownership. You can find information at www.gruabcn.cat.

CYCLING

There's a network of bike lanes (*carrils bici*) along major avenues and alongside the seafront. For information see www. bcn.cat/bicicleta.

TOURS

By bike
Un Cotxe Menys *C/Esparteria 3, Born (93 268 21 05, www.bicicletabarcelona. com). Metro Jaume I.* **Open** *10am-7pm daily.* **Tours** *11am daily, plus Apr-Sept 4.30pm Mon, Fri-Sun.* **Tickets** *€23. Hire €5/1hr; €10/4hrs; €12/1-day; €60/wk. No cards.* **Map** *p87 J10.*

Meet in Plaça Sant Jaume and then head to the shop for bikes and helmets followed by a 3hr English-speaking tour.

Fat Tire Bike Tours *C/Marlet 4 (93 342 92 75, fattirebiketours.com/barcelona). Metro Drassanes. **Tours** Feb-mid Apr, Nov-mid Dec 11am daily. Mid Apr-Oct 11am, 4pm daily. Rates €24. **Map** p70 H9.*

Tours meet in Plaça Sant Jaume and last over 4hrs, taking in the Old City, Sagrada Família, Ciutadella park and the beach.

By bus

Barcelona City Tours

*93 317 64 54, www.barcelonacity tour. cat. **Tours** Oct-Jan 11am-6pm daily; every 15-20mins. June-Oct 11am-8pm daily; every 8-10mins. **Tickets** 1 day €28; 2 days €39. Free under-4s.*

There are 2 routes: the East route takes in Sagrada Família, Park Güell and Port Olímpic; the West route takes in the seafront and the Fòrum, Montjuïc and Camp Nou. Both circuits take around 2hrs.

Bus Turístic *93 285 38 32, www.tmb. net. **Tours** Apr-Oct 9am-8pm daily; every 5-10mins. Nov-Mar 9am-7pm daily; every 25mins. **Tickets** 1 day €28; 2 days €39. Free under-4s. Available from tourist office or on bus. No cards.*

Bus Turístic (white and blue, with colourful images of the sights) runs 3 circular routes. Tickets are valid for all routes and ticket-holders get discount vouchers for a range of attractions.

On foot

Barcelona Walking Tours *93 285 38 32, www.barcelonaturisme.com. **Tours** (in English) Gothic 9.30am daily. Picasso Apr-Oct 3pm Tue-Sat; Nov-Mar 3pm Tue, Thur, Sat. Modernisme April-Oct 6pm Wed, Fri; Nov-Mar 3.30pm Wed, Fri. Gourmet 10.30am Mon-Fri. Tickets Gothic, Modernisme €16. Picasso, Gourmet (reservations essential) €22.*

Tours take 90mins-2hrs, excluding the museum trip. There is a 10% discount for booking online; check website for details.

My Favourite Things *mobile 637 265 405, www.myft.net.*

Unusual outings (€26) that include walking tours for families with children, urban design tours, and romantic tours, plus a 1-day wine tasting tour in the Priorat (€155).

Telefèric de Montjuïc

Resources A-Z

ACCIDENT & EMERGENCY

Emergency numbers
Emergency services *112*.
Police, fire or ambulance.
Ambulance *Ambulància 061*.
For hospitals *see below* and other health
services, *see p181* Health.
Fire service *Bombers/Bomberos 080*.
Police *Mossos d'Esquadra 088*.
Catalan police force.

A&E departments
In a medical emergency, go to the
casualty department (*Urgències*) of any
of the main public hospitals in the city.
All are open 24hrs daily.

Centre d'Urgències Perecamps
*Avda Drassanes 13-15, Raval (93 441 06
00). Metro Drassanes or Parallel.* **Map**
p101 G10.

Hospital Clínic *C/Villarroel 170,
Eixample (93 227 54 00). Metro Hospital
Clínic.* **Map** *p134 F5.*

Hospital Dos de Maig *C/Dos de Maig
301, Eixample (93 507 27 00). Metro Sant
Pau-Dos de Maig.* **Map** *p134 N5.*

Hospital del Mar *Passeig Marítim
25-29, Barceloneta (93 248 30 00). Metro
Ciutadella-Vila Olímpica.* **Map** *p112
L10.*

Hospital de Sant Pau *C/Sant Quintí
89, Eixample (93 291 90 00). Metro
Hospital de Sant Pau-Guinardó.* **Map**
p134 N4.

AGE RESTRICTIONS

Buying/drinking alcohol 18.
Driving 18.
Smoking 18.
Sex *(hetero- and homosexual)* 16.

CLIMATE

Barcelona is usually agreeable year-
round. Spring is unpredictable: warm,
sunny days can alternate with winds
and showers. Temperatures in May and
June are pretty much perfect and 23
June marks the beginning of summer.
July and Aug can be unpleasant, as
the summer heat kicks in and many
locals leave town. Autumn weather is
generally warm and fresh, with heavy
downpours common around Oct. Crisp,
cool sunshine is normal Dec-Feb. Snow
is very rare.

Travel Advice

For up-to-date information on travel to a specific country contact your home
country government's department of foreign affairs.

Australia
www.smartraveller.gov.au

Republic of Ireland
foreignaffairs.gov.ie

Canada
www.voyage.gc.ca

UK
www.fco.gov.uk/travel

New Zealand
www.safetravel.govt.nz

USA
www.state.gov/travel

EMBASSIES & CONSULATES

The contact details for all embassies are available on embassy.goabroad.com. Embassies are located in Madrid, but several countries also have consulates in Barcelona.

British Consulate *Avda Diagonal 477, 13º, Eixample (93 366 62 00, www.gov. uk/government/world/spain). Metro Hospital Clínic.* **Map** *p134 F4.*

Canadian Consulate *Plaça Catalunya 9, 1º, Eixample (93 270 36 14, www. espana.gc.ca). Metro Catalunya.* **Map** *p134 H7.*

Irish Consulate *Gran Via Carles III 94, 10º, Les Corts (93 491 50 21, www. embassyofireland.es). Metro Maria Cristina.*

New Zealand Consulate *Travessera de Gràcia 64, 2º, Gràcia (93 209 50 48). Metro Diagonal.*

US Consulate *Passeig Reina Elisenda 23, Sarrià (93 280 22 27, barcelona. usconsulate.gov). FGC Reina Elisenda.*

CUSTOMS

Custom declarations are not usually necessary if you arrive from another EU country and are carrying legal goods for personal use (regardless of whether you are an EU citizen). The amounts given below are guidelines only.

• 800 cigarettes, 400 small cigars, 200 cigars or 1kg loose tobacco.
• 10 litres of spirits (more than 22% alcohol), 20 litres of spirits (less than 22% alcohol), 90 litres of wine (or 60 litres of sparkling wine) or 110 litres of beer.

Coming from a non-EU country or the Canary Islands, you can bring:

• 200 cigarettes, 100 small cigars, 50 regular cigars or 250g (8.82oz) of tobacco.
• 1 litre of spirits (more than 22% alcohol) or 2 litres of spirits or similar beverages (less than 22% alcohol) or 4 litres of wine (less than 22% alcohol) or 16 litres of beer.
• Personal goods to a value of €430.

Climate

Average temperatures and monthly rainfall in Barcelona

	Temp (°C/°F)	Rainfall (mm/in)	Sun (hrs/day)
January	10/50	44/1.7	5
February	10/50	36/1.4	7
March	12/54	48/1.9	7
April	13/55	51/2.0	8
May	16/61	57/2.2	8
June	20/68	38/1.5	9
July	23/73	22/0.9	10
August	24/75	66/2.6	9
September	22/72	79/3.1	8
October	18/64	94/3.7	6
November	13/55	74/2.9	5
December	11/52	50/2.0	4

Visitors can also carry up to €10,000 in cash without having to declare it. Non-EU residents can reclaim VAT (IVA) on some large purchases when they leave. For details, *see p182.*

DISABLED

A useful resource is the Catalan government's website www. turismeperatothom.com.
Institut Municipal de Persones amb Discapacitat *C/València 344, Eixample (93 413 27 75, ajuntament. barcelona.cat/accessible). Metro Girona.* **Map** *p134K6.*
The official city organisation for the disabled has information on access to venues and transport, and can provide a map with wheelchair-friendly itineraries. Call in advance to make an appointment.

Transport

Access for disabled people to local transport is improving but still leaves much to be desired. For wheelchair-users, buses and taxis are usually the best bet. For transport information, call **TMB** (902 075 027) or 010.

Buses All the Aerobús airport buses, night buses, standard buses and the open-topped tourist buses are fully accessible, though you may need assistance with the steep ramps. Visual and audio assistance is also in place for blind passengers.

FGC Accessible FGC stations include Provença, Muntaner and Avda Tibidabo. The Montjuïc funicular railway is fully wheelchair-adapted.

Metro For a list of accessible metro stations and bus lines, check www.tmb. cat/en/barcelona/metro/lines.

RENFE trains Sants and Plaça Catalunya stations are wheelchair-accessible, but the trains are not. Go to the Atenció al Viajero office ahead of time, to arrange help on the platform.

Taxis All taxi drivers are officially required to transport wheelchairs and guide dogs for no extra charge, but cars can be small, and the willingness of drivers to co-operate varies widely. Special minibus taxis adapted for wheelchairs can be ordered from the **Taxi Amic** service (93 420 80 88, www. taxi-amic-adaptat.com).

Wheelchair-friendly museums & galleries

All of the below should be accessible to wheelchair-users:
CCCB; CaixaForum; La Pedrera; Fundació Joan Miró; Fundacío Antoni Tàpies; MNAC; Museu Frederic Marès; Museu d'Arqueologia de Catalunya; Museu d'Història de Catalunya; Museu d'Història de Barcelona; Museu de la Xocolata; Museu Picasso; Palau de la Música; Palau de la Virreina.

DRUGS

Many people smoke cannabis fairly openly in Spain, but possession or consumption in public is illegal. In private, the law is contradictory: smoking is OK, but you can be nabbed for possession or distribution. Enforcement is often not the highest of police priorities, but you could theoretically receive a fine. Larger amounts entail a fine and, in extreme cases, prison. Smoking in bars is also prohibited. Cocaine is also common in Spain, but if you are caught in possession of this or any other Class A drug, you are looking at a hefty fine, and possibly a long prison sentence.

ELECTRICITY

The standard voltage in Spain is 220V. Plugs are of the 2-round-pin type. You'll need a plug adaptor to use British-bought electrical devices. If you have US (110V) equipment, you will need a current transformer as well as an adaptor.

HEALTH

For general details on healthcare, see catsalut.gencat.cat or call 061. Visitors can obtain emergency care through the public health service (*see p178* Accident & emergency). EU nationals are entitled to free basic medical attention if they have the European Health Insurance Card (EHIC). Contact the health service in your country of residence for details. Citizens of certain other countries that have a special agreement with Spain can also have access to free care.

For non-emergencies it's usually quicker to use private travel insurance rather than the state system.

Tap water is drinkable in Barcelona, but tastes faintly of chlorine.

Contraception

All pharmacies sell condoms (*condoms/ preservativos*) and other forms of contraception including pills (*la píndola/la píldora*), which can be bought without a prescription, as can the morning-after pill (*la píndola de l'endemà/la píldora del día siguiente*) but some health centres will dispense it free themselves.

Centre Jove d'Anticoncepció i Sexualitat *C/La Granja 19-21, Gràcia (93 415 10 00, www.centrejove.org). Metro Lesseps.* **Open** *11am-7pm Mon-Thur; 10am-5pm Fri. Closed 2wks Aug.* **Map** *p157 K2.*

A family-planning centre aimed at young people (under-25s).

Dentists

Most dentistry is not covered by the Spanish public health service (to which EU citizens have access). Check the classified ads in *Metropolitan* for English-speaking dentists.

Hospitals

See p178 Accident & emergency.

Opticians

+Visión El Triangle *Plaça Catalunya 4, Eixample (93 304 16 40, www.masvision. es). Metro Catalunya.* **Open** *10am-10pm Mon-Sat.* **Map** *p134 H8.*

There are some English-speaking staff at this handy optical superstore.

Pharmacies

Pharmacies (*farmàcies/farmàcias*) are signalled by large green and red neon crosses. About a dozen operate around the clock, while more have late opening hours. Call two helplines, 010 and 098, for information.

STDs, HIV & AIDS

Free, anonymous blood tests for HIV and other STDs are given at the Unidad de Infección de Transmisión Sexual at **CAP Drassanes** (Avda Drassanes 17-21, Raval). HIV tests are also available at the Asociació Ciutadana Antisida de Catalunya (C/Lluna 11, Raval, 93 317 05 05, www.acasc.info) and at BCN Checkpoint (C/Comte Borrell 164-166, 93 318 20 56, www.bcncheckpoint.com).

ID

From the age of 14, Spaniards are legally obliged to carry their DNI (identity card). Foreigners are also meant to carry an ID card or passport, and are in theory subject to a fine for not doing so – in practice, you're more likely to get a warning. If you don't want to carry it around with you carry a photocopy or a driver's licence instead: it's usually acceptable.

LANGUAGE

Over a 3rd of Barcelona residents prefer to speak Catalan as their everyday language, around 70% speak it fluently, and more than 90% understand it. Everyone in the city can also speak Spanish. If you take an interest and learn a few phrases in Catalan, it is likely to be appreciated. *See p186* Spanish Vocabulary and *p187* Catalan Vocabulary.

LEFT LUGGAGE

Look for signs to the *consigna*.
Aeroport del Prat *Open Terminal 1 24hrs daily; Terminal 2 6am-10pm daily.*
Estació d'Autobusos *Barcelona-Nord C/Alí Bei 80, Eixample. Metro Arc de Triomf. Open 24hrs daily. Map p134 L8.*
Sants-Estació *Open 24hrs daily.*
Some smaller railway stations also have left-luggage lockers.

LGBT

Casal Lambda *Avda Marques de Argentera 22, Born (93 319 55 50, www. lambda.cat). Metro Barceloneta. Open 5-9pm Mon-Sat. Closed Aug. Map p87 K10.*
Gay cultural organisation.
Front d'Alliberament Gai de Catalunya *C/Verdi 88, Gràcia (93 217 26 69, www.fagc.org). Metro Fontana. Open 7-9pm Mon-Fri. Map p157 J3.*
A vocal group that produces the *Debat Gai* information bulletin.

LOST PROPERTY

If you lose something at the airport, report it to the lost property centre (Oficina d'Objectes Perduts, in T1, 93 259 64 40). If you have mislaid anything on a train, look for the Atenció al Passatger desk or Cap d'Estació office at the nearest station.

Oficina de Trobelles *Plaça Carles Pi i Sunyer 8-10, Barri Gòtic (010). Metro Catalunya or Jaume I. Open 9am-2pm Mon-Fri. Map p70 H8.*
All documentation or valuables found on city public transport and taxis, or picked up by the police in the street, should eventually find their way to this Ajuntament office, just off Avda Portal de l'Àngel.

TMB Lost Property Office *Diagonal metro station L5 entrance (902 075 027, www.tmb.cat). Open 8am-8pm Mon-Fri. Map p134 H5.*

Items found on most public transport services are sent to this office, then transferred to the above office on Wed. If the item was lost on a tram, call 900 701 181; on FGC trains, 93 205 15 15; for taxis, call 902 101 564.

MONEY

Spain's currency is the euro. Each euro (€) is divided into 100 cents (¢), known as *céntims/céntimos*. Notes come in denominations of €500, €200, €100, €50, €20, €10 and €5. Smaller businesses may be reluctant to accept anything larger than €50.

Banks & currency exchanges

Obtaining money through ATMs with a debit or credit card is the easiest option, despite the fees often charged.
Bank hours Banks are normally open 8.30am-2pm Mon-Fri. Oct-Apr, most branches also open 8.30am-1pm Sat.
Out-of-hours banking Foreign exchange offices at the airport are in T1 (open 7am-10pm) and T2B (open 7am-8.30pm). Others in the centre open late: some on La Rambla open until midnight.

Credit & debit cards

Major credit cards are accepted in hotels, shops, restaurants and other places. American Express cards are less frequently accepted than MasterCard and Visa. You can withdraw cash with major cards from ATMs.

Tax

The standard rate for sales tax (IVA) is 21%; this drops to 10% in hotels and restaurants, and 4% on some books. IVA may or may not be included in listed prices at restaurants, and it usually isn't included in rates quoted at hotels. If it's not, the expression *IVA no inclòs/ incluido* (sales tax not included) should appear after the price.

In shops displaying a 'Tax-Free Shopping' sticker, non-EU residents can reclaim tax on large purchases when leaving the country.

The *tasa turística* ('tourist tax') is now levied on hotel stays, and varies from 65¢ to €2.25 a night, depending on the star rating of the hotel. Children under 16 are exempt, and the tax is applicable for a maximum of 7 nights.

OPENING TIMES

Note that in summer, many of Barcelona's shops and restaurants shut for all or part of Aug. Some businesses also work a shortened day June-Sept, 8/9am-3pm. Many museums close one day each week, usually Mon.

Most shops are open 9/10am-1/2pm, and then 4/5pm-8/9pm Mon-Sat. Many smaller businesses don't reopen on Sat pm. All-day opening (10am-8/9pm) is becoming more common, especially for larger and more central establishments.

Markets open at 7/8am; most stalls are shut by 2pm, although many stay open on Fri and Sat until 8pm.

POLICE

Barcelona has several police forces: the **Mossos d'Esquadra** (in a uniform of navy and light blue with red trim), the **Guàrdia Urbana** (municipal police – navy and pale blue), the **Policía Nacional** (national police – darker blue uniforms and white shirts, or blue, combat-style gear).

The **Guàrdia Civil** is a paramilitary force with green uniforms, policing highways and government buildings.

Reporting a crime

If you're robbed or attacked, report the incident as soon as possible at the nearest police station (*comisaría*), or dial 112. In the centre, the most convenient is the 24-hr **Guàrdia Urbana** station (La Rambla 43, Barri Gòtic, 112 or 93 300 22 96); they may transfer you to the **Mossos d'Esquadra** (C/Nou de la Rambla 76-80, Raval, 088 or 93 306 23 00) to report the crime formally. You can also make this

statement over the phone or online (902 102 112, www.policia.es), apart from for crimes involving violence, or if the perpetrator has been identified. You'll still have to go to the *comisaría* within 72 hrs to sign the *denuncia*, but you'll be able to skip some queues.

POSTAL SERVICES

Letters and postcards weighing up to 20g cost 45¢ within Spain; €1.15 to the rest of Europe; €1.30 to the rest of the world; prices normally rise on 1 Jan. It's easiest to buy stamps at *estancs* (government-run tobacco shops, with brown and yellow signs). Postboxes in the street are yellow. For information on postal services, see www.correos.es.

Correus Central *Plaça Antonio López, Barri Gòtic (93 486 83 02). Metro Barceloneta or Jaume I.* **Open** *8.30am-9.30pm Mon-Fri; 8.30am-2pm Sat.* **Map** *p70 J10.*
Take a ticket from the machine as you enter and wait your turn. To send something express delivery, ask for *urgente*.

PUBLIC HOLIDAYS

Most shops, banks and offices, and many bars and restaurants, close on public holidays (*festius/festivos*), and public transport is limited.

New Year's Day *Any Nou* 1 Jan
Epiphany/Three Kings *Reis Mags* 6 Jan
Good Friday *Divendres Sant*
Easter Monday *Dilluns de Pasqua*
May (Labour) Day *Festa del Treball* 1 May
Whit Monday *Segona Pascua* 1 June
Sant Joan 24 June
Assumption *Verge de l'Assumpció* 15 Aug
Diada de Catalunya 11 Sept
La Mercè 24 Sept
Dia de la Hispanitat 12 Oct
All Saints' Day *Tots Sants* 1 Nov
Constitution Day *Día de la Constitución* 6 Dec

La Immaculada 8 Dec
Christmas Day *Nadal* 25 Dec
Boxing Day *Sant Esteve* 26 Dec

SAFETY & SECURITY

Pickpocketing and bag-snatching are epidemic in Barcelona. Be especially careful around the Old City, as well as at stations and on public transport. Most street crime can be avoided by taking precautions:
• Don't keep wallets in accessible pockets, keep your bags closed and in front of you.
• Don't flash wads of cash, fancy cameras and phones.
• Avoid deserted streets in the city centre if you're on your own at night.
• Don't carry more money than you need: use your hotel's safe deposit facilities, and take out travel insurance.

SMOKING

Smoking is banned in enclosed public areas. Most hotels have a non-smoking policy.

TELEPHONES

Dialling & codes

Normal Spanish phone numbers have 9 digits; the area code (93 in the province of Barcelona) must be dialled with all calls, both local and long-distance. Spanish mobile numbers usually begin with 6, and, very occasionally, 7. Numbers starting 900 are freephone lines, while other 90 numbers are special-rate services.

International & long-distance calls

To phone Spain from abroad, dial 0034, followed by the number. To make an international call from Spain, dial 00 and then the country code, followed by the area code (omitting the first 0 in UK numbers), and then the number. Country codes:

Australia 61.
Canada 1.
Irish Republic 353.
New Zealand 64.
South Africa 27.
United Kingdom 44.
USA 1.

Mobile phones

Most mobiles from other European countries can be used in Spain, but you may need to set this up before you leave.

If you're staying more than a few weeks, it may work out cheaper to buy a local SIM card for your own phone.

Phone centres & phonecards

Phonecards and phone centres give cheaper call rates, especially for international calls. Phone centres (*locutoris*) are full of small booths where you can sit down and pay at the end. Find them in streets such as C/ Sant Pau and C/Hospital in the Raval, and along C/Carders-C/Corders in Sant Pere. Telefónica phonecards (*targetes telefónica/tarjetas telefónica*) are sold at newsstands and *estancs*. Other cards sold at phone centres, shops and newsstands give cheaper rates on all but local calls.

TIME

The local time is Central European Time: 1 hr ahead of Greenwich Mean Time, 6 hrs ahead of US Eastern Standard Time and 9 hrs ahead of Pacific Standard Time. Daylight saving time runs concurrently with the United Kingdom: clocks go back in Oct and forward in Mar.

TIPPING

There are no rules for tipping in Barcelona, but locals don't tip much. It's fair to leave 5-10% in restaurants. In taxis, tipping is not standard, but many people round up to the nearest 50¢. It's usual to tip hotel porters.

TOURIST INFORMATION

010 phoneline *Open 24hrs daily.*
This city-run information line is aimed mainly at locals, but it does an impeccable job of answering all kinds of queries. There are sometimes English-speaking operators available.

Centre d'Informació de la Virreina *Palau de la Virreina, La Rambla 99, Barri Gòtic (93 316 10 00, www.barcelona.cat/barcelonacultura). Metro Liceu. Open 10am-8.30pm daily (information office and ticket sales). Map p70 G9.*
The information office of the city's culture department has details of shows, exhibitions and special events.

Oficines d'Informació Turística *Plaça Catalunya 17, Eixample (information 93 285 38 34, bookings 93 285 38 33, www.bcn.cat, www.barcelonaturisme. com). Metro Catalunya. Open 8.30am-8.30pm daily. Map p134 H8.*
The main office of the city tourist board is underground on the El Corte Inglés/south side of the square: look for the big red signs with 'i' superimposed in white.

Palau Robert *Passeig de Gràcia 107, Eixample (93 238 80 91/ 92/93, www. gencat.net/probert, www.catalunya. com). Metro Diagonal. Open 10am-7pm Mon-Sat; 10am-2.30pm Sun. Map p134 H5.*
The Generalitat's centre for tourists is at the junction of Passeig de Gràcia and Avda Diagonal. Its speciality is a huge range of information in different media for attractions to be found elsewhere in Catalonia.

VISAS & IMMIGRATION

UK and Irish nationals will need a valid passport to enter Spain. Due to the Schengen Agreement, most other European Union citizens, as well as Norwegian and Icelandic nationals, need only a national identity card.

Visas are not required for citizens of the United States, Canada, Australia and New Zealand who are arriving for stays of up to 90 days and not for work or study. Citizens of South Africa and other countries need visas to enter Spain; approach Spanish embassies in your home country for information (see embassy.goabroad.com). Visa regulations do change, so check before leaving home.

EU citizens
EU citizens living in Spain for more than 3 mths need a resident's card (*tarjeta de residencia*), as well as ID or a passport from their own country.

Non-EU citizens
While in Spain on a tourist visa, you are not legally allowed to work. Those wanting a work permit officially need to be made a job offer while still in their home country. The process is lengthy and not all applications are successful.

Spanish Vocabulary

Although many locals prefer to speak Catalan, everyone in the city can speak Spanish. The Spanish familiar form for 'you' (tú) is used very freely, but it's safer to use the more formal usted with older people and strangers (verbs below are given in the used form).

Useful expressions

hello hola; **good morning** buenos días; **good afternoon, good evening** buenas tardes; **good evening** (after dark); **good night** buenas noches; **goodbye** adiós; **please** por favor; **very good/OK** muy bien; **thank you (very much)** (muchas) gracias; **you're welcome** de nada; **do you speak English?** ¿habla inglés?; **I don't speak Spanish** no hablo castellano; **I don't understand** no lo entiendo; **OK/fine** vale; **what's your name?** ¿cómo se llama?; **Sir/Mr** señor (sr); **Madam/Mrs** señora (sra); **Miss** señorita (srta); **excuse me/sorry** perdón; **excuse me, please** oiga (to attract someone's attention, politely; literally, 'hear me'); **where is...?** ¿dónde está...?; **why?** ¿por qué?; **when?** ¿cuándo?; **who?** ¿quién?; **what?** ¿qué?; **where?** ¿dónde?; **how?** ¿cómo?; **who is it?** ¿quién es?; **is/are there any...?** ¿hay...?; **very** muy; **and** y; **or** o; **with** con; **without** sin; **enough** bastante; **open** abierto; **closed** cerrado; **entrance** entrada; **exit** salida; **I would like** quiero; **how many would you like?** ¿cuántos quiere?; **how much is it?** ¿cuánto es?; **I like** me gusta; **I don't like** no me gusta; **good** bueno/a; **bad** malo/a; **well/badly** bien/mal; **small** pequeño/a; **big** gran, grande; **expensive** caro/a; **cheap** barato/a; **hot** (food, drink) caliente; **cold** frío/a; **something** algo; **nothing** nada; **more/less** más/menos; **more or less** más o menos; **toilets** los baños/los servicios/los lavabos

Getting around

a ticket un billete; **return** de ida y vuelta; **the next stop** la próxima parada; **left** izquierda; **right** derecha; **here** aquí; **there** allí; **straight on** todo recto; **to the end of the street** al final de la calle; **as far as** hasta; **towards** hacia; **near** cerca; **far** lejos

Time

now ahora; **later** más tarde; **yesterday** ayer; **today** hoy; **tomorrow** mañana; **morning** la mañana; **midday** mediodía; **afternoon/evening** la tarde; **night** la noche; **late night** (roughly 1-6am) la madrugada; **at what time...?** ¿a qué hora...?; **at 2** a las dos; **at 8pm** a las ocho de la tarde; **at 1.30** a la una y media; **at 5.15** a las cinco y cuarto; **in an hour** en una hora

Numbers

0 cero; **1** un, uno, una; **2** dos; **3** tres; **4** cuatro; **5** cinco; **6** seis; **7** siete; **8** ocho; **9** nueve; **10** diez; **11** once; **12** doce; **13** trece; **14** catorce; **15** quince; **16** dieciséis; **17** diecisiete; **18** dieciocho; **19** diecinueve; **20** veinte; **21** veintiuno; **22** veintidós; **30** treinta; **40** cuarenta; **50** cincuenta; **60** sesenta; **70** setenta; **80** ochenta; **90** noventa; **100** cien; **200** doscientos; **1,000** mil

Days & months

Monday lunes; **Tuesday** martes; **Wednesday** miércoles; **Thursday** jueves; **Friday** viernes; **Saturday** sábado; **Sunday** domingo **January** enero; **February** febrero; **March** marzo; **April** abril; **May** mayo; **June** junio; **July** julio; **August** agosto; **September** septiembre; **October** octubre; **November** noviembre; **December** diciembre

Catalan Vocabulary

Catalan phonetics are significantly different from those of Spanish, with a wider range of vowel sounds and soft consonants. Catalans use the familiar (*tu*) rather than the polite (*vosté*) second-person forms very freely, but for convenience verbs are given here in the polite form.

Useful expressions

hello *hola*; **good morning** *bon dia*; **good afternoon** *bona tarda*; **good evening/night** *bona nit*; **goodbye** *adéu*; **please** *sisplau*; **very good/OK** *molt bé*; **thank you (very much)** *(moltes) gràcies*; **you're welcome** *de res*; **do you speak English?** *parla anglés?*; **I'm sorry, I don't speak Catalan** *ho sento, no parlo català*; **I don't understand** *no ho entenc*; **what's your name?** *com es diu?*; **Sir/Mr** *senyor (sr)*; **Madam/Mrs** *senyora (sra)*; **Miss** *senyoreta (srta)*; **excuse me/sorry** *perdoni/disculpi*; **excuse me, please** *escolti* (literally, 'listen to me'); **OK/fine** *val/d'acord*; **how much is it?** *quant val?*; **why?** *perqué?*; **when?** *quan?*; **who?** *qui?*; **what?** *qué?*; **where?** *on?*; **how?** *com?*; **where is...?** *on és...?*; **is/are there any...?** *hi ha...?/n'hi ha de...?*; **very** *molt*; **and** *i* or *o*; **with** *amb*; **without** *sense*; **enough** *prou* **open** *obert*; **closed** *tancat*; **entrance** *entrada*; **exit** *sortida*; **I would like** *vull*; **how many would you like?** *quants en vol?*; **I like** *m'agrada*; **I don't like** *no m'agrada*; **good** *bo/bona*; **bad** *dolent/a*; **well/badly** *bé/malament*; **small** *petit/a*; **big** *gran*; **expensive** *car/a*; **cheap** *barat/a*; **hot** (food, drink) *calent/a*; **cold** *fred/a*; **something** *alguna cosa*; **nothing** *res*; **more** *més*; **less** *menys*; **more or less** *més o menys*; **toilets** *els banys/els serveis/els lavabos*

Getting around

a ticket *un bitllet*; **return** *de anada i tornada*; **left** *esquerra*; **right** *dreta*; **here** *aquí*; **there** *allí*; **straight on** *tot recte*; **at the corner** *a la cantonada*; **as far as** *fins a*; **towards** *cap a*; **near** *a prop*; **far** *lluny*; **is it far?** *és lluny?*

Time

now *ara*; **later** *més tard*; **yesterday** *ahir*; **today** *avui*; **tomorrow** *demà*; **morning** *el matí*; **midday** *migdía*; **afternoon** *la tarda*; **evening** *el vespre*; **night** *la nit*; **late night** (roughly, from 1-6am) *la matinada*; **at what time...?** *a quina hora...?*; **in an hour** *en una hora*; **at 2** *a les dues*; **at 8pm** *a les vuit del vespre*; **at 1.30** *a dos quarts de dues*; **at 5.15** *a un quart de sis/a les cinc i quart*; **at 22.30** *a vint-i-dos-trenta*

Numbers

0 *zero*; **1** *u, un, una*; **2** *dos, dues*; **3** *tres*; **4** *quatre*; **5** *cinc*; **6** *sis*; **7** *set*; **8** *vuit*; **9** *nou*; **10** *deu*; **11** *onze*; **12** *dotze*; **13** *tretze*; **14** *catorze*; **15** *quinze*; **16** *setze*; **17** *disset*; **18** *divuit*; **19** *dinou*; **20** *vint*; **21** *vint-i-u*; **22** *vint-i-dos, vint-i-dues*; **30** *trenta*; **40** *quaranta*; **50** *cinquanta*; **60** *seixanta*; **70** *setanta*; **80** *vuitanta*; **90** *noranta*; **100** *cent*; **200** *dos-cents, dues-centes*; **1,000** *mil*

Days & months

Monday *dilluns*; **Tuesday** *dimarts*; **Wednesday** *dimecres*; **Thursday** *dijous*; **Friday** *divendres*; **Saturday** *dissabte*; **Sunday** *diumenge*; **January** *gener*; **February** *febrer*; **March** *març*; **April** *abril*; **May** *maig*; **June** *juny*; **July** *juliol*; **August** *agost*; **September** *setembre*; **October** *octubre*; **November** *novembre*; **December** *desembre*

Index

23 Robadors 110
1881 118

A
accident &
  emergency 178
**Accommodation
168–173**
A&E 178
age restrictions 178
Agua 117
Aire 152
airport 174
air travel 174
Ajuntament 69
Almacenes del
  Pilar 80
Alonso 80
Altaïr 144
ambulance 178
Antic Hospital de la
  Santa Creu & La
  Capella 102
antiques 33, 35
L' Aquàrium 114
Arena 44, 148
Las Arenas 32
Arlequí Màscares
  96
art galleries 32
L'Auditori 148
autumn 178

B
Bacoa 91
Bacon Bear Bar
  152
Balius 166
Bangkok Café 159
banks 182
Bar Calders 130
Bar Cañete 105
Barcelona City Tours
  177
Barcelona-Sants
  station 175
Barcelona Walking
  Tours 177
**Barceloneta & the
  Ports 111–120**
Bar Celta 91
Bar del Convent 94
Bar del Pla 94
Bar Kasparo 106
Bar Lobo 106
Bar Mendizábal
  106
Bar Pastís 110
Bar Pinotxo 77
**Barri Gòtic & La
  Rambla 67–84**
bars
  Barri Gòtic 77
  Born & Sant
    Pere 94

Dreta 141
Esquerra 150
Gràcia & Park
  Güell 156
Horta & around
  165
Montjuïc 129
Poblenou,
  Diagional Mar &
  the Fòrum 166
Poble Sec & Sant
  Antoni 130
Raval 106
BARTS 131
Báscula de la
  Cererìa 94
Base Nàutica de la
  Mar Bella 119
B&Bs 168
BCN Books 144
beaches 12, 116.
  See also platja
beach libraries 117
Belmonte 74
Bestial 117
biblioplatges 117
bicycles. See cycling
El Bitxo 94
Black Lab 118
The Black Room 44
boat trips 119
Bodega Quimet 156
La Bodegueta 141
Bonic Guesthouse
  173
La Boqueria 17,
  78, 81
Bormuth 94
**Born & Sant Pere
  85–98**
  shopping 35
Born Centre de
  Cultura i Memòria
  89
boutiques 32,
  35, 36
British Consulate
  179
budget travel 49
Bulevard dels
  Antiquaris 144
bus travel 174, 175,
  180
Bus Turístic 177

C
Caelum 80
Cafè de l'Acadèmia
  74
Cafè del Centre 141
Cafè de les Delicies
  108
Cafè de l'Opera
  77, 79
Café Godot 156

Café Royale 82
cafés
  Barceloneta 118
  Barri Gòtic 77
  Born & Sant
    Pere 94
  Dreta 141
  Esquerra 150
  Gràcia & Park
    Güell 156
  Horta & around
    165
  Montjuïc 129
  Poblenou,
    Diagional Mar &
    the Fòrum 166
  Poble Sec & Sant
    Antoni 130
  Raval 106
CaixaForum 35,
  122
C/Banys Nous 35
Cal Pep 93
Camper 144
Camp Nou
  Experience 12,
  159
Canadian Consulate
  179
Can Culleretes 74
Can Majó 117
Can Paixano 118
Can Travi Nou 164
La Capella 103
Capricho de Muñeca
  96
Caravelle 105
car hire 176
Carnaval 60
car parks 176
Casa Almirall 108
Casa Àmatller 137
Casa Batlló 12, 138
Casa Calvet 139
Casa Camper 171
Casa de les Punxes
  137
Casa Delfín 93
Casa Fuster 170
Casa Gispert 33, 96
Casa Gràcia 173
Casa Lleó Morera
  136
Casa Lolea 94
Casa Milà 140. See
  also La Pedrera
La Caseta del Migdia
  129
Castell de Montjuïc
  122
castellers 59
Catalan language
  187
Catamaran Orsom
  119

Catedral de
  Barcelona 14, 73
CCCB 103
CDLC 42, 120
Centre de Cultura
  Contemporània
  de Barcelona.
  See CCCB
Cereria Subirà 80
Chic&Basic Born
  173
Chicken Shop 74
children 50
Cinema Maldà 83
Cinemes Méliès
  152
City Hall 149
Ciutat de Barcelona
  172
climate 178, 179
Club de Natació
  Atlètic
  Barceloneta 119
coffee 27
Collserola 160
La Concha 110
La Confitería 108
consulates 179
contraception 181
Convent de Sant
  Agustí 94
correfoc 59
Correus Central
  183
El Corte Inglés 146
Les Corts 158
CosmoCaixa 161
Cotton House Hotel
  170
Un Cotxe Menys
  176
La Cova Fumada
  119
credit & debit cards
  182
crime 183
currency exchanges
  182
Custo Barcelona 96
customs 179
cycling 174, 176

D
dentists 181
Diagonal Mar 165
Diary 53–60
disabled travellers
  180
discount schemes
  66
Domènech i
  Montaner, Lluís
  23, 98
Dos Trece 105
dressmakers 32

Dreta 136
driving 176
drugs 180
Dry Martini 150
Du Pareil au Même
147

E
**Eating & Drinking
25–30**
**Eixample 36,
133–152**
electricity 180
Elisabets 105
embassies 179
emergency services
178
En Aparté 93
Els Encants flea
market 33, 146
**Entertainment
37–44**
Barceloneta 120
Barri Gòtic 82
Born & Sant
Pere 97
Dreta 148
Esquerra 152
Gràcia & Park
Güell 158
Poblenou,
Diagional Mar &
the Fòrum 166
Poble Sec 131
Raval 110
Sants & Les Corts
160
Tibidabo &
Collserola 161
Escribà 151
Esquerra de
l'Eixample
149–152
L'Esquinica 165
Estació d'Autobusos
Barcelona-Nord
174
Èstro 96
European Health
Insurance Card
181
Euskal Etxea 28, 95

F
families 50
fashion 33, 35, 36
Fat Tire Bike Tours
177
FC Barcelona 159
Federal 77, 130
Festes de la Mercè
57
festivals 59
FGC train 174, 175,
180
fire service 178
Flors Navarro 146
Font de Canaletes
78
Font Màgica de
Montjuïc 122

football 159
Formatgeria La
Seu 82
Fòrum 165
Fundació Antoni
Tàpies 137
Fundació Foto
Colectania 89
Fundació Gaspar 89
Fundació Joan Miró
14, 127
Fundación Mapfre
139
Funicular de
Tibidabo 160

G
Gaig 150
Gaixample 44
Galeria Estrany · De
La Mota 146
Garage Beer Co
150
Gaudí, Antoni 22,
107, 155
Gaudí Exhibition
Center 71
Gaudí Experiència
154
gay festivals 44
Gay Pride 44
gegants 59
Gelateria Caffetteria
Italiana 156
**Getting Around
174–177**
**Getting Started
62–66**
Las Golondrinas
119
Gothic 92
Gothic Quarter.
See Barri Gòtic
**Gràcia & Other
Districts 36,
153–166**
Gran Café 74
Grand Hotel Central
171
Granja 1872 77
Granja M Viader
109
Granja Petitbó 144
Gran Teatre del
Liceu 79, 83
Gresca 150
Güell, Eusebi 107,
155
Guitar Shop 109
Guzzo 95

H
Harlem Jazz Club
84
Hash Marihuana
Cáñamo & Hash
Museum 71
health 181
Heliogàbal 158
Hibernian Books
158

Highlights 10–18
Hisop 163
Holalà! Plaza +
Gallery 109
Horta & around
164–165
hospitals 178
hostales 168
Hostal Girona 173
Hostal Grau
Barcelona 173
Hostal Sol y K 173
Hotel Claris 171
Hotel Constanza
172
Hotel Duquesa de
Cardona 171
Hotel España 172
Hotel Granados
83 172
Hotel Mesón Castilla
172
Hotel Neri 171
Hotel Petit Palace
Boqueria 172
Hotel Pulitzer 172
hotels 168–173

I
ID cards 181
El Ingenio 82
Irish Consulate 179
Itineraries 46–51

J
Jamboree/Los
Tarantos 84
El Jardí 109
Jardí Botànic 122
Jazz Sí Club 110
jewellery 33, 36
Jujol, Josep Maria
155

K
Kaiku 118

L
Ladyloquita 158
Lando 131
language 181, 186,
187
Lascar 74 130
left luggage 182
LGBT 44, 182
La Llotja 90
Loisaida 97
lost property 182
Luz de Gas 152

M
MACBA 15, 104
Mam i Teca 105
Mandarin Oriental
Barcelona 171
La Manual
Alpargatera 82
Manzana de la
Discòrdia 136
Mar Bella 44

Maremagnum 36,
120
Market Hotel 173
markets 33
Marsella 109
Martinez 129
Marula Café 84
Maumau 131
Med Winds 109
Mercat de la
Boqueria. See La
Boqueria
Mercat de les Flors
132
La Mercè 57.
See Festes de la
Mercè
Mercè Vins 76
metro 174, 175,
180
Metro 44, 152
Milk 77
Mirablau 161
The Mix 97
MNAC 126
mobile phones 184
Modernisme 21–23
Monestir de
Pedralbes 162
money 182
**Montjuïc & Around
121–132**
Monument a Colom
114
motorbikes
hire 176
MUHBA 14, 35, 75
Mundial Bar 93
Museu Blau 165
Museu d'Art
Contemporani de
Barcelona 104
Museu de Cera 71
Museu de Cultures
del Món 89
Museu de la Màgia
91
Museu de la
Xocolata 91
Museu del Disseny
166
Museu del
Modernisme
Català 139, 150
Museu d'Història
de Barcelona.
See MUHBA
Museu d'Història de
Catalunya 114
Museu Diocesà 71
Museu Etnològic
128
Museu Frederic
Marès 71
Museu Marítim 115
museums
access for
disabled visitors
180
Barri Gòtic 69

Born & Sant
   Pere 89
Dreta 137
Esquerra 150
Gràcia & Park
   Güell 154
Horta & around
   164
Montjuïc 122
Poblenou,
   Diagional Mar &
   the Fòrum 165
Poble Sec &
   beyond 130
Port Vell 114
Raval 102
shops 35
Tibidabo 160
Zona Alta 161
Museu Nacional
   d'Art de
   Catalunya.
   See MNAC
Museu Olímpic i de
   l'Esport 128
Museu Picasso
   11, 90
My Favourite Things
   177

N
New Zealand
   Consulate 179

O
On Land 97
opening hours 183
Oplum Mar 120
opticians 181

P
Palau de la
   Generalitat 72
Palau de la Música
   Catalana 13,
   94, 98
Palau de la Virreina
   72
Palau Güell 17,
   79, 107
La Panxa del Bisbe
   156
Paradeta 93
Paradiso 95
El Paraigua 84
Parc de la Ciutadella
   18, 88
Parc del Laberint
   164
Park Güell 13, 155
parking 176
La Parra 159
Passeig de Gràcia
   31, 32, 36, 175
Passeig del Born 35
Pavellons de la
   Finca Güell 162
La Pedrera 18, 140
Penedès 27
pensiones 169
People Lounge 152
pharmacies 181

Picasso, Pablo
   51, 90
Picnic 94
pintxo 28
Plaça dels Àngels
   36
Plaça Espanya 32
Platja de Bogatell
   116
Platja de la
   Barceloneta 116
Platja del
   Somorrostro 116
Platja de Mar Bella
   116
Platja de Nova Icària
   116
Platja de Sant
   Miquel 116
Platja de Sant
   Sebastià 116
Platja Llevant 116
Platja Nova Mar
   Bella 116
Poble Espanyol 128
Poblenou & Sant
   Antoni 165
Poble Sec 129
police 178, 183
Portal de l'Àngel 32
Portalón 80
Port Vell 113
postal services 183
ProEixample 148
public holidays 183
public transport
   175
Punto BCN 152

Q
Quatre Gats 76
Queviures Múrria
   147
Quimet i Quimet
   28, 131
Quinze Nits 76

R
rail travel 175
La Rambla 13, 79
Rambla de
   Catalunya 32, 36
Rambla de les
   Flors 79
Rambla dels Ocells
   78
Rasoterra 76
Razzmatazz 44,
   166
Recinte Modernista
   de Sant Pau 16,
   145
Refugi 307 130
Rei de la Màgia 97
RENFE 175, 180
Resolis 109
**Resources A-Z
   178-185**
restaurants
   Barceloneta 117

Barri Gòtic 74
Born & Sant
   Pere 91
Dreta 139
Esquerra 150
Gràcia 156
Horta & Around
   164
Montjuïc 129
Poble Sec & Sant
   Antoni 130
Raval 105
Sants & Les Corts
   159
Zona Alta 163
Room Mate Emma
   173
Rubí 97

S
safety & security
   64, 184
Sagrada Família
   10, 142
Sala Apolo 44, 132
Sala Beckett 166
Sala BeCool 160
Sala Parés 82
Sala Phenomena
   149
sales 35
Santa Eulàlia 73,
   147
Santa Maria del Mar
   15, 92
Sant Antoni 129
Sant Pau del Camp
   103
Sants & Les Corts
   158
sardana 59
Sésamo 105
Set Portes 118
Shopping 31-36
Barri Gòtic 80
Born & Sant
   Pere 95
Dreta 144
Esquerra 151
Gràcia 158
Port Vell 120
Raval 109
Sidecar Factory
   Club 84
Sightseeing 19-24
Barri Gòtic 69
Born & Sant
   Pere 89
Dreta 137
Esquerra 150
Gràcia 154
Horta & around
   164
Montjuïc 122
Poblenou,
   Diagional Mar &
   the Fòrum 165
Poble Sec & Sant
   Antoni 130
Raval 102

Tibidabo &
   Collserola 160
Zona Alta 161
Silenus 106
smoking 184
Soho House
   Barcelona 171
Spanish language
   186
spring 178
STDs, HIV & AIDS
   181
Suculent 106
summer 178
El Suquet de
   l'Almiral 118

T
Taller de Tapas 80
tapas 28
Barri Gòtic 77
Born & Sant
   Pere 94
Dreta 141
Esquerra 150
Gràcia & Park
   Güell 156
Horta & around
   165
Montjuïc 129
Poblenou,
   Diagional Mar &
   the Fòrum 166
Raval 106
Tapas 24 28, 144
targetes 175-176
tax. See sales tax
taxis 174, 176, 180
Teatre Lliure 132
Teatre Nacional de
   Catalunya 149
Telefèric del Port
   115
Telefèric de Montjuïc
   129
telephones 184
Temple Romà
   d'August 72
La Terrrazza 132
Texas 158
Tibidabo 160
Tibidabo Funfair
   161
Tickets 130
time zone 184
tipping 184
TMB 175, 180
Torre Bellesguard
   163
Torre de Collserola
   160
Torres (shop) 110
tourist information
   66, 175, 185
tours 176
Tragaluz 139
trains 175
Tramvia Blau 163
transport 64, 174
Barri Gòtic 69,
   86, 100, 113,
   123, 137, 154

disabled travellers
180
travel advice 178
Les Tres a la Cuina
156
Twenty One by
Esther Llongueras
148

U
Universal 160
Universal Exhibition
88
US Consulate 179

V
El Vaso de Oro 120
Velódromo 151
Ven Tú! 43
Verdi 158
Vermouth
43
viewpoints 160
Vila Viniteca 97
vintage clothes
shops 32, 33, 34
Vinya del Senyor 95
visas & immigration
185
vocabulary 186

W
watersports 119

X
Xampanyet 95
Xix Bar 131

Z
Zona Alta 161
zoo 91

Picture credits

Pages 2 (top left), 111 Ingus Kruklitis/Shutterstock.com; 2 (bottom), 12 (bottom) CCat82/Shutterstock, Inc.; 3, 162 Olivia Rutherford/Time Out; 5 Roglopes/Shutterstock. com; 7, 17 (top), 153 Yury Dmitrienko/Shutterstock.com; 11 (bottom) Vlad G/Shutterstock.com; 11 (top) EQRoy/Shutterstock.com; 12 (top) Resul Muslu/Shutterstock. com; 13 (bottom), 155 JeniFoto/Shutterstock.com; 13 (top), 81 (bottom) Arsenie Krasnevsky/Shutterstock.com; 14 (top), 19, 22, 127 alionabirukova/Shutterstock.com; 14 (bottom), 96 Alfred Abad/SuperStock.com; 15 (bottom) Cubo Images/SuperStock.com; 15 (top), 107 Luciano Mortula - LGM/Shutterstock.com; 16 (bottom), 83, 90, 130 Lucas Vallecillos/SuperStock.com; 16 (top) Felix Lipov/Shutterstock.com; 17 (bottom) itsmejust/Shutterstock.com; 18 (top) Alberto Zamorano/Shutterstock.com; 18 (bottom) Joseph Sohm/Shutterstock.com; 21 engineervoshkin/Shutterstock.com; 23, 75 Greg Gladman/Time Out; 25 AForlenza/Shutterstock.com; 27 Korke/Shutterstock. com; 28 Hans Geel/Shutterstock.com; 30 Olaf Speier/Shutterstock.com; 31 Kaesler Media/Shutterstock.com; 33, 73, 177 Kiev.Victor/Shutterstock.com; 34 ksl/Shutterstock. com; 37, 42, 132 Christian Bertrand/Shutterstock.com; 39 age fotostock/SuperStock.com; 40 Veniamin Kraskov/Shutterstock.com; 43 Gemma Martz/www.ventubcn.es; 45, 55, 57, 126, 151 Iakov Filiminov/Shutterstock.com; 46 Isa Fernandez Fernandez/Shutterstock.com; 47, 49 Natalie Pecht/Time Out; 48 alionabirukova/Shutterstock.com; 49 TTstudio/Shutterstock.com; 50 Alex Tihonovs/Shutterstock. com; 51 Marc Soler/SuperStock.com; 53 Hans Blossey/SuperStock.com; 58 Xavier For,s/SuperStock.com; 59 Jos, Enrique Molina/SuperStock.com; 60 Nejron Photo/Shutterstock.com; 61 OShuma/Shutterstock.com; 62, 167 Mark.Pelf/Shutterstock.com; 64 LuisPinaPhotography/Shutterstock.com; 67 Boris Stroujko/Shutterstock.com; 69 Inu/Shutterstock.com; 79 Takashi Images/Shutterstock.com; 81 (top) cornfield/Shutterstock.com; 85, 121 Ale Argentieri/Shutterstock.com; 89 Bestravelvideo/Shutterstock.com; 92 Sergio TB/Shutterstock.com; 98, 128 Sopotnicki/Shutterstock.com; 99, 102 joan_bautista/Shutterstock. com; 104 J2R/Shutterstock.com; 108 Holala! Plaza + Gallery; 114 kavalenkava/Shutterstock.com; 116 Valery Bareta/Shutterstock.com; 123 feliks/Shuttestock.com; 133 Alessandro Colle/Shutterstock.com; 138 Brian Kinney/Shutterstock.com; 141 Vlada Photo/Shutterstock.com; 143 (top) Rodrigo Garrido/Shutterstock.com; 143 (bottom) wjarek/Shutterstock.com; 145 Dino Geromella/Shutterstock. com; 147 Konstantin Tronin/Shutterstock.com; 153 Darya Mamulchenko/Shutterstock.com; 164 nito/Shutterstock. com; 167 Sergii Zinko/Shutterstock.com; 177 Kiev.Victor/Shutterstock.com.

Credits

Crimson credits

Author Sally Davies
Editor Beth Bishop
Listings editors Emilie Crabb,
Mary-Ann Gallagher
Proofreader Ros Sales
Layouts Emilie Crabb, Patrick Dawson
Cartography Gail Armstrong, Simonetta Giori

Series Editor Sophie Blacksell Jones
Production Manager Kate Michell
Design Mytton Williams

Chairman David Lester
Managing Director Andy Riddle

Advertising Media Sales House
Marketing Lyndsey Mayhew-Dehaney
Sales Molly Keel

Writers

This guide was written and researched by
Sally Davies, along with Colman Andrews,
Stephen Burgen, Gijs van Hensbergen and
Nick Rider.

Acknowledgements

The author would like to thank Barbara
Berraondo, Maria Parrilla, Montse Planas
and Tess O'Donovan, plus all contributors
to previous editions of *Time Out Barcelona*,
whose work forms the basis of this guide.

Photography credits

Front cover
alionabirukova/Shutterstock.com
Back cover Boule/Shutterstock.com
Interior Photography credits, see *p191*.

Publishing information

Time Out Barcelona Shortlist 8th edition
© TIME OUT ENGLAND LIMITED 2017
July 2017

ISBN 978-1-78059-252-7
CIP DATA: A catalogue record for this book is
available from the British Library

Published by Crimson Publishing
19-21c Charles Street, Bath, BA1 1HX
(01225 584 950, www.crimsonpublishing.
co.uk) on behalf of Time Out England.

Distributed by Grantham Book Services
Distributed in the US and Canada by
Publishers Group West (1-510-809-3700)

Printed by Grafostil

While every effort has been made by the
authors and the publishers to ensure that
the information contained in this guide is
accurate and up to date as at the date of
publication, they accept no responsibility
or liability in contract, tort, negligence,
breach of statutory duty or otherwise for
any inconvenience, loss, damage, costs or
expenses of any nature whatsoever incurred
or suffered by anyone as a result of any
advice or information contained in the guide
(except to the extent that such liability may
not be excluded or limited as a matter of law.